IZP Hir

Free Frank

FREE FRANK

A Black Pioneer on the
Antebellum Frontier

Juliet E.K. Walker

THE UNIVERSITY PRESS OF KENTUCKY

401436

Copyright © 1983 by The University Press of Kentucky

Scholarly publisher for the Commonwealth,
serving Bellarmine College, Berea College, Centre
College of Kentucky, Eastern Kentucky University,
The Filson Club, Georgetown College, Kentucky
Historical Society, Kentucky State University,
Morehead State University, Murray State University,
Northern Kentucky University, Transylvania University,
University of Kentucky, University of Louisville,
and Western Kentucky University.

Editorial and Sales Offices: Lexington, Kentucky 40506-0024

Library of Congress Cataloging in Publication Data

Walker, Juliet E.K., 1940-
   Free Frank.

   Bibliography: p.
   Includes index.
   1. Frank, Free, 1777-1854. 2. Afro-Americans—
Kentucky—History. 3. Afro-Americans—Illinois—
History. 4. New Philadelphia (Ill.)—History.
5. Afro-Americans—Kentucky—Biography. 6. Afro-
Americans—Illinois—Biography. 7. Kentucky—
Biography. 8. Illinois—Biography. I. Title.
F460.N4F728   1983   976.9'00496073'0924   82-40181
ISBN 0-8131-1472-1

To Free Frank's Great-Granddaughter—My Mother
Thelma McWorter Kirkpatrick Wheaton

Contents

Illustrations

Tables

Acknowledgments

In writing this book I have had the support and encouragement of many people, and I am pleased to acknowledge the many kindnesses they have shown. The study of Free Frank grew out of my work as a graduate student at the University of Chicago, where three people particularly, have earned my gratitude. Dean Charles O'Connell was especially supportive of my work, and I would like to express my thanks to him for that support. The germ of this book emerged from discussion of New Philadelphia with Professor Peter Goheen in his classes in urban geography. Professor John Hope Franklin encouraged me to undertake the study of Free Frank's life as my dissertation. His criticism and insights as my dissertation adviser constantly enlarged my perspectives. His continuing support of my work since completion of the dissertation is gratefully acknowledged.

Preparing the manuscript for publication has been an unforgettable experience. Of course, I can convey only my gratitude for the generous assistance received. I have benefited from conversations and correspondence with many colleagues. Barbara Flint offered her critical insights and has helped clarify my ideas at every stage of the manuscript. Darlene Clark Hine called attention to Free Frank's perspectives of the frontier. An early draft of the first chapters was read by James Anderson, Richard Barksdale, Chester Fontenot, and Alton Hornsby, Jr., who offered useful comments on style and interpretation. My discussion of Free Frank's saltpeter activities benefited from comments made by Stanley Engerman. Mary F. Berry, John W. Blassingame, Willard B. Gatewood, and Nell I. Painter read the entire manuscript and provided their encouragement through support of various aspects of my interpretation of Free Frank's life. My largest debt undoubtedly extends to Professor Gatewood, who provided many useful criticisms of the manuscript and offered many suggestions for its improvement.

I also welcome the opportunity to note the generous support and encouragement that I received from my colleagues in the History Department at the University of Illinois, especially during the final stage. I can never hope to thank adequately Clark C. Spence, Robert M. Sutton, Robert McColley, William Widenor, Mary Lee Spence, Ralph Fisher, Caroline Hibbard, Ronald Jennings, John McKay, and John Pruett. I can only trust that in some small degree I have justified the help so generously given. I am also indebted to Walter Arnstein, Natalia Belting, Richard Burkhardt, Donald Crummey, John Dahl, C. Ernest Dawn, Bennett Hill, Keith Hitchens, Thomas Krueger, Richard Mitchell, Winton Solberg, and Robert Waller. I would also like to thank Gwen Varnell for her careful typing of an earlier draft of the manuscript.

I am particularly grateful for the assistance I received at the Pulaski County Clerk's Office in Somerset, Kentucky, and at the Pike County Clerk's Office in Pittsfield, Illinois, while researching the dissertation. A University of Illinois Scholar's Travel Grant enabled me to return to South Carolina and Kentucky while preparing the manuscript for publication. A Newberry Library Fellowship for the Study of State and Local History allowed time for organizing my research on New Philadelphia's development after the Civil War. Vera Mitchell of the University of Illinois Library's Afro-Americana Bibliography Section brought important research material to my attention.

At every stage in the preparation of this book I have had the support of my family and friends. Gloria Valentine, who typed the dissertation and an earlier draft of the manuscript, provided useful commentary from her family history. She was also an unfailing source of encouragement, as was Juanita Walters, who worked in the History Department at the University of Chicago, and James E. Walker, Sr. Ernest and Edwina Beavers, Helen and Thomas Terrell, Marye K. Taylor, Allen and Deloris Kirkpatrick, David and Lorraine Kirkpatrick, Ellen McWorter Yates, Bernice McWorter Hawkins, Cordell McWorter, LaVere and Alberta McWorter Ewing, and Gladys McWorter Crushon also provided their encouragement.

My largest debts extend to my sons, James E. Walker, Jr., and Jeffrey E. Walker, and my mother. Without their sacrifices, love, and support, this study would have remained unfinished. My mother gave extraordinary support at times when I was most discouraged. She was always a source of inspiration. It is to her that this book is dedicated.

Free Frank

Introduction

No aspect of America's history has so captured the nation's imagination as the frontier experience. From the beginning of the seventeenth century, the new American challenged and conquered a vast continent, spectacularly rich in land and natural resources. Black pioneers shared in building the new country, but a national image which portrays successive waves of westward-moving pioneers fails to reflect the full extent of black participation in the development of America's frontiers. The subject of this book—Free Frank, a black pioneer—played an active role in the development of three successive frontiers as the new nation moved westward in the era between the Revolutionary War and the Civil War. Few contemporaries shared his distinctive experiences—an Afro-American frontiersman who as a slave established his own extractive mining operation and then, after purchasing his own freedom, was a frontier land speculator, commercial farmer, stockraiser, town founder, and town developer. Free Frank's diverse business activities were motivated by an overwhelming drive to buy his family's freedom. Over a period of forty years he purchased sixteen family members, including himself, from slavery. The total cost—some $15,000—Free Frank earned during his lifetime as a pioneer entrepreneur on the new nation's western frontiers.

Free Frank lived as a slave for forty-two years. In the South Carolina Piedmont frontier where he was born in 1777 he experienced the turmoil of the Revolutionary War and its aftermath. Before the turn of the century he was taken to the new Kentucky Pennyroyal frontier, where he labored for fifteen years to subdue a desolate wilderness land and to develop his owner's pioneer farm homestead. By 1810 Free Frank began hiring his own time, and with markedly shrewd enterprise he set up a saltpeter manufactory during the War of 1812. From the profits which remained after paying his owner for allowing him to hire his own time, he purchased first his wife's freedom in 1817 and then his own in 1819.

With freedom came the expansion of Free Frank's entrepreneurial activities on the Kentucky frontier. While he continued to manufacture saltpeter, frontier land speculation and commercial farming were added to the growing list of his enterprises. Then in 1830 he made the westward move to

Illinois, where he established a pioneer homestead on the highly productive but undeveloped and sparsely populated frontier of the Illinois-Mississippi River Valley. In Pike County the black pioneer continued his speculation in land, and stockraising broadened the scope of his commercial farm enterprise. Caught up in the Illinois town-platting boom of the mid-1830s, Free Frank founded his town, New Philadelphia, and as its proprietor promoted its development until his death in 1854 at the age of seventy-seven.

Free Frank's life story provides new evidence that Afro-American economic activities where they existed on the nation's antebellum frontiers contributed to the transformation of wilderness areas into established communities. From another perspective, his activities as a black pioneer entrepreneur provide additional insights into the multiplicity of responses by Afro-Americans as they contended with life in the new nation before the Emancipation Proclamation's promise of freedom. Few historical studies fully document the wide range of activities of the pioneer slaves who developed the southern frontiers. Nor has serious historical inquiry been directed to the lives of those comparatively few free blacks whose experiences differed little from those of the white pioneers who forged the Old Northwest frontiers. Although free blacks averaged 10 percent of the Afro-American population from 1790 on, plantation slavery, urban slavery, and industrial slavery have been the areas of paramount interest for students of the Afro-American historical experience. Recently free blacks in the cities of the new nation have also become a subject of historical research. This examination of the life of Free Frank appraises a seriously neglected but important area in Afro-American and western frontier history.

Free Frank's life on the nineteenth-century Kentucky and Illinois frontiers provides the focus of this study. The documentary evidence required to detail specific events in his early life as a pioneer slave on the late eighteenth-century South Carolina and Kentucky frontiers just does not exist. Recordkeeping on these frontiers at that time was limited, and existing records are many times inaccurate. The use of important scholarly studies that detail the slave experience, however, provides insights that allow for a historical reconstruction of the impact of frontier conditions on this young slave. Liberal land laws influenced the slaveowner's westward move to the new state of Kentucky. His land acquisitions thus provide an important perspective from which to reconstruct Free Frank's early years in that state. The hardships of frontier life for a pioneer slave who worked to develop his owner's Pulaski County pioneer farm homestead, and proscriptive slave laws in force, seen in Kentucky's 1798 Slave Code, provide the basis for interpreting Free Frank's life at the turn of the new century as he moved to circumvent the constraints of his slavery.

Sufficient evidence does exist to reconstruct the sequence of events and the patterns inherent in the process which saw Free Frank become a slave entrepreneur on the Kentucky frontier. Available sources also allow for discussion of his other business enterprises once he became free. His land purchasing activities in Kentucky and Illinois comprise an important area of this study. From 1790 to 1860 America's urban population increased from only 5 percent to 20 percent. In a predominantly agrarian-based economy, land ownership offered economic independence for the majority of white Americans. That Free Frank had access to land through federal and state laws was therefore important. Land ownership was perhaps the most important factor that enabled this black pioneer to buy the majority of his family members from slavery.

Free Frank's use of the law provides another area of discussion. He was involved as a litigant in several court cases in Kentucky and Illinois, and I have provided a detailed analysis of the records of these cases. These court cases are important, for they show most clearly a theme that runs through each of Free Frank's activities—his astute assessment of American civil and common law. In their intent and design, antebellum laws were constructed to encourage economic opportunities for whites, and, when in force, were exclusionary of blacks. However carefully Free Frank provided for the efficient and profitable organization of his productive resources, the discretionary enforcement of these laws exerted a more powerful determining influence on the success or failure of his enterprises than did his business acumen and obvious entrepreneurial abilities. Taking advantage of frontier conditions, first as a slave and then as a freedman, Free Frank shrewdly used the law to promote the profitable expansion of his economic activities and as a means to protect his ownership rights in his land and property.

The origin and development of Free Frank's town, New Philadelphia, comprise another important part of this study. The New Philadelphia town records provide the only documented case of a town founded by a black man in antebellum America. Thus Free Frank's activities as an Afro-American town founder, proprietor, promoter, and developer are important. His pioneering role foreshadowed the direction that would be taken by other blacks who founded or promoted towns on the nation's frontiers after the Civil War. Certainly it appears that for black town founders throughout the nineteenth century, America's frontiers provided less restraint of economic activities than did life in established, densely populated communities. With the increasing interest in black town founding in Afro-American historiography, New Philadelphia's development into a biracial antebellum frontier town provides a distinct contrast with most black towns founded after the Civil War.

Free Frank's life therefore generates a new perspective from which to examine an alternate black experience. Before the Civil War only a small percentage of blacks in the nation's work force were entrepreneurs. But a vacuum existed, particularly in the urban South, and, as Free Frank's business enterprises suggest, also on the newly opening frontiers that did not preclude active black participation in the economy. Consumer demand in those developing economies was invariably met more efficiently and at less cost in the market place, especially when black businessmen at the local level were allowed a degree of entrepreneurial freedom in managing their own enterprises. Innovation, risk-taking, the ability to sense the wants of the consumer—entrepreneurial expertise—distinguished the business activities of Free Frank.

Entrepreneurial success requires the ability to organize business ventures in a rational manner. From the perspective of production, management, organization, and marketing, Free Frank's relative success as a saltpeter manufacturer, small land speculator, commercial farmer, and town founder and developer places him in the tradition of creative capitalism on America's developing frontiers. Thus while Afro-American history has focused on the agricultural, unskilled, service, and craft occupational participation of blacks, and American business history has emphasized those black business enterprises peripheral to the developing economy, Free Frank's diverse business activities, while limited in scope, provide examples of the parallel between black and mainstream business activity in nineteenth-century America. Free Frank's entrepreneurship provides an unprecedented perspective on the multi-faceted dynamics of race relations on the antebellum frontiers.

As my analysis of Free Frank's life shows, the extent to which this black pioneer participated in the commercial life of the developing communities where he lived was determined, not so much by his status as a slave or a freedman, as by the conditions of freedom allowed by the whites who shared the frontiers with him. And these conditions were limited. Despite Free Frank's relative success as a pioneer slave entrepreneur, Pulaski County manumission records show that few slaves were able to purchase their freedom in this Kentucky frontier community. That most antebellum free blacks lived in towns and cities shows that for blacks, access to land on the frontiers was also difficult. Free Frank's experiences suggest that some blacks were allowed to develop entrepreneurial activities in frontier communities because the sparse population demanded an elastic labor supply and greater occupational diversity. Once the frontier period came to a close, however, racism set limits to Free Frank's profitable pursuits, notwithstanding his ingenuity, resourcefulness, immeasurable determination, and subtle aggressiveness. Free Frank's life, his successes and failures, his limitations and his options, thus illuminate the harsh reality of frontier life for blacks.

Fortunately, the life of this remarkable black man has been preserved in the oral history of his descendants. Free Frank never learned to read or write, and because he is a relatively obscure historical figure, the family oral tradition is important. That his life is even now a subject of serious historical inquiry results from the fact that in addition to the family's oral record there exists a limited but important collection of documents—the Free Frank Papers. In the antebellum period, few blacks, slave or freed, failed to realize the importance of preserving every paper that came into their possession. The earliest extant document in the Free Frank Papers is the 1817 manumission paper that certified the free status of Lucy, Free Frank's wife of fifty-five years. As the family gradually became free, their continuous struggle for survival in a racially hostile slave society required that any written record attesting to their manumission, good character, or property ownership be carefully guarded and preserved. These papers were symbolic, the badges of their freedom. That some one hundred documents collected by the family before the Civil War were preserved by Free Frank's descendants marked the initial step that allowed corroboration of the family's oral tradition.

The Free Frank Papers represent traditional types of historical sources, but for Afro-American history they are invaluable, one of the few collections of papers of illiterate ex-slaves dating back almost two centuries. More important, the Free Frank Papers provided a repository of information that suggested the existence of published sources, especially federal, state, and county records, which comprise the most substantial part of the diverse source materials used in this study. The use of related primary and secondary sources which underscore conditions on the three frontiers where Free Frank lived provided a judicious mix of detail and thus generated thoughtful appraisals which rescued an important figure from obscurity and charged his life with historical significance. While this method allows for serious historical inquiry and provides the basis for capturing the significance of Free Frank as a historical figure, it also reveals the difficulties historians encounter as they attempt to reconstruct the lives of the masses of Afro-Americans. Unfortunately, until new sources are made available and new methodologies are developed, the lives of most antebellum Afro-Americans and their contribution to American life and thought will continue to be absent from the historical record.

In the absence of any personally written accounts, this black pioneer's own assessments, experiences, personal feelings, and concerns, whether as a slave or as a freedman, are noticeably absent from the record. The historiography of this subject thus imposes strict limitations. The detailed biographical analysis which distinguishes the studies of prominent antebellum Afro-

Americans whose prolific testimonies remain available for examination is impossible to attain in the case of Free Frank. Yet a biography is as much a commentary on the human spirit as is the subject's own assessment of his ideas, concerns, and experiences. For an antebellum black who lived much of his life on undeveloped frontiers, where few pioneers, white or black, kept detailed accounts of their lives, a biography is especially a commentary on the resiliency of the human spirit. As a black pioneer, then, Free Frank's life becomes not only a statement of the time in which he lived but also a record of the conditions of the frontiers where he lived, especially as these conditions affected the lives of black pioneers.

In the American mind, the frontier was more than just a place, the wilderness area beyond the constraints of an established society. It was also a process involving man's physical and psychological conquest of his environment. Aggressiveness, self-reliance, and boundless energy were qualities that made for survival in wilderness communities, where individual courage and resourcefulness, as much as prowess with an axe, plow, and rifle, encouraged respect and made for success. The tactics and strategies required for Free Frank to survive on America's frontiers met a daily testing against hardship and adversity. Free Frank's entrepreneurial activities to purchase his family from slavery displayed a resolute but resilient militance sustained by a strong-willed determination and a tough-minded intelligence. From this perspective Free Frank's life takes on heroic qualities, for heroism has much to do with the struggle to endure and to transcend the circumstances of life that would discourage another individual in his efforts to survive and especially to be free.

Thus the historical reconstruction of Free Frank's life is as much a study of the conditions of the frontiers on which he lived as it is of the experience and activities of a black pioneer in antebellum America. Free Frank's life as a slave, his activities to free himself and his family, the westward move to settle an undeveloped wilderness, and his establishment of a town take on a new historical significance when seen within the context of the broader society in which he lived. This study is one of the few biographies of an illiterate black man whose life began in the last quarter of the eighteenth century with the birth of this nation, and whose experiences bridged not only two centuries but two worlds—slave and free.

CHAPTER ONE

A Slave Who Would Be Free

When his mother became sick she was sent to the woods
after the cows late at night in ordor that the child might
die, the child was born in the wood that night and his
mother brought him home alive next morning.[1]

Free Frank was born a slave in 1777 near the Pacolet River in South Carolina's Union County.[2] In an age marked by revolution and war, his birthplace differed little from other desolate outpost settlements on the upcoun-
try frontier, where few pioneers failed to escape the conflict that quickly dev-
astated the newly developing Piedmont region in the late 1770s.[3] The American Revolutionary War had moved into its second year at the time the slave
was born. Union County, located in the old Ninety-Six District, South Carolina's last frontier, was isolated from the densely populated Tidewater low
country, a fact that seemed only to heighten the county's vulnerability to
the chaos and violence of that era.

As the new Americans forced their claim for freedom, Free Frank's
mother, the West African-born Juda, fought to assure the survival of her
son. She was determined to counter the hostility of a slaveholder anxious
that the new slave not survive his birth. Her Scotch-Irish owner, George
McWhorter, from all available evidence, was Free Frank's father.[4] The family's oral tradition recognizes his paternity but remains deliberately vague,
an obvious attempt to obscure any familial relationship. Since written
sources that could offer irrefutable proof of the slaveholder's paternity do
not exist, the Free Frank family only openly acknowledged that George
McWhorter was Free Frank's Kentucky owner, information which they knew
could not be refuted from the available evidence.[5] Thus, in the family's
painful attempt to disassociate his relationship from the slaveholder, Free
Frank's grandson Arthur McWorter noted only that Free Frank "was so
closely related to his master['s] children he was sold or sent to Pulaski
County Kentucky."[6]

In the family's oral tradition, George McWhorter's paternity is not important. Sensitive scholars of the Afro-American historical experience have
observed that, with the bitter legacy from their recent past in slavery, few
black families retain particularly fond memories of slaveowning whites who
held their ancestors in bondage.[7] As Free Frank's grandson John McWorter

emphasized in 1919, recalling the family's tragic history in slavery, "When I think of what my own family has suffered, the suffering endured by millions of other former slaves. . . . How can this fair land of ours ever fully atone for the crime of human slavery?"[8] From this perspective, it is highly significant, considering the many events in Free Frank's early life, irretrievably lost in the family record, that the circumstances of his birth remain a persistent historical memory, a singular event which continues to preface the family's historical tradition.

Yet the circumstances of Free Frank's birth provide some anxious afterthoughts that are not so readily apparent in the family's oral tradition. The South Carolina slaveholder's response to the child's birth was, after all, not what one would expect, at least not on the South Carolina frontier. On the eve of the Revolution, blatant immorality plagued the frontier communities. The church reports of Charles Woodmason include commentaries which scathingly denounce what the Anglican itinerant considered a breakdown in societal constraints. In one instance, completely outraged by the behavior of the South Carolina backwoodsmen, Woodmason wrote, "There are rather more Bastards [white], more Mullatoes born than before."[9] Such moral recriminations disturbed few slaveholding whites, but there were economic considerations which they could not ignore when it came to their chattel holdings. A slave was a valuable commodity who represented an increase in the property holdings of the owner. With each year the value of a newborn slave and the productivity of his labor represented significant capital gains. The primary economic interest of the slaveowner in his chattel property at the very least required the protection of his investments. Yet slaveholders often pursued a course of action decidedly irrational as it affected their slaves.

Then, too, the wives of slaveholders often bitterly resented their husbands' passions for the black women, and sometimes viciously abused the mulatto children and their mothers. In an 1843 autobiography, the former slave Moses Roper described the events which followed his birth. Once the slave mistress ascertained that he was her husband's son, she "got a large club, stick, and knife, and hastened to the place in which my mother was confined. . . . She went into my mother's room with full intention to murder me with her knife and club, but as she was going to stick the knife into me, my grandmother happening to come in, caught the knife and saved my life."[10]

Without venturing to consider the whole nature of the violence inherent in the Afro-American slave system, it must be noted that, while the circumstances of Free Frank's birth were unusual, the intent of the slaveholder was not uncommon. In his incisive analysis of racial attitudes in eighteenth-century America, Winthrop Jordan explains that in a society which often condoned the "simultaneous embracing of Negro women and the rejection of the ensuing offspring," the abuse of slave women was tolerated with few recriminations.[11] The moral exigencies that distinguished American slavery thus offer more than subjective insights as one attempts to grasp the discontinuities suggested by Free Frank's birth. Perhaps the already tense conditions existing in the decidedly hostile environment of the South Carolina frontier provoked the startling response. Still it is difficult to grasp the moral tone of historical behavior so contrary to economic concerns.

Another explanation may be advanced for the circumstances of Free Frank's birth. For a black woman under slavery, the birth of a child imposed critical emotional and moral choices. In this instance, the possibility exists that Free Frank's West African mother did not want a child fathered by a white man. But if this had been the case, being sent to the woods alone to deliver her baby would have provided her ample opportunity to end Free Frank's life once he was born, rather than to bring him home alive, obviously with great defiance, the next morning. Even before his birth, in fact, Free Frank's African mother could have terminated her pregnancy. In his impressive study of slavery in colonial South Carolina, Peter Wood found that "African cultures place a high priority on their extensive pharmacopoeia, and since details were known through the oral tradition, they were readily transported to the New World . . . including such specific acts as abortion."[12]

In another sense, too, it was not unusual for slave women to choose deliberately to deliver their children alone. A child born in slavery would thus have his freedom, if only for a moment. While little information is available on childbearing practices among slave women on the South Carolina frontier in the late 1770s, studies of Africans brought into Virginia and Maryland after 1750 show that most were assimilated into a developing African-European culture.[13] Although certain societies have cultural dictates that require their women to bear their children in isolation, few West African societies made childbirth a solitary ritual, nor was this a European practice. In eighteenth-century American slave society, it seems unlikely that this practice would have been encouraged, especially when the slave woman's new baby marked an increase in the chattel holdings of the slaveowner.

Until recently, historians have ignored the challenging crucial dilemmas which confronted the black woman under slavery. Increasingly, recorded oral family histories, slave autobiographies, and slave narratives which detail the sexual abuse and physical exploitation of the slave women have sustained serious critical attack as objective historical records. As sources for reconstructing the Afro-American historical experience under slavery, their va-

lidity has become unduly suspect. In his use of slave autobiographies and
narratives, however, John Blassingame has found that in reconstructing the
devastating effects of slavery on the black family these sources are invaluable.[14] Slave autobiographies, narratives, and family oral histories underscore the importance of the family and its role in preserving the integrity of
Afro-Americans under slavery, and in assuring their survival in a society that
actively encouraged their dehumanization. The horror and brutality of the
slave experience do not require the construction of deliberately contrived
stories. In the oral history of Free Frank's family, as his grandson Arthur
McWorter indicates, "I just writen [sic] what was handed to me."[15]

In the absence of documented sources, recycled family memories provide important insights for biographical analysis of a subject's early life, as
Robert Abzug suggests. In a relatively restricted sense, oral tradition becomes important in reconstructing early childhood experiences, which can
have a profound impact on the development of the special character that
distinguishes an individual in his adult life. In a provocative discussion of his
reconstruction of the early life of the antislavery spokesman Theodore Weld,
Abzug emphasizes that Weld's difficult birth and a tenuous hold on life
during the first months provided the basis for an especially close relationship
with his mother. "The struggle of those early months left its own legacy in a
particularly strong bond between mother and son, as well as a sense of spe-
cialness growing out of the retelling of the birth story itself."[16]

From this perspective, the recycled family memories of the circumstances of Free Frank's birth become important. The mother-infant bond is
one of great intensity. Independence in a child develops slowly. During the
child's period of dependence, skills and behavior patterns necessary to function as an adult are learned. A child also acquires the knowledge for survival
through observation and imitation. In particular, the attitudes expressed by
the mother in response to the conditions of her life have a profound influence on the child's development. How could Free Frank forget the record of
his birth or the conditions of his mother's slavery? As they endured the in-
dignities perpetrated on them simply because they were black, outrage, bit-
terness, and frustration were constant realities in the life of Afro-American
slave women.

Blassingame, in his intensive analysis of the slave community, affirms
the preeminent influence of the slave mother. He carefully details the complex family structures, strong kinship ties, and powerful bonds of love and
affection that encouraged family cohesion. "The degree to which slaves were
able to give their children hope in the midst of adversity is reflected in the
attitudes that black autobiographers held toward their parents." He particularly emphasizes that "Slave mothers, were, of course, held in even greater

esteem by their children."[17] In the oral historical record of Free Frank's descendants, his mother has been regarded as an important force who, during his formative years, shaped the indomitable will that was to mark his character.

In a larger sense, too, because Free Frank succeeded in freeing himself and his family from slavery, his mother's influence cannot be rejected as an imaginative representation in the family's oral record. Certainly the jarring discontinuities that would mark Free Frank's life as a pioneer slave required a formidable determination just to survive. But as Blassingame emphasizes, "The love and affection blacks received in infancy and early childhood initially determined how much self-esteem and sense of security they would have as young adults."[18] Juda's role as a mother obviously transcended her slavery. The Free Frank family historical tradition, including their "screen memories," thus broaden their frame of reference as they probe the complex character of this ingenious and perceptive man whose whole life is a testament to the struggle to be free.

While Free Frank's birth became part of the oral record of his descendants, documentary evidence which details his mother's early life or the conditions under which she lived on the Union County frontier during the Revolutionary War era just does not exist. But Peter Wood provides some insight into the physical exploitation of slave women in the South Carolina low country during the settlement period. In his discussion of the back-breaking labor extracted from female slaves during the early eighteenth century, he notes that they were "equipped with the appropriate 'Hoes, Hatchets, Broad Axes, . . . and other necessary Tools' [and] were expected, like black and white men, to clear and cultivate the equivalent of three acres annually."[19] Wood's study is limited in scope, but when combined with other information available on the field work required of antebellum slave women, there is little to suggest that the labor expectations were any less demanding for Free Frank's mother in Union County. With the birth of her son, the tumultuous conditions on the rugged Piedmont wilderness during the Revolutionary War only added to the desperation of her life. Doubtless, the devastating conditions of her slavery more than challenged her will to survive.

Sources that provide information on Free Frank's early life in South Carolina are also noticeably absent. On the other hand, sufficient evidence exists to document the experiences of George McWhorter in both Union and Pulaski counties. Reconstructing the slaveholder's life during this period is thus valuable. In a relatively restricted way, several distinctive events in George McWhorter's life illuminate Free Frank's early life on the South Carolina and Kentucky frontiers. Certainly the conditions of slavery in the

Piedmont Plateau region point to sources of tension and conflict which doubtless exerted a marked influence on an owner in his relationship to his slaves. One might expect, too, that the military hostilities on the South Carolina frontier during the Revolution, and the social and economic dislocation that shaped the Union County frontier in the aftermath of the war, also had an impact on a slaveholder, and on a young slave who grew to manhood in that era.

CHAPTER TWO

The Formative Years

A man must be hard as well as ingenious to survive and to
keep his own in an iron age.[1]

By the time of Free Frank's birth, Union County, South Carolina, already
had a history of conflict and protest. Until 1761 it was the home of the Cherokee nation and the scene of several decisive battles in the Anglo-Cherokee
wars which forced the Indians to relinquish their land. The threat from the
Cherokees had been largely removed when the family of George McWhorter, who became Free Frank's owners, settled the undeveloped up-country of
Union County in 1763. George was one of four sons of John and Eleanor
McWhorter. John, who was Scotch-Irish, had immigrated early from Ireland
to the American colonies, where he married. His name is found in county
deed records and on the tax list for land ownership in what is now Cumberland County, Pennsylvania. Sometime around 1743 the family moved to
Albemarle County, Virginia, apparently following the back country movement of other Scotch-Irish who settled the western Piedmont region of Virginia and the Carolinas. John must have died around 1758, since that is
when the inventory of his estate was settled. Some five years later his widow
Eleanor and her four sons, including George, moved to South Carolina. In
Union County the family settled what was virtually a wilderness outpost on
the Pacolet River near the present town of Jonesville.[2]

The McWhorters were representative of the Scotch-Irish presence in the
settlement of the nation's early frontiers. The contribution of this group to
the development of wilderness areas had a decided impact on the westward
movement, and the determination of the Scotch-Irish to succeed in the new
land added to the distinctive character of the Americans as a new people.
James Leyburn points to the importance of this group in the history of the
American frontier, but emphasizes that their determination to succeed did
much to intensify the violence that was a part of life on the early western
frontiers. In his study, which includes an important discussion of the eighteenth-century Piedmont frontier, Leyburn shows that the Scotch-Irish were
usually "first on the fringe of settlement, of making small farms in the forest
. . . [which] called for self-reliance, [and] ingenuity." He also contends that
their heritage from the historic settlement of Ulster "left a streak of cruelty"
which found expression on the early American frontier. As much as the En-

glish might deprecate this group's refusal to comply with colonial laws, Leyburn emphasizes that during the Revolution the Scotch-Irish in the frontier up-country were "the most whole-hearted supporters of the American cause."[3]

During the Revolutionary War, Union County and the surrounding area were the site of several important battles that would lead to the ultimate defeat of the British. Even before full-scale fighting with veteran British forces shifted the theater of war to the South Carolina frontier in 1780, virtual anarchy had destroyed any semblance of peace or stability in the region, as outlaw gangs of renegade whites terrorized the backwoods settlements. British authority was always noticeably absent on the colonial frontier. As hostilities escalated between Tories and rebels, the extra-legal bands of vigilante law enforcers, including the Regulators, organized in the late 1760s, no longer existed to suppress lawlessness and disorder. After 1776, the possibility of containing the renegades was effectively eliminated, with devastating consequences. "Rapine, outrage, and murder became common," as Ramsay subsequently recalled in his discussion of this era.[4] From 1776 on, Tory intrigues added chaos and turmoil to the already unsettled conditions. On the frontier, loyalists met with ruthless acts of resistance from the disparate rebels and their forces, who throughout the conflict more than countered their defenses with relentless hit-and-run guerrilla attacks in their fight for freedom.

Blacks, slave and free, also raided and plundered as they relentlessly fought their own war of independence on the South Carolina frontier. The wartime turmoil provided space for this discontented group to express their rage against the racist slave society in which they lived. Free blacks were motivated as much by the philosophy which had pushed the colonists to move for independence as by the desire to retain the relative freedom they had found in the frontier up-country. Their open resistance was not lost on South Carolina whites. White resentment of free blacks who defiantly resisted all attempts to limit their freedom was perhaps best expressed by one South Carolina Regulator: "Is it not Slavery to be subject to the Impudence, Impertinence and Insults of Free Negroes and Mullatoes who greatly abound here?—and who have taken Refuge in these Parts from the Northern Colonies?"[5] Some free blacks had joined the outlaws in attacking the isolated frontier settlements, and it appears that these outcast white frontiersmen did not resent their presence. In a study of the violence on the South Carolina frontier, Richard M. Brown suggests that "the outlaws and lower people apparently accepted the colored men [free blacks] as equals."[6] Other free blacks, however, joined their slave brothers who had escaped to the frontier and carved out an existence apart from whites.

From the beginning of the eighteenth century, South Carolina's slaves outnumbered whites, although by 1775 some 90 percent of the slave population still lived in the Tidewater region, where almost half the colony's white population was settled. The remaining slaves were unevenly dispersed on the up-country frontiers, but there were districts where slaves accounted for as much as 30 percent of the population.[7] Once the war began, however, the back-country slave population was continuously augmented by fugitive slaves who fled the low country seeking freedom in the sparsely populated Piedmont. Others joined or established maroon communities, isolated strongholds where blacks, slave and free, lived and which were also used as bases to attack up-country white settlements.[8] By the time of the Revolution, while the slave force was still concentrated in the low country, where the threat of their resistance was greater, isolated frontier communities also felt that threat, and it intensified during the early years of the war.

Frontier slaveholders found it difficult to contain their slaves, and extreme measures were often taken to prevent bondsmen from running away. Only a few slaveholders, however, acted to free themselves from an increasingly hostile and restive slave force, although the unusual circumstances of Free Frank's birth provide at least one instance when a slaveholder in the region apparently found the addition of another slave only an unwelcome burden. Violence and devastation thus marked the era of Free Frank's birth in 1777, and his birthplace, although a remote outpost, suffered the full force of the Revolutionary War.

During the Revolution, George McWhorter volunteered and served in Colonel Henry Hampton's regiment of light dragoons, which was part of General Thomas Sumter's South Carolina Brigade and which fought at Camden. There the Americans, despite superior forces, suffered an overwhelming and humiliating defeat in August 1780.[9] The impact of this defeat in the South Carolina up-country was disastrous, as Robert Remini explains. While American resistance would continue, the back-country settlers were completely demoralized, many no longer caring which side won. As Remini says, after Camden "the Carolina countryside was one vast charnel house of butchered Tories and Patriots. It was no longer a revolution, but a civil war, with brother fighting brother, father against son, and neighbor killing neighbor."[10] Then in October 1780, at York, in the county northeast of Union, the Americans won a singular victory at the Battle of King's Mountain. They won again at Spartanburg in the county west of Union, where the Battle of Cowpens was fought in early 1781. Both were decisive victories and marked the turning point of the war, but not the end of hostilities in the Piedmont.[11]

South Carolina's Indian territory was located on the fringe of the Blue

Ridge Mountains, placing the Cherokee nation only forty miles west of Union County, less than two days' distance. The Cherokees, capitalizing on the manpower shortage in the back country, resumed their raids on the isolated settlements in the Old Ninety-Six.[12] As the American armies turned toward Charleston in the summer of 1781, the outlaws returned, adding to the devastation in the up-country. Even with the British defeat on the frontier in 1781, when Free Frank was four years old, the violence continued. The turmoil from the outlaw raids and sporadic Cherokee attacks only diminished in intensity two years later, when Charleston saw the final removal of the British forces. More than 25,000 slaves had escaped from their owners in the period from 1775 to 1783, and in such an inflamed atmosphere there was always the fear, verging on panic among South Carolina whites, that slaves would stage a successful massive attack. Not surprisingly, South Carolina was one of the two new American states that did not allow the enlistment of blacks in its military forces during the Revolutionary War, although South Carolina blacks, slave and free, served in the militias of other states, as well as the Continental Army. Their services in the navy were especially valued because of their skills as pilots. And, as Herbert Aptheker emphasizes, "The feats of Francis Marion, the guerrilla fighter of South Carolina, have long been celebrated, but rarely is it mentioned that among his original group of fighters were Negroes."[13]

Afro-Americans felt a powerful sense of community, and throughout the new nation took pride in those blacks who had served in the American armies and contributed to the defeat of the British. Doubtless few slaves on the South Carolina up-country frontier would readily forget the successful threats made by their brothers, slave and free, in their rebellion against slavery during the war years. One should not underestimate the imprint of black resistance on the minds of South Carolina slaves, especially on young slaves who experienced the aftermath of that war in a frontier community. The conflict in the South Carolina up-country had an unsettling effect on whites, as well. Remini points to the profound impact of the Revolution on the young Andrew Jackson, who at the age of thirteen was imprisoned by the British at Camden. With particular emphasis, the noted Jacksonian scholar added: "In later years, Jackson remembered the fury of those days."[14]

Preparations for defense and movements of troops surrounded Free Frank during his early childhood, and the young slave's awareness of the war, and of the hostility and tension stemming from its aftermath cannot be discounted as factors that influenced his later life. The war was a disruptive force in the lives of the new Americans, and in South Carolina few up-country settlers remained untouched by the violence of that era. In the aftermath of the war, most settlers rapidly adjusted to a life free from the uncertainties of wartime, but others never really suppressed the need to live constantly on the threshold of danger, violence, and, for some, new adventures. Few whites had escaped the threat of slave resistance, and it too was a heritage not likely to be forgotten by either the whites or the slaves who shared the frontiers with them.

While the Revolution marked the beginning of the end of slavery in the new states to the north, the institution remained solidly entrenched throughout the South. In South Carolina slaves suffered the most severe form of repression, as a young Irishman who traveled in the state in 1780 later recalled. His impression of the dehumanizing effects of slavery underscores its brutality and its effect on the slaves, for as he said, "The very ground is damp with the sweat and tears of the unhappy Africans. . . . Here may be seen every day, and all day long, thousands of our fellow creatures, branded, chained, and treated like cattle in every respect, but that of humanity."[15] Whatever childhood experiences Free Frank had as he lived through the Revolutionary War era were doubtless filled with fear and terror.

That childhood came to an abrupt end in the mid-1780s. In 1785 Free Frank was eight years old, and slave children assumed the burdens of adult work at a very early age. While little information is available about the lives of slave children on the late eighteenth-century South Carolina frontiers, studies of antebellum slavery in other areas provide some insight into their work patterns. In his seminal study of the slave community, Blassingame notes the responsibilities of slave children. "Many began working irregularly at light tasks before they were ten. After that age, they usually started working in the fields."[16] Eugene Genovese's comprehensive study of plantation slavery also emphasizes the early work responsibilities of the slave children: "Before the age of eight most children did little or no work apart from looking after ('nursing') those younger than themselves, although in every part of the South, some masters worked the little ones unmercifully from the time they could toddle."[17] Given the conditions of land development and settlement on the frontiers, obviously much more labor was demanded from the slave child who lived there than from one who lived on the plantations. Pioneer slave children could be expected not only to work the fields but also to help clear and prepare the undeveloped land for cultivation, and then to participate in the harvest.

In the late 1780s Union County was a general farming community in which intensive labor was required to make the land pay. Much of the Piedmont uplands presented a rugged terrain of hills, swampy grounds, and densely wooded thickets. Even before the development of large farms or the more substantial plantations, extensive cattle raising was an important activ-

ity in the region. In those areas that allowed for productive cultivation, tobacco and wheat were principal crops, although in some areas hemp was cultivated as a cash crop, as well. By the mid-1780s improved transportation
provided easier access to the Charleston market, prompting the slaveholders
to push their slaves with even greater severity to meet the new market demands. The 1787 Constitutional Convention only intensified their concerns,
and the future of slavery was a critical issue even while the upland slaveholders watched the growing consolidation of large landholding estates.[18]

By the late eighteenth century, however, the full development of a
plantation economy in the South Carolina Piedmont was still a generation
away, especially since only about one-fourth of the whites had slaves to help
them work the land. In Union County, the total white population in 1790
was 6,430; the slave population was 1,236. Of the 1,058 heads of household
in the county, only 231 were slaveholders and over half held fewer than four
slaves. George McWhorter and his brother John stood in that class of small
slaveholders: George is listed in the 1790 federal manuscript census as owning five slaves, while his brother John held three.[19] From the 1790s on, the
South Carolina up-country showed a rapid increase in population, as Tidewater planters and small slaveholders moved in to settle the increasingly desirable yet undeveloped frontier. Up-country land costs rose to almost prohibitive rates, and the price of slaves increased, as well. For many non-slaveholding whites and small slaveholders, including George and his brother
John, the only recourse, as they considered their economic future, was to
move west, especially to Kentucky, where good land was cheap and still
available.

Kentucky land records show that the brothers were in that state in 1795.
In that year George McWhorter purchased land south of the Green River in
Lincoln County, one of the three original counties organized in Kentucky,[20]
in the central part of the Pennyroyal region. Contemporary travel accounts
describe the area, especially the land between the Green and Cumberland
rivers, as "in general rich, and finely watered."[21] The Pennyroyal was also
covered by dense, almost impenetrable forests, and the "Barrens," desolate
burned-away areas full of sinkholes and swamps and once used as buffalo
grazing lands, dotted a large part of this region. While few prospective settlers in the late eighteenth century were interested in locating in this region,
even fewer could afford the highly desirable land in the Bluegrass country,
where the state's first plantations were established. In his discussion of the
early settlement of Kentucky, Thomas Abernethy indicates that even in the
early 1790s, "prices as high as one hundred dollars per acre were paid [in the
Bluegrass], and even the wealthier planters held no more than a hundred
acres."[22]

George McWhorter, however, acquired his Pennyroyal holdings under Kentucky's new Head Rights Claim System, which required the claimant to pay only $30.00 for every 100 acres surveyed. The act creating this land distribution policy was passed by the Kentucky legislature in December 1795. By design it applied only to those people living in Kentucky at the time, requiring that any individual applying for a grant had to "have actually settled himself or herself . . . on or before the first day of January next [1796]."[23] The applicants could claim up to 200 acres, but the survey had to be completed by August 1796 and the plat registered six months from that day. George McWhorter filed a claim for a survey of 57 acres on August 2, 1796. To qualify, he must have settled his Lincoln County land before the end of December 1795.[24]

Free Frank was also in Kentucky in 1795 according to the *Pike County* (Illinois) *Atlas,* which provides a brief biographical note on his life. Based on the family's publicly acknowledged oral history, this 1872 source confuses the question of his paternity, but the *Atlas* is an important source, since it provides a record of the specific year that Free Frank first settled in Kentucky: "Owing to the peculiar relationship existing between himself and his master, he was sold at the age of eighteen to a planter in Kentucky."[25] That would have been in 1795. Historically, sending a slave away was one method slave owners used to sever paternity, although in the westward move slaves usually accompanied their owners. It was also a common practice for slaveowners who settled the wilderness to send their slaves ahead to clear the land and build cabins before the slaveholders moved their own families west.[26] As the parallel circumstances in the lives of Free Frank and George McWhorter suggest, and based on the family's private oral record, George McWhorter was Free Frank's South Carolina owner, who sent the slave ahead to Kentucky. Whether Free Frank was sold by an unknown South Carolina owner with whom he had a "peculiar relationship," as the *Atlas* noted, or because he was "so closely related to his master's children," as his grandson Arthur McWorter said, is not important. What is important is that the record definitely shows that McWhorter was Free Frank's Kentucky owner and that Free Frank first settled in Kentucky in 1795.

Free Frank and George McWhorter were among some 5,000 new settlers who entered Kentucky by way of the Wilderness Trace during 1795.[27] The journey west was difficult and dangerous. Most pioneers traveled in wagon trains because few dared to go it alone. The westward move took almost a month, although the distance was only 200 miles from South Carolina's western Piedmont region through the Cumberland Gap to Crab Orchard, the first white settlement in Kentucky beyond the Appalachian Mountains. Harry Toulmin, who traveled the Wilderness Trace in the 1790, described it as only a path, "hardly possible for a carriage to pass, great parts of the way being over high steep hills, upon the banks of the rivers and along defiles which in some places seem to threaten you at every step with danger."

The pioneers also suffered heavy losses from Indians, who fiercely resisted their westward advances. At Hazel Patch, less than a half-day's ride from where Free Frank and George McWhorter settled, a band of white pioneers were brutally massacred by "a strong party of Indians" in 1793. Lewis Collins tells us that "a portion of the men fought bravely, and several of them were killed. The others ran away and left the women and children to be made captives."[28] Discouraged by the hardships of travel, the dangers from Indian attacks, and what appeared to be insurmountable obstacles in developing the new frontier, few easterners were willing to make the move west to settle the desolate Kentucky Pennyroyal in the 1790s. Thus the 1795 migration did not mark the beginning of any appreciable population increase in the region, even when Kentucky opened up new land for sale in that area with the passage of more liberal land laws.

George McWhorter, however, owned four slaves who would be used to develop his holding. In 1796 he took advantage of the new land laws by purchasing additional land in Lincoln County.[29] In 1798 he acquired another 170 acres on Fishing Creek in recently established Pulaski County, in a place called Flat Lick, described by the early settlers as a beautiful, rolling wooded area.[30] McWhorter obtained this land under the 1797 Kentucky Head Rights Claim Act, which required that each claimant actually live on the land, fence two acres, and cultivate a crop of corn in order to secure title to the property.[31] From the beginning of settlement, Free Frank was actively involved in establishing his owner's Pulaski County farm homestead.

That a slave was the primary instrument of settlement on the Pennyroyal frontier was not unusual. In his discussion of the early settlement of the Pennyroyal, Thomas D. Clark found that "The Negro proved himself an excellent frontiersman. . . . Slaves chopped down the heavy timber, helped build the cabins, planted the crops, and performed a thousand and one tasks which had to do with settling people on the western waters."[32] In every respect, then, the work of pioneer slaves contributed to the survival of the first settlers.

Life on the trans-Appalachian frontier was hard for all. Trade and transportation just did not exist, and even well into the first decades of the nineteenth century many frontiersmen on the Pennyroyal had yet to move beyond self-sufficiency. As William Savage, a contemporary, observed, the early settlers continued to "subsist without those comforts that they have been in the habit of enjoying in their preceding life society."[33] For slaves life was even harder. They were forced to live under the most primitive and brutal conditions, enduring innumerable hardships and even greater deprivations. Penlike structures, hastily thrown together, provided them shelter, and these makeshift huts served as their homes until conditions improved for the slaveholders. For many slaves, up to ten years passed before "these hovels were abandoned for the hewed log cabins of their masters." For household furnishings the general practice was that, as conditions improved for their owners, "the extremely coarse furniture was moved out gradually to the negro cabins or the wood piles."[34]

Frontier life on the early Pennyroyal was not only rough but dangerous. The slaves were required to protect the frontier homesteads as well as set them up. In his brief historical sketch of early Pulaski County, W.H. Perrin reports that Indians continued to resist white settlement of their lands even into the early 1800s, when "numerous depredations . . . and slight skirmishes occurred now and then."[35] The Pennyroyal Barrens, especially between the Green and Cumberland rivers, where George McWhorter's holdings were located, had also become a hideout for renegades, who used this region as a base from which to launch devastating raids on the isolated settlements.[36] Fear of Indian attacks and outlaw raids found the Kentucky frontiersmen relying on their slaves to join in defense of the backwoods settlements.

The significance of slaves as a force in conquering the Kentucky wilderness has been noted by J. Winston Coleman. "Master and slave in the earlier days worked together in the fields, [and] marched together against the Indians."[37] The 1798 Kentucky Comprehensive Act regarding "Slaves, Free Negroes, Mulattoes and Indians" provides an even more forceful recognition of the need for blacks, slave and free, to take an active part in defending the frontier. "All negroes, mulattoes, and Indians, bond or free, living at any frontier plantation [are] permitted to keep and use guns, powder, shot, and weapons, offensive and defensive."[38] Only a license issued by the county justice of the peace, upon application by free blacks or Indians or by the owners of slaves, was required for blacks to carry weapons on the frontier.

The implications of this act offer a startling contrast to the conditions of control that existed in the settled areas of the Southeast. Statutory provisions there made it illegal for blacks even to assume a defensive posture, much less an armed, offensive one. In the old Southeast especially, where the black population was much greater, whites consistently suppressed any form of black defiance. Military and quasimilitary forces stood ready to put down expressions of black discontent and to counter any acts of resistance.[39] In the rural countryside a patrol system provided the force to control the slaves. This method of containing blacks was carried over onto the Kentucky frontier, but in Pulaski County patrols were not statutorily instituted until 1809, and appropriations for their operations were not granted until 1844.[40]

Pulaski's failure to establish a legally constituted patrol system from the beginning was due in part to the small numbers of blacks living in the county. The Pulaski tax list for 1799 shows only 121 slaves owned by 49 landholders out of a total of 235 heads of household.[41] Numerically Pulaski's slaves did not constitute a threat to the county's white population. Moreover, a developing general farming community actually required a greater degree of mobility for slaves than did a settled area. Pioneer slaveholders more often than not owned land in several separate locations. If the full extent of their slaves' labor was to be efficiently utilized, the slaves would need greater mobility than the patrol system would permit. Kentucky's legislators early recognized the need for the unrestricted mobility of pioneer slaves, and the 1798 Slave Code included a provision which prevented undue restrictions on their movement in frontier areas, stipulating "that nothing herein contained shall be construed to prohibit the negro or slaves of one and the same owner, though seated at different quarters from meeting, with their owner's or overseer's leave, . . . nor to restrain the meeting of such slaves."[42]

At the same time, the state acted to suppress clandestine slave activities on the frontier. The Slave Code also included a provision designed to discourage pioneer slaves from using their mobility in devious ways that might threaten whites, for the statute made it illegal for slaves "to presume to come and be upon the plantation of any person whatsoever, without leave in writing from his or her owner or overseer, not being sent on lawful business."[43] Slaves easily discovered the loopholes in this provision. Some masters were lax, failing to provide a slave with written permission, and other slaveholders could not write. Taking advantage of their owners' laxity or incompetence, the pioneer slaves increased their mobility without the threat of serious reprisals, providing their own opportunities for the clandestine meetings feared by the slaveholding whites. If apprehended, they sometimes escaped punishment by claiming that they were attending to their masters' business as they understood some instructions given them.

In addition to their relatively unrestricted mobility on the Kentucky frontier, participation in religious activities afforded pioneer slaves further opportunities for developing a sense of community. The Kentucky Slave Code did not restrict religious activities among slaves, emphasizing that they should not be prohibited "from going to church and attending divine service on the Lord's day or on any other day of public worship."[44] Pulaski County's Sinking Creek Baptist Church was established in 1799, and slaves were allowed to attend, but only as long as they sat in the gallery.[45] Their own religious services, often surreptitiously conducted, however, provided a more meaningful religious experience.

Harvest time offered slaves in general farming communities an additional opportunity to relieve the sense of isolation from other blacks that was common in frontier areas where small slaveholders settled. Customarily, as Francis Frederic recalled, slaves were sent, "with letters to the other planters around asking them to allow their slaves to come and help with the corn shuckings."[46] He notes that while slaves, male and female, young and old, found little relief from the demanding work usually required, the corn shuckings provided one of the few social occasions allowed them. Thus on Kentucky's Pennyroyal frontier, by evading some laws and taking advantage of others, pioneer slaves provided themselves with a greater degree of mobility than the system found desirable. Consequently, even while living in isolated backwoods settlements, they quickly developed a sense of community and created new kinship and familial ties to replace those broken by their move west.

During his first year of settlement in Pulaski County, Free Frank met Lucy, who became his wife in 1799.[47] Lucy was born a slave in 1771.[48] Her Pulaski County owner, William Denham, lived in a settlement on Fishing Creek, although his holdings were located at some distance from George McWhorter's. Denham's daughter had married George McWhorter's brother John in Lincoln County in December 1795, and they too settled in Pulaski County.[49] (Pulaski County, created from part of Lincoln County, was established in 1798.) The Denham-McWhorter family ties undoubtedly provided the opportunity for the two slaves to meet and then marry. Although Lucy and Free Frank did take each other as husband and wife, Coleman notes that as far as whites were concerned, "Legally there were no binding marriages among slaves. They were not citizens but mere property."[50]

Free Frank and Lucy, however, cared for each other with remarkable feeling and a loving concern, and even without a formal religious ceremony or the legal vows that the state allowed whites, morally and spiritually the two slaves considered their marriage binding. Eventually they married formally under Illinois law in 1839. Their marriage at that time conveyed the intensity of Free Frank's deep and long-lasting commitment to Lucy. In the Pike County history, which reported the ceremony, it was said that "When McWhorter was asked if he would live with, cherish and support, etc., his wife, he replied, 'Why, God bless your soul! I've done that thing for the last 40 years.'"[51] From 1799, their vows—a deep and powerful love for each other—sustained them for the fifty-five years which marked Free Frank's and Lucy's life as husband and wife.

Because their owners lived in distant settlements, Free Frank and Lucy were married for almost twenty years before they lived together in one household, and then they were able to do so only because they were free. Nevertheless, both were able to fulfill their responsibilities without undue loss of time, since both of their owners lived in the same area. Married slaves who lived at great distances from each other created distress for their owners,

Table 1. Approximate Birth and Death Dates of Free Frank's Surviving Children

Name	Grave Marker	Approximate Birth Date	Age at 1850 Census	Age at 1860 Census
Juda	"b. May 13, 1800 d. Mar. 12, 1906 aged 105 yrs. 10 months"	May 1800	47	(Not listed)
Frank	"d. June 21, 1851 46 yrs. 9 months"	September 1804	45	(Dead)
Sally	"d. Mar. 22, 1891 aged 77 yrs."	1811	39	49
Solomon	"d. Jan. 7, 1879 aged 63 yrs. 11 mths 3 days"	February 1815	35	46
Squire[1]	"d. Dec. 18, 1855 aged 38 yrs. 3 mths"	September 1817	33	(Dead)
Commodore[1]	"d. Mar. 15, 1855 aged 32 yrs. 3 mths"	January 1823	27	(Dead)
Lucy Ann[1]	"b. Sept. 22, 1825 d. April 16, 1902"	September 1825	23	34

SOURCES: Gravestones in New Philadelphia, Illinois, cemetery; U.S., Bureau of the Census, "Population Schedules of the Seventh Census of the United States, 1850, Illinois, Pike County" (Washington, D.C.: National Archives and Records Service, Manuscript Microcopy M-432, reel 124); idem, "Population Schedules of the Eighth Census of the United States, 1860, Illinois, Pike County, Hadley Township" (Washington, D.C.: National Archives and Records Service, Manuscript Microcopy M-653, reel 219).

1. Born free.

who claimed literally every moment of their time. Other than the most limited conjugal visits, any attempts by married slaves to see each other beyond the time allotted were strictly limited and severely discouraged. Slave marriages represented strictly economic alliances between their chattel property. Despite these restrictions, many slaves displayed a strong determination to improve the quality of their family life.

Lucy and Free Frank's 1799 marriage was advantageous to their respective owners. They knew that greater productivity could be expected from both the man and the woman once they were married. More important, especially for the owner of the female slave, any children born would belong to him, thus increasing the value of his property. Certainly Denham's property holdings increased. One year after Free Frank and Lucy's marriage, their first child was born. Free Frank named her Juda, his mother's name,[52] and her birth in 1800 represented the third generation of slaves in the Free Frank family. Within the next seventeen years Lucy and Free Frank would have twelve more slave-born children, only four of whom would live to adulthood and freedom.[53] Later only three of their four freeborn children survived the Pulaski County frontier and lived to adulthood (see Table 1). This was the harsh reality of frontier life for slaves, but Free Frank and Lucy struggled persistently to hold their family together. The efforts of slaves to improve the quality of their family life were limited by the economy of the slave system—in particular, the tenuous financial situation of pioneer slave owners, for whom heavy investments in land and the absence of venture capital to develop their new holdings often militated against the survival of slave families.[54]

The break-up and separation of black families were very much parts of the slave system. That slaves felt it imperative to keep their families together and provide for them within the limitations of their slavery, however, strengthened their positions as husband and wife, mother and father, and also strengthened the familial bonds of love and affection. Thus for Free Frank to remain with his owner in the area where his wife and daughter lived, it was to his advantage to make himself useful, if not indispensable. The ultimate threat was that he could be sold. A slave on the Pennyroyal frontier whose existence required an almost arrogant defense of the wilderness with rifle and shot must have found it advantageous to his family's survival to present himself as reliable, trustworthy, and responsible. Perhaps from that time on, as Free Frank sought a means to achieve his goals, "the singleness of purpose, persistence, and determination that marked his life was etched on his face," according to a great-granddaughter who remembered him from a family daguerreotype.[55]

On first glance, as she recalled, "There was little of the Irish that showed in his face, but one was also reminded of Frederick Douglass: there were remarkable similarities in their appearance." His great-granddaughter explained that Free Frank was remembered by the family as a man of tremendous energy and robust vitality. Older family members, she said, also spoke often of his constrained self-assuredness and tremendous charisma: "He possessed that indefinable quality of presence." As he assumed maturity, he commanded respect from some and fear from others, but there was never an air of open defiance or hostility about him, "just a quiet sense of power." He was also an easy man, but once he began to act a thoughtful deliberateness was there. For those who finally came to know him there was the realization that he would not be stopped. Free Frank was fiercely determined but had an air of gentleness. Seldom did he openly express anger, and his friendly, resonant voice never changed. "You would have to know Free Frank quite well to read his thoughts and assess his intent, and even then you could never be sure just what he was thinking," she explained.

Free Frank was of average height and build, erect and straight-backed. Even though he was past seventy when the daguerreotype was taken, his still sinewy frame showed strength and vigor. "Free Frank had an implacable will," his great-granddaughter said. Even today she recalls that he was a man with piercing dark eyes, alert and intelligent. "The indomitable set of his face, however, expressed a cautious self-restraint and control that marked the inner reserves of energy and perseverance that sustained him." The Pike County history notes that Free Frank was a "live, enterprising man, a reputable, worthy citizen, kind, benevolent, and honest." And, with particularly great emphasis, the county history notes: "He labored hard to free his family from the galling yoke of southern slavery."[56]

Admittedly, the complexity and force of Free Frank's character and personality from 1800 on do not lend themselves to easy analysis. But the subsequent events in his life, as he responded to the conditions of slavery and freedom, show caution and self-restraint on the one hand, and on the other, shrewdness and ingeniousness as he moved to free himself and his family from slavery. In 1800, when he became a father at the age of twenty-three, Free Frank faced life as a slave for nineteen more years. On the Pennyroyal frontier, in a new, hostile, and desolate land, the survival of pioneer slaves required not only raw courage and dogged willpower, but also ingenuity and deliberate restraint. Doubtless the force of Free Frank's character was shaped in part by the experiences of his formative years on the South Carolina and Kentucky frontiers.

Free Frank's first adult years saw him participate in the westward movement to settle the Kentucky Pennyroyal wilderness, where he was actively involved in developing and defending his owner's land. In a real sense, however, his contribution to the development of the frontier was recognized as only a function of the organized system of labor. Coleman, in his assessment of slavery on the Kentucky frontier, notes that "probably few of these sturdy pioneers realized as they accepted slavery to provide the additional labor required to clear their lands, to build cabins and to aid them in wresting a livelihood from the back woods, that they were introducing an economic and social factor that would later go far to shape and mould Kentucky's system of agriculture and to determine the texture and tendencies of her society."[57] Even fewer whites considered the challenges of the frontier from a pioneer slave's point of view, a perspective which perhaps explains Free Frank's make-up and pragmatic cast of mind.

In the late eighteenth century, life for a pioneer slave in a wilderness area was unrelenting, unrewarding, back-breaking drudgery. It was also accountably less cruel and less debilitating than plantation life, where slaves were rigorously restricted and stringently controlled. As Wood emphasizes in explaining those distinctions, "white slaveholders, whose descendants could impose a pattern of mannered docility upon their Negroes, were themselves dependent upon a pioneer pattern of versatility and competence among their workers in the early years."[58] Certainly whites on the frontiers, both in up-country South Carolina and in the Kentucky Pennyroyal, encountered greater difficulty in subjugating their slaves. Frontier life provided slaves a more effective position to circumvent the constraints of their forced subordination. Nevertheless, in 1800 Free Frank and his new family, as they began their lives in a new century, were still in bondage. As he assumed a new maturity on the Pulaski County frontier, Free Frank was doubtless determined to free his family.

In a society where expectations of profit underlay the economic system, most slaves needed "cash money to buy their way out of bondage," as Ira Berlin explains. "Iron determination alone was not enough."[59] In the undeveloped areas of the Pennyroyal, where there were few whites and even fewer blacks, some slaves were permitted to participate in occupations which would allow them to become wage earners, a first step to freedom. These were the slaves who hired their own time, but "this mode of struggle," as Herbert Aptheker explains, "while usually unobtrusive and rarely spectacular, nevertheless required great perseverance and a deliberate, cool courage."[60]

Having assumed the responsibilities of an adult at an early age, by 1800 Free Frank was fully aware that his labor had helped to build a new home and to provide a livelihood for his owner. Doubtless he knew, too, that he could do the same for himself and his family if only he were free.

CHAPTER THREE

"For a Valuable Consideration"

After working for his master for a number of years, [Free Frank] hired his time, agreeing to pay a certain amount per annum. He then engaged in the manufacture of saltpeter, which he sold for good prices, and in that way, by hard work and strict economy for a number of years, he saved enough money, after paying his master for hire, to purchase his freedom.[1]

In the early years of the nineteenth century, George McWhorter hired Free Frank out as a farm laborer and jack-of-all-trades. Sheer raw labor was required to develop the new wilderness land, and agricultural work and farm life were neither simple nor easy. A white settler who had spent his young life on the early Pennyroyal recalled, "Everything was done by main strength. The heavy lifting made men stoop-shouldered and old at forty and fifty. . . . [and] there seemed to be no ingenuity to lessen or lighten labor."[2] Labor resources were shared on that sparsely populated frontier, but access to a more permanent labor supply was essential for farmers who wished to move quickly beyond self-sufficiency. As François Michaux observed early in the nineteenth century, Pennyroyal farmers "never have more than the twentieth, thirtieth, or even the fortieth of what they might produce." Moving west with limited cash reserves left many first settlers unable to meet even minimal installment payments for their new landholdings, much less to pay the hired labor so desperately needed to work it. Others, however, carefully planned their move west. They had anticipated that hired labor, specifically hired slave labor, would be an initial step required for the development of their new holdings, for Michaux also noted in his commentaries that even in the early years, "Some [farmers] who are in more easy circumstances employ negro-slaves in the cultivation of their ground."[3] With the energies of most early Pennyroyal farmers spent in attempting to move beyond subsistence and to develop their farm homesteads, hired slave labor, an almost indispensable investment, was crucial, especially during the first years of settlement.

While a competitive market existed for hired slaves on the Pennyroyal, few slaves were available for hire on Pulaski County's newly developing frontier (see Table 2). After the initial settlement period in the late 1790s, dur-

Table 2. Kentucky and Pulaski County Population, 1800-1830

	Free Blacks		Slave Blacks		Whites	
Year	Kentucky	Pulaski	Kentucky	Pulaski	Kentucky	Pulaski
1800	741	1	40,343	232	179,873	2,928
1810	1,713	0	80,561	450	324,237	6,447
1820	2,759	9	126,732	635	434,644	6,953
1830	4,917	20	165,213	1,017	517,787	8,463

SOURCE: U.S., Bureau of the Census, *A Century of Population Growth from the First Census of the United States to the Twelfth, 1790-1900* (Washington, D.C., 1909).

ing which time the best land for plantation development was taken up, Pulaski offered little attraction for small slaveholders, although for non-slaveholding whites, good land was still available for establishing small but profitable commercial farms. By 1800, Kentucky's new land laws, designed to encourage settlement on the rugged Pennyroyal, allowed the purchase of a 100-acre tract for only twenty dollars.[4] As a result, Pulaski showed a substantial population increase in the early years as compared to the period after 1810, when few new pioneers attempted settlement there. With the steady influx of new settlers before 1810, then, there was a constant need for hired slaves, and as Michaux suggests, there were those who could afford to hire them.

While the monetary value of slave hiring was sufficient inducement for many owners to hire out their slaves, the smooth and efficient operation of their own farms was paramount. The slaveholder's own house had to be built, the land cleared, and food crops cultivated first, before a frontier slaveholder was in a position to hire out his slaves for any extended period of time. Three years appear to have been the minimum length of time required to establish a self-sufficient farm homestead, and ten years seems to have been the maximum for a small farm to become productive beyond the subsistence level.[5] As a late eighteenth-century traveler commented, on observing the rapid development in many areas of the Pennyroyal, "From dirty stations, or forts, and smoky huts, Kentucky has expanded into fertile fields, blushing orchards, rising villages and trading towns. Ten years have produced a difference in the population and comforts of the country."[6]

Within the first years of settlement, slaveholders, having a permanently assured labor force, more often than not increased their landholdings as they attempted to develop more profitable agricultural units.[7] George McWhorter conformed to this pattern. In 1802 he acquired an additional 200 acres of land, and then another 300 acres in 1807.[8] His land purchases were intended for future speculation rather than immediate development, however, as were many other Pennyroyal land purchases acquired from the state after 1800. In this region land was cheap. But it was not particularly productive, and profitable development was both labor-intensive and capital-intensive. Rather than attempt even limited development of this "waste" land—an expensive, difficult, and time-consuming process—some slaveholders found that hiring out their slaves provided a much more profitable and less demanding enterprise.

In the process of establishing their owners' farm homesteads, pioneer slaves developed many highly marketable skills, and in wilderness farming communities, as in settled rural areas, their labor was not limited to cultivation and harvesting.[9] A pioneer slave such as Free Frank invariably developed a variety of farm-related skills which included animal husbandry, dairying, land improvement, the use, maintenance, and repair of farm tools and equipment, and building construction. The skills and services provided by a jack-of-all-trades slave were in demand throughout the year, as were those of skilled slave craftsmen. In the developing economy of the trans-Appalachian West, the services of the slave blacksmith, carpenter, wheelwright, cabinetmaker, and other craftsmen proved important from the beginning of settlement. Often labor constraints and economies of scale worked to the competitive exclusion of white workers, especially for the jack-of-all-trades. As Thomas Abernethy explains, "Social conditions were never favorable for them in the [region] where slavery existed."[10] For this reason, too, pioneer slaves also participated in early manufacturing activities. Even before Pulaski County became a settled community, several manufacturing works were set up along the south fork of the Cumberland River. Alma Owens Tibbals describes one owner who, "with the help of thirty slaves ran a carding machine, a grist mill, a tannery and a distillery."[11]

During his first years of settlement in Pulaski, George McWhorter, too, considered setting up a gristmill. On August 1, 1799, he petitioned the Pulaski County Court for "leave to errect a water grist mill on Cold Water Creek, he owning the land on both sides."[12] In February 1800, in another petition, he asked the county to allow him to build another water gristmill on Fishing Creek, where he had established his farm settlement. County records fail to show that he followed through on building either of the mills, however. Certainly his slaves provided an available work force, a labor base for him to undertake such an enterprise, since slaves could also work as millers. What is important to recognize is that even with slave labor on the frontier, as Robert Fogel and Stanley Engerman indicate, "Participation in a variety of activities was the rule rather than the exception."[13] Furthermore, the services and skills that pioneer slaves could provide were in demand throughout the year. Thomas D. Clark, while sometimes critical in his discussion of slavery in Kentucky's agricultural development in the late antebellum period, nevertheless notes that "So long as pioneer conditions prevailed, slavery was a valuable asset to Kentuckians."[14]

From the beginning of settlement, then, slave-hiring developed into a common and well-organized practice in Kentucky. Slaves were hired out either for special jobs on short-term contracts, or for the year on annual contracts. On the Pennyroyal, with its sparse population, slave hiring on short-term contracts was especially important, affording greater flexibility in the labor supply. Although Pulaski slaves averaged only 8 percent of the population between 1800 and 1810, the labor base was expanded when they were hired out on short-term contracts because of the rapid market turnover. Before 1810, with less than 20 percent of Pulaski's heads of household owning slaves, the county's slave owners, like those in the settled areas, were well aware of this additional source of income. In the early 1800s, with his Fishing Creek farm established and no longer requiring the full-time, year-round labor of his four slaves, George McWhorter moved to capitalize on the highly developed skills of his slave Free Frank. Before 1810 he hired Free Frank out as a farm laborer and jack-of-all-trades for other Pulaski County farmers.[15]

Admittedly, a brief review of the circumstances that sometimes prompted a frontier slaveholder to hire out his slaves does not shed light on a number of key interpretive issues in the slave-hiring process. But one factor was fundamental in sustaining the slave-hiring system, especially as it relates to Free Frank: the profit expectations of the three principals involved, the slaveholder, the slave hirer, and the slave. Slave hiring was profitable for the hirer. Slave labor could be bought at cheaper rates than free labor, and there were also social and psychological rewards. As Coleman indicates, "Many a small farmer, mechanic or country storekeeper, leading away his first hired slave, swelled with pride as he assumed that enviable position in society known as a slaveholder. He was now a member, even though in a small way, of that much respected and influential class who favored the institution."[16] As for the slave, he sometimes gained the advantage of greater mobility and less supervision than when working only for his owner. A hired slave was also in a position to earn money for himself beyond that paid the slaveowner. More important, slave hiring marked the initial stage in the process by which slaves could put themselves in a position to hire their own time and become wage earners—a first step toward buying their way out of slavery.[17]

While the practice of slave hiring was encouraged and sanctioned under the law, paradoxically slaveholders who allowed their slaves to hire out their own time stood in violation of the law. In the early period of statehood Kentucky sought to repress this practice, and the 1798 Slave Code provided that slaves who hired their own time were to be sold "forthwith." The law was changed four years later, when in 1802 only a £10 fine was to be levied on both the hirer and the owner.[18] As one might expect, on the frontier generally, and in Pulaski County particularly, the law was easily circumvented. "The practice was grounded on fundamental economic necessity," notes a specialist in southern agricultural history. This was true not only because a diversified labor force was needed to develop a frontier society into settled communities, but also because the slaveholder's own economic interest sometimes required that his slaves hire out their own time.[19] Hired slaves provided their owners with financial returns of from $.50 to $1.50 per day, or from $80 to $100 if hired out by the year. But a slave who hired his own time paid his owner from $10 to $12 or more per month. When weighing long-term cost benefits and capital gains, some slaveholders consequently found it more profitable to allow their slaves to hire their own time. George McWhorter was among them, for before 1810 Free Frank, "after working for his master for a number of years, . . . hired his time agreeing to pay a certain amount per annum."[20]

It is not clear exactly what McWhorter's economic interests were at this time. He had established a productive, well-running farm, had attempted to set up a gristmill, and had expanded his landholdings, yet by 1810 he left his Fishing Creek homestead and moved to Wayne County, directly south of Pulaski. Within five years he moved again, this time to Lincoln County, Tennessee, directly north of the Alabama border.[21] It was a common practice for frontiersmen to move several times before they died or established permanent homesteads. Slaveowners who had greater stakes in their holdings, as well as greater chance for the successful development of their land, moved less frequently, and when they did move they usually sold their holdings and took their slaves with them. Free Frank's owner did neither. Instead, he left the slave in Pulaski County to work his Fishing Creek farm. During his absence, McWhorter would continue not only to earn full profits from his farm, but also to draw the annual payment from Free Frank for the privilege of hiring his own time.

When he left Pulaski County, George McWhorter was fairly secure in thinking that Free Frank would remain in the county. Strong family attachments among slaves were most effective in restricting their mobility, as Coleman emphasizes. "So long as a black family remained together . . . the love of its members for one another operated as the strongest bond to prevent their unceremoniously leaving." But slaveholders also recognized that "upon the breaking up or separation of families, with no prospect of reunion, the firmest and often sole tie which held them together was severed.

There was then little left to hold them back."[22] When McWhorter left Free Frank in Pulaski County, there is little reason to believe that his intention was to preserve the integrity of Free Frank's family, but he must have realized that if he took his slave with him he faced the risk of losing not only his valuable slave but also the slave's future labor value, since there was every possibility that Free Frank would attempt to rejoin his family.

By 1810 it was apparently clear to George McWhorter that Free Frank was motivated by one paramount goal—to buy his family's freedom. But remaining with his family without at the same time being allowed to earn money would have provided little economic advantage for Free Frank, so from 1800 on he was doubtless as systematic in developing strategies that would enable him to become a wage earner as McWhorter was in calculating how he could most profitably exploit the labor of his slaves. Even before his owner hired him out in the early 1800s, Free Frank's strategy required that he convince McWhorter that his eagerness, industry, and reliability made him indispensable; these were the qualities slaveholders considered important when taking into account the various ways they could capitalize on their slaves' labor or skills.[23]

Hired-out slaves had to be resourceful, too, but initially it could be disastrous for a slave to show either abilities or ambitions beyond those that furthered the slaveholder's interests. Frederick Douglass, once a hired slave who "bought" his freedom by taking to the road, said, "Ignorance is a high virtue in a human chattel; and as the master studies to keep the slave ignorant, the slave is cunning enough to make the master think he succeeds."[24] It is not difficult to imagine that before 1810 Free Frank masked his determination to succeed as a wage earner. He had to be hired out first. But once this was achieved, he used those very qualities of industriousness and resourcefulness to convince his owner that he would realize more income by allowing his slave to hire his own time.

For George McWhorter, leaving Free Frank to hire out his own time while also working the farm was a rational, even a shrewd, economic decision. By 1810 the conditions of settlement in Pulaski County appeared to offer little opportunity for Free Frank to earn his way out of slavery. The county was attracting few new settlers now, and the competitive demands for hired slave labor were virtually nil. As Berlin found, "In the countryside, where there were few opportunities to hire out, the most skilled slaves had little chance of earning the money necessary to buy their way out of bondage even if their owner had granted permission to try."[25]

Nevertheless, the services of a slave jack-of-all-trades were always needed in a frontier community. Free Frank could be assured of some demand for his services, although he could not expect to earn much more than an unskilled slave, and after paying his owner the annual sum he would have little if any left to save for his freedom. Fogel and Engerman note that "some skilled slaves were able to accumulate enough capital to purchase their own freedom within a decade, for others, the period extended two decades or more."[26] Free Frank knew this, and George McWhorter knew this. As an extra incentive, when the slaveholder left he promised the slave his freedom. Yet for Free Frank, promises of freedom were not good enough. There was little assurance that they would ever be fulfilled.

Free Frank's situation must have placed an almost impossible burden on him. Running his owner's farm required enormous expenditures of time, energy, and labor. As Tibbals indicates, tobacco, corn, and wheat, rather than cotton, became the leading agricultural products in Pulaski County. Productive farm labor in the South required intensive work for nine to ten months, as compared to four to six months in the mixed-grain areas of the North. In both sections, however, farm maintenance work was required throughout the year. In the South, depending on the season, farm workers averaged ten to sixteen hours a day.[27] In addition to working his owner's farm, Free Frank had to develop some profitable enterprise to meet the annual payments required by his owner and still have enough left over to buy his family's freedom.

That he eventually succeeded leads one to consider that Free Frank's motivation and energy after 1810 were derived not only from the satisfaction of being able to remain near his family and earn money for their freedom, but also from being now directly involved in an activity that judiciously weakened the social and economic fabric of the slave system. Frederick Bancroft, in his perceptive assessment of the realities of slave labor, points out the profound implications of the practice of allowing slaves to hire their own time, by which the slave "might choose his hirer, save his master all expenses, and be, in this respect, a free agent."[28] The survival of slavery rested on absolute control over the slave and his labor. Yet in frontier areas the diversification of labor needed for the development of an established community required the participation of slaves in the commercial life of the community.

For Free Frank's purposes, George McWhorter could not have left at a more opportune time. There was every likelihood that the United States would soon be at war, and the demand for saltpeter, the principal ingredient in gunpowder, would soon reach monumental proportions. Kentucky was the nation's leading producer of saltpeter. The Mammoth Cave in western Kentucky and the "Big Cave" in Rockcastle, the county directly east of Pulaski, were principal centers of saltpeter production in the state. Blacks, slave and free, were employed in both saltpeter caves. Collins, writing in

1848, commented on the extensive saltpeter production carried out at the "Big Cave," noting that "the saltpeter manufactured here, before and during the late war [of 1812], gave employment to some sixty or seventy laborers." Collins also noted that "among the hills of Rockcastle there . . . [were other] numerous salt petre caves, at which large quantities of saltpetre were manufactured during the late war." [29]

Crude niter, the principal natural resource used in making saltpeter, was also available in large quantities in the numerous caves in central and western Pulaski, especially in the area around Fishing Creek where George McWhorter's farm was located. [30] The availability of this natural resource obviously suggested to Free Frank the possibility of setting up a saltpeter works as a way of making money. Certainly the demand was there. In 1810 there were 63 gunpowder mills producing 115,716 pounds of gunpowder and 210,937 pounds of saltpeter, and during the War of 1812 both the production of saltpeter and its price increased. [31] Only ten years earlier, in 1802, Michaux had reported that "saltpeter of the first evaporation is sold for the eighth of a dollar per pound." [32] By 1810 the price had increased to $.17 a pound, but beginning in 1812 a precipitous price increase found saltpeter selling for the almost phenomenal amount of $.75 to $1.00 a pound. [33] The market was wide open, although war inflation was probably reflected in the price increase. As Horace Hovey noted, "The nitre fever of 1812 rivaled the subsequent gold fever of 1849." [34] R.W. Bird recalled that "profits [during the war] were so great as to set half the Western world gadding after nitre caves. Cave hunting, in fact, became a kind of mania." [35]

With the highly productive Rockcastle saltpeter caves only a short distance away, the numerous limestone caves of Pulaski County also became a major area for saltpeter exploration. But apparently overhead production costs for setting up a saltpeter works in Pulaski far outweighed the kinds of profits anticipated by potential investors. Published sources provide no instances of saltpeter works in the county other than the one set up by Free Frank. For a pioneer slave, Free Frank's activities as a businessman proved extremely profitable. Within nine years after hiring his own time, he earned $1,600 in addition to the annual fees paid his owner. [36]

Free Frank's profit expectations were not as great, to be sure, as those of the owners of large and extensive saltpeter manufactories, although he did have an initial investment advantage over the professional cave hunters. By 1812 he had lived in Pulaski County for almost fifteen years and was in a better position to identify the limestone caves which offered the best prospects for successful mining of saltpeter. The existence of crude niter was easy to determine, as an 1806 report on saltpeter mining indicated. "Proof of the presence of nitre [is seen] when the impression made on the dust by the

hand or foot is in a very short time effaced. Where the nitre is very abun-
dant, the impression made today will be scarcely visible tomorrow." It was
also easy to ascertain the grade of the crude niter by trusting to taste: "high
grade saltpeter earth has a slightly bitter taste."[37] Also, if the dirt is sprin-
kled on a fire, it will ignite and sparkle. Given the rudimentary mining tech-
niques of the time, once Free Frank had ascertained the grade of crude niter
in one of the nearby limestone caves, he could begin to produce saltpeter.
The activity was to consume at least seven years of his life as a pioneer slave.

A shovel for digging and a mattock to break up the dirt were the basic
tools used in saltpeter mining. The saltpeter dirt was dredged out of the
earth to a depth of no more than two or three feet. In the larger works the
saltpeter was manufactured right in the caves. Collins described the "Big
Cave" saltpeter works in Rockcastle County: "There is a fine bold running
stream of water in the cave and works were constructed inside for the manufacture of saltpeter by torchlight."[38] Oxcarts were used to bring up dirt from
the interior of the caves, or the miners carried it out in sacks. Hovey details a
three-stage process used in Mammoth Cave: first the saltpeter dirt, crude
nitre, was leached in vats within the cave; then the solution was piped out to
open-air boilers; finally the concentrated solution was run through hoppers
filled with wood ashes and boiled a second time. Crystals of potassium ni-
trate—saltpeter—were the end product.[39]

Free Frank's saltpeter manufactory was not as extensive nor as sophisti-
cated as these larger ones. Yet in the basic equipment and the production
process, his operations differed little because of the limited technology available at the time. The production of saltpeter was so simple that even while a
slave, Free Frank could acquire the necessary equipment for processing it on
a small scale. These items were commonly available in frontier households in
the early nineteenth century. There is sufficient evidence to show that Free
Frank's saltpeter works, as it expanded in the 1820s, included "two still[s],
. . . 24 still Tubbs, Two Stake stands, two singling and one doubling
kegs."[40] The steel tubs served as vats to boil the saltpeter water, the still
served as an open air boiler to provide the percolating effect necessary for the
leaching process which activated the crystallization of the crude niter, and
the residue was saltpeter.

Free Frank's initial investment costs, then, were minimal—ingenuity,
energy, industriousness, resourcefulness, and a formidable business acumen. He was able to set up a saltpeter works also because he had not been
encumbered with any stipulations that limited his activities while hiring out
his own time. That farm work was generally done during the day allowed
him to work at his saltpeter enterprise at night. In the absence of a patrol
that could control his movements, and doubtless with few whites objecting

if, after a day's labor in the fields, Free Frank chose to take a torch to go digging about in caves and boiling crude niter, the slave perhaps encountered only limited opposition to the enterprise. In his discussion of the work patterns of blacks, Berlin makes the point that blacks, both slave and free, were able to work in certain occupations because they were stigmatized as "nigger work." He emphasizes too that "Southern society identified labor with blacks, and whites disdained jobs at which blacks worked. The more closely blacks were connected with a trade, the greater the scorn of whites."[41] Saltpeter manufacturing was classified under mining, which was one of the major nonagricultural occupations in which blacks worked in the slave South. So as Free Frank began to manufacture saltpeter, he could expect little resistance from whites. In fact, by purchasing his saltpeter, whites indirectly encouraged his economic activities.

The military activities of a nation at war encouraged the production of saltpeter, and the conditions of frontier life made this commodity a necessity for the early pioneers, as well. Saltpeter, salt, and lead were the only three items in daily use on the frontier that could not be produced on the self-sufficient pioneer farm. More important, the limited economy of the Pennyroyal communities did not preclude Free Frank's getting cash from the sale of his saltpeter. As Allan Bogue indicates, "Capital flowed into the frontier community in a variety of ways—as savings brought by newcomers, in the form of loans made by residents of older states, in the shape of goods sold to the frontier merchants on credit," and in other ways.[42] Rolla Tryon emphasizes that the huckster or peddler system was also common on the frontier.[43] Thus, even if cash sales were not always possible, Free Frank could trade or barter his saltpeter for other commodities, which could subsequently be sold.

Sulphur from Philadelphia was sold in frontier areas and would be a commodity of particular interest to Free Frank: when combined with charcoal and saltpeter, the finished product was gunpowder. That slaves and free blacks in frontier areas were allowed to own both rifles and powder suggests that the Pulaski community may not have been averse to a slave making gunpowder. And the military activities in Kentucky at this time would have been an added encouragement. On the market, consumers, more concerned with prices than with producers, rarely complained when slaves sold goods and other commodities, especially when those items could be bought at cost. The prospects of producing not only for wholesale and retail markets but even for an illegal black market, would not be overlooked by this enterprising slave. The family's oral history provides no specific evidence that Free Frank produced gunpowder, but considering his shrewdness, versatility, resourcefulness, and especially the motivation for his enterprise, this probability cannot be discounted.

The organized system of trade that existed in Pulaski County during this period was another important factor which encouraged Free Frank's production of saltpeter. The transportation network developed in the county in the early 1800s provided him access to the New Orleans market via the Cumberland River, which formed Pulaski's southern border and which flowed into the Mississippi. Goods were also hauled by mule-drawn freight wagons, ox carts, and horse-drawn wagons to Louisville, thence shipped down the Ohio and Mississippi rivers to New Orleans.[44] During the War of 1812, however, Lexington, eighty miles north, with its six gunpowder mills, was where saltpeter from the "Big Cave" in Rockcastle was shipped, while the Mammoth Cave's saltpeter was transported to the DuPont gunpowder mills in Wilmington, Delaware.[45]

Records show that a bushel of crude niter was sufficient to produce from three to five pounds of saltpeter, and that a bushel of high-grade niter could be made into almost ten pounds of saltpeter. In the Mammoth Cave, Hovey found that with a full work force of sixty to seventy laborers, over 500 pounds of saltpeter were produced each day. If Free Frank produced only four pounds of saltpeter each day and sold it for $.35 to $.50 per pound (half the market price), his earnings could amount to as much as two dollars a day. Running his saltpeter works seven days a week would thus offer him the possibility of making as much as $728 a year. Even earning less than half that amount, the slave could still pay his owner the stipulated price of ten or twelve dollars a month for hiring out his own time and have as much or more in reserve to add to his savings. It appears, too, that in addition to his manufacturing skills, Free Frank had a genius for marketing, for the record shows that he was able to sell his saltpeter "for good prices."

The war ended in 1815, but the impact on saltpeter production for military purposes would not be felt until the following year. Free Frank intensified his saltpeter production efforts after 1815, however. His owner died that year without making any provisions for Free Frank's manumission. While manumission was not encouraged, Kentucky imposed no legal encumbrance that either restricted or prevented a slaveowner from freeing his slaves. The law of manumission was quite clear, stipulating only that "It shall be lawful for any person by his last will and testament, or by any other instrument in writing under his or her hand and seal to emancipate or set free his or her slave or slaves."[46]

George McWhorter had intended to emancipate Free Frank, as his heirs, two sons and two sons-in-law, subsequently admitted, "it being to our knowledge the will and desire of our late father and father-in-law to liberate from slavery a certain Negro man named Frank."[47] Yet under Kentucky law, on the death of an intestate owner, slaves were deemed real estate and, under the laws of descent, could not be emancipated by oral wills.[48] So George McWhorter's "will and desire to liberate" Free Frank could not legally become a reality simply because for some reason he had failed to provide for it in writing. Certainly it could not be said that it was due to any failing on Free Frank's part, for it was later recalled in Pulaski County that "Frank was formerly a slave of George McWhorter and served him faithfully as such."

Instead, notwithstanding their father's wish, the heirs qualified Free Frank's manumission, indicating that they would "set at liberty and give freedom to a Negro slave named Frank, in the state of Kentucky late the property of George McWhorter Dec' if said Negro gave said Abner McWhorter the sum of five hundred Dollars as the price of his freedom."[49] At the same time, because they lived in Tennessee and did not want to sell McWhorter's prosperous farm, which Free Frank had maintained so efficiently and profitably for the past five years, the heirs made another qualification on his manumission. Free Frank was also "to do all things concerning the premises in as if we were personally present at the doing of." Thus, with his owner's death, it would appear that Free Frank was no closer to freedom than he was in 1810 when George McWhorter left the county, promising to manumit him.

Recognizing that Free Frank might be somewhat reluctant to accept their offer, and in order to show their good intentions, the heirs recorded and filed the document in the Pulaski County Court. The significance of the document's being recorded offers unusual insight not only into the dynamics of the master-slave relationship, but also into the extent of the state's interest in the institution of slavery. A slave was legally incapacitated from making contractual agreements. Yet the offer made by the new owners constituted a contractual agreement which surprisingly found protection under cover of law. The slave was thus afforded a degree of assurance that the state would protect his interest, since under the law "an agreement to emancipate [was] specifically enforced in equity; whereas a promise or declaration of emancipation made to a slave, or for his benefit cannot be enforced in a court of law or equity."[50] At the same time, this law indirectly expanded the state's control over the slave, an obvious infringement of the property rights of the slave owner.

Yet in 1815, when McWhorter's heirs filed their "agreement to emancipate," they had every reason to believe that in their slave Free Frank they had a "blue chip" investment that would pay dividends for years to come. They were aware of his saltpeter manufacturing activities, but to their knowledge Free Frank had not yet earned the $500 to purchase his freedom. They were also aware of the length of time it generally took a slave to buy his freedom. From the slaveholders' perspective, then, Free Frank would be around to manage their farm for another five to fifteen years before he earned the $500 they had demanded as the cost of freedom.

In retrospect, Free Frank could have had no way of knowing in 1810, when George McWhorter left Pulaski County, promising to manumit him, that the law made a distinction between a slaveholder's "promise" to emancipate and an "agreement" between a slave and his owner that tendered emancipation upon the slave's fulfillment of certain conditions. It was a harsh lesson. Yet, given any realistic consideration, in their expectations for their own survival slaves could never really depend on the owners, and rarely did they place any great reliance on their promises. While Free Frank's new owners might consider the agreement a crushing defeat for their slave, for Free Frank it was only a continued challenge in his fight to be free. The heirs apparently had failed to consider his resiliency and determination, and particularly his shrewdness. From the beginning, Free Frank had never really given them or George McWhorter any indication of the amount of money he was making or, even more important, that he intended to buy his wife Lucy's freedom before his own.

The recorded oral history of the Free Frank family has it that after 1815, while still a slave, Free Frank "soon became the owner of a small farm."[51] While he was not in fact the owner, he did have full responsibility to work the farm in the absence of the owners, and had to make all of the decisions inherent in farm management, so that his activities went beyond the usual responsibilities of slaves in rural communities. But, as Fogel and Engerman show, "with the exception of entrepreneurial decisions regarding the allocation of resources among alternative uses and the marketing of crops, slaves engaged in the full range of agricultural duties."[52] Free Frank had to make just such entrepreneurial decisions in managing the slaveholders' farm. Profits had to be earned or he risked the chance of not being allowed to continue with his own economic activities.

Little information seems to exist respecting Free Frank's farm activities during this period, which suggests that they were similar to those of other Pulaski County farmers. Since whiskey distilling was one of the common home manufacturing activities on the frontier, the likelihood that Free Frank was not only involved in this activity but that he also surreptitiously marketed this product for his own profit cannot be discounted. Thomas D. Clark shows that Kentucky's soils "were conducive to the manufacture of fine liquor in two ways: first, the soil produced good yields of high grade cereals; and, second, the water used in distilling came from a limestone source." Free Frank had access to the land to produce the grain crops, and limestone water was available from the county's many caves and springs.

Many early settlers who moved west already knew the secret of successful distilling, and "most families had their own stills, and when their fields yielded more grain than could be disposed of profitably, they converted it into whiskey which could be shipped from the state in jugs and barrels."[53]

Making salt was another profitable enterprise that offered Free Frank a way to make money during his owners' absence. Brine was found in abundance on Fishing Creek, and the site of the first commercial salt manufactory in Pulaski County, established in 1849, was on Fishing Creek.[54] Before its establishment, as Tibbals indicates, "men rode horseback or in crude wagons to Middlesboro, a distance of seventy-five miles, and brought back enough to last a community for weeks or perhaps months."[55] By 1815, however, the need for salt was so great that the state passed a law encouraging its manufacture.[56] As a slave, Free Frank could not benefit directly from this legislation, but passage of the law indicates the existence of a market for this commodity, and in Pulaski County as Ramey notes, "the price of it was high and the necessity of it very great."[57] Michaux found that the early settlers felt "it was necessary to give salt to the cattle," otherwise "whatever food is given them, they will not fatten."[58] The settlers also used salt as a preservative for their own meat supply and for meat that was shipped out for sale on the eastern market. Early salt-making on a small-scale was a fairly easy process.[59] For a man of Free Frank's considerable versatility and resourcefulness, the probability is great that he included salt-making in his business activities.

Free Frank's economic activities, both before and after 1815, were clearly profitable. In 1817, within two years of George McWhorter's death, Free Frank purchased his wife Lucy's freedom: "He bought his wife first so all children born after would be free."[60] Lucy was then forty-six years old. Free Frank paid $800 for her freedom, a substantial sum at that time.[61] It had taken him seven years of hiring out his own time to accumulate that amount of money. His efforts did not go unnoticed, for it was recalled by several Pulaski county men in 1830 that "Frank by his industry purchased his wife Lucy . . . for which he paid a valuable consideration."[62]

The rapidity with which Free Frank did so was prompted by the birth of their thirteenth slave child, Solomon, in February 1815. Since Lucy was forty-four at that time, the likelihood of subsequent pregnancies seemed small, but in 1817 she was expecting again. Since she was purchased in April 1817, the child (Squire) born that September was free.[63] It is not known whether Lucy's owner knew that she was expecting at the time Free Frank purchased her freedom. If so, that could account for the "valuable consideration" of $800. Perhaps her owner, William Denham, required payment for two slaves rather than one. Free Frank willingly paid the sum rather than have another child born in slavery. Solomon was to remain a slave for twenty years before Free Frank could purchase him. Their first child, Juda, would remain a slave until she was almost fifty.[64]

Although Free Frank paid for Lucy's freedom, there is nothing in her manumission paper, recorded in the county courthouse, to indicate that she was purchased or, even more remarkably, that the purchaser was a slave. The document only states: "Know all men by these presents that I William Denham of the County of Pulaski and State of Kentucky, being desirous for Certain Reasons to liberate from a state of slavery my Negro woman Lucy, a yellow or mulatto woman. . . . Therefore I the said William Denham, do by these presents Emancipate and set free my said Negro woman Lucy from my services as a slave."[65]

The law concerning emancipation stated that the sale of slaves need not be recorded.[66] This was a private chattel property transaction between a buyer and a seller, even though in this instance the buyer was a slave who was legally incapacitated from making contracts and who, in addition, also had no legal recourse in the courts if the slave owner took the agreed-on sum and then refused to manumit the slave. In Kentucky, the law of emancipation simply did not provide for one slave to own another, nor did the law empower one slave to free another. Thus a slave, in making a bargain with a slave owner to purchase himself or another slave, had to rely on the good faith of an owner not to renege on the manumission once the purchase price was paid. Or a slave with some knowledge of the law could require the slave owner to file a document in the court that promised emancipation once the sum agreed on was paid, as Free Frank's owners did. The court itself had no right to manumit a slave. Under the law of manumission, "the only act for the court to perform, is to receive proof of the execution of the will or deed by which the manumission may be effected." The court's only other power regarding emancipation was that it could demand bond from the former slaveholder if it appeared that the newly emancipated slaves could not maintain themselves as freedmen. The emancipation law also required that the instrument by which a slave was manumitted had to be presented to the county court in writing.[67]

In 1817, Free Frank accomplished what was most important to him—the purchase of his wife. Lucy was now free, and the child born in that year was also free, marking the beginning of freedom for his family. With the purchase of Lucy's freedom, moreover, the Free Frank family could expand its economic activities. Lucy was now in a position to participate in any business transaction that Free Frank might find difficult to consummate because of his status as a slave. Even more, now that she was established in her own home on the farm that Free Frank worked, she could use her time to engage in household manufacturing. The family's oral history emphasizes that Lucy

Fig. 1. Lucy McWorter (1771-1870), wife of Free Frank. Painted by George Neal from a daguerreotype taken about 1870. Courtesy of Thelma McWorter Kirkpatrick Wheaton. No photograph of Free Frank has survived.

"did her full share to assist her husband in all his undertakings."[68] She was described by the family as a woman of extraordinary courage who also possessed a shrewd intelligence and a gentle strength that was concealed by her soft voice and a deliberate outward restraint. Just as Free Frank had become a jack-of-all-trades by his slave labor on the frontier, so Lucy, in addition to her field work, had developed equal facility in household handicrafts as part of her pioneer slave labor. That she continued these activities once freed is not surprising—for the first time Lucy's work could benefit her own family, as she added her labor resources to those of her husband.

Spinning, weaving, and knitting were among the skills Lucy put to good use while she lived on the Pulaski County frontier, for as Tibbals explains, "Every family raised flax from which linens were made, and every farm had its patch of cotton which was carded and spun into cloth."[69] Candle- and soap-making were other household manufactures in which pioneer women such as Lucy were involved. These household goods, along with cloth, were among Kentucky's major exports during this period. Thus, as a free black woman, Lucy was in a position to help Free Frank earn money to buy his freedom. Lucy's economic activities could also be extended beyond home handicrafts, for in rural areas of the slave South, as Berlin explains, it was not unusual to find that free black women "generally worked as laundresses, housekeepers, and seamstresses, although doubtless they too spent considerable time in the fields."[70]

Saltpeter continued to be an important commodity after the War of 1812. Even in 1818, the year before Free Frank purchased his own freedom, it ranked ninth among Kentucky's major exports. From the beginning Free Frank profited from the steady demand for saltpeter and continued selling it for good prices, and as the *Pike County Atlas* notes: "In that way, by hard work and strict economy for a number of years, he [Free Frank] had saved money enough, after paying his master for hire, to purchase his freedom."[71] Remarkably, Free Frank purchased his own freedom only two years after he purchased Lucy's. Four years had elapsed from the time of the original agreement, however, and the owners, perhaps not surprisingly, now demanded that Free Frank pay $800 instead of the $500 initially stipulated. No cost-of-living increase had been stipulated in the original agreement, and while 1819 found Kentucky in a state of depression, even an inflated economy or a general rise in the slave index price listings, as Engerman suggests,[72] cannot explain the owners' demand for an additional $300.

That the owners even allowed Free Frank to hire out his own time and earn money to buy his freedom might be regarded by some as an example of benevolence, paternalism, and humanitarianism. Studies of American slavery, however, reveal that the underlying structure of the institution was more readily apparent during times of personal and historical crisis. Free Frank's attempt to purchase his freedom provides an illuminating instance in which his owners, with apparent benevolence, offered their slave a chance for freedom, yet at the same time, made every effort to undermine his chance for success. Free Frank's self-purchase is therefore important for analysis. The evidence establishes unequivocally that his manumission was strictly an economic arrangement. The owners definitely profited from his labor and enterprise. That Free Frank manipulated the conditions of his servitude so that he too profited from his labor cannot be dismissed, rationalized, or explained as resulting from paternalism. Free Frank provides an example of a slave who shrewdly capitalized on the slaveowners' miscalculated allocation of their labor force. Neither can his manumission be explained as the result of "particularly fortunate factors, such as perhaps the particular interests of certain members of the families who had been his owners and so on," as August Meier suggests. Yet Meier agrees that Free Frank's personality and abilities were important to his success: "A key factor in Free Frank's career was the kind of personality he had. I simply don't think that an exceptional man like this can be explained in any other way."[73]

In the beginning, Free Frank carried out his strategies with a shrewd cautiousness, but by 1815 the precariousness of his manumission and the future of his family required him to be extremely calculating and bold if he would be free. Doubtless in the period from 1815 to 1819 he showed a certain unrestrained ruthlessness. After George McWhorter's death, it would appear that Free Frank took a calculated risk when he agreed to the conditions of his freedom. He could not rely on the owners to live up to their part of the agreement, nor could he depend on the protection that the law promised slaves when they made agreements with their masters. Nevertheless, even if it was the slaveholders' intent from the beginning to renege on the agreement, in retrospect, it was at this point that they lost the last element of control over their slave. Had the owners sold both Free Frank and the farm, or sold the farm and taken Free Frank back to Tennessee with them, they might have defeated him. Four years later time was no longer on the owners' side.

There is every reason to believe that Free Frank could have purchased his own freedom for $500 in 1817, since he bought Lucy's freedom first, and for $800. Perhaps it was for this reason that his owners felt that their slave should pay the same amount for his own freedom. In 1819 Free Frank was still a strong and vigorous man, and his potential productivity did not escape the owners. Had they refused the $800 at that time, he could have used the money to buy some of his slave-born children. Had the owners demanded that he continue to run their farm while allowing him to continue his other economic activities, any future money earned could be used to buy his other slave-born children until all were free. Lucy could then move north, and there was every reason for the owners to believe that nothing short of death would stop Free Frank from following his family.

It would be a mistake to assume that Free Frank's owners were unaware that their slave had outmaneuvered them. When he put up the $800, the owners must have known that he had presented them with his final ultimatum. Had they refused his offer, they probably could not have made $800 by selling the supposedly unskilled slave on the slave market. Even Free Frank's death would have offered little capital satisfaction. And as an uncooperative slave, his labor value to the owners would have been virtually nil. Of their alternatives, then, accepting the money was the most rational economic decision. The gain of $800 apparently far outweighed any psychological satisfaction they would have gotten by refusing the money and keeping Free Frank as a slave.

So the owners took the $800 and manumitted the slave on September 15, 1819. As with Lucy, however, his emancipation paper did not state that he had purchased his own freedom. Free Frank's owners noted only that they "Do by these present Emancipate set free the said Negro man Frank from our service as a slave and from the service of all and every person or persons whatever (it being also the wish and desire of our father as above named) as a slave aforesaid to do and act for himself as a person hereby Freed agreeably to the laws of the Commonwealth of Kentucky or the laws of any other state."[74] It was, of course, recognized in Pulaski County by those who knew him that "Frank was formerly a slave of George McWhorter and served him faithfully as such until he purchased his Freedom from his master."[75] That Free Frank had earned $1,600 in less than ten years was no mean accomplishment, for, with only three manumissions in Pulaski County before 1820, it appears that slaveholders there were not inclined to free their slaves.[76] In a relatively poor frontier community in the trans-Appalachian West, especially on the Pennyroyal, conditions were such that few pioneer slaves could become wage earners of any significance.

It is also important to recognize that Free Frank's commercial activities, first as a slave who hired his own time and then as a tradesman who marketed goods, were by law considered illegal. The state had no objections to hired slaves who provided goods and services under the direction of their owners, but marketing and trading by slaves who hired their own time were statutorily defined as criminal activities, surreptitiously carried out under the guise of legitimate business activities. The statute proscribing trading and business activities by slaves was quite specific on this issue, even indicting the slaveholder who allowed his slave to hire out his own time. It stated that "In consideration of stipulated wages to be paid by such slaves, [to] license them to go at large and trade as free man . . . [which] is found to be a great encouragement to the commission of thefts and other such practices by such slaves. . . . the master or owner shall forfeit and pay the sum of ten pounds current money." [77]

Black market activities by slaves who hired their own time indeed existed, yet it seems obvious that the intent of the lawmakers was not simply to suppress those activities. The state legislators found it intolerable that slaves should be allowed, much less encouraged, to exist in a condition of quasi-freedom and, more important, to be successful in the process. Yet few attempts were made to suppress the economic activities of those few slaves who hired their own time and who acted as tradesmen, especially during the frontier period. Doubtless the state found it inimical to its interest to force compliance with a law that was disadvantageous to its development. The goods and services provided by those slaves were a necessary and integral part of the state's economy. In this instance, Free Frank's production of saltpeter during the War of 1812 contributed to the war effort, if only indirectly, as well as to the development of Kentucky.

While Free Frank, as he stood in relation to his owners, was only a slave who hired his own time, and while his business enterprises were statutorily defined as illegal, in the development of his saltpeter manufactory he was an entrepreneur, and a skillful one. Entrepreneurship is "the ability to make unusual amounts of money using commonly available resources." [78] Free Frank recognized the market potential of saltpeter in a frontier community and moved to produce and supply this commodity from crude nitre, a natural resource found in the area where he lived. In the process of arranging for its production and distribution, for all practical purposes he acted as an independent businessman. The pattern of his commercial transactions differed little from that of his free counterparts—advertising services, negotiating contracts, receiving payments, assuming debts, and setting up places of business. [79] His ingenuity in exploiting the wilderness environment to his own economic advantage was vital to his success. So too was the fact that he involved himself in an activity in which few whites were engaged. Most important, however, were his indomitable will, unconquerable determination, resourcefulness, and shrewd business ability, which would have gone unrealized had he not hired out his own time. Free Frank's enviable record as a businessman was recognized in Pulaski County. In 1830, some thirty Pulaski whites who said they had known Free Frank "for many years some of us upwards of twenty years" recalled that in his business enterprises he "has always been an honest industrious man punctual to his word in all his dealings." [80]

Free Frank's entrepreneurship was not just a response to the diversification of labor needed to develop the new country. Entrepreneurship also involves the accumulation of funds for future investment, and for a slave the most desirable investment was in his freedom. As Coleman emphasizes, "It was a courageous undertaking for a slave of comparatively little earning power to attempt the purchase, either of himself or some member of his family."[81] Slavery rested upon economic exploitation of the slave's involuntary labor. While for the owners of slaves the institution may have been viewed as resting on mutual social obligations and a paternalistic accommodation, it lacked any meaningful reciprocal benefits for the slaves. Freedom was their ultimate goal, and its achievement found little encouragement from slaveholders. Rather than accept a paternalistic ethos fashioned by the slaveholder, slaves structured their own kind of freedom, their liberation expressed either in the distinctive character of the Afro-American community they developed or when possible, in the acquisition of money to buy their way out of slavery.[82]

Since 1800, Free Frank had seen the births and deaths of several of his slave-born children. As a slave father, the tragedy and despair of his family's life must have affected him in a way experienced by few fathers who were free and in a better position to provide for the survival of their children. Free Frank's prodigious efforts therefore had the sole purpose of buying his family from slavery. In 1817 he succeeded in buying his wife Lucy's freedom, and in 1819 his own—a goal accomplished through determined and systematic effort on the part of both. They had worked together, encouraged each other, and provided each other with the support necessary to sustain them as they labored to secure their freedom. The importance Free Frank attached to his freedom can be seen from the 1820 federal manuscript census. In it the former slave Frank, rather than choosing a surname, had his name listed for the first time as Free Frank.[83]

CHAPTER FOUR

Speculation in Freedom

I obediah Denham of the County of Pulaski have for and in consideration of two stills—the one got of John Denham and the other got in Danville by Free Frank. . . . bargained sold and delivered to said Free Frank . . . one mulatto boy named Frank who has runaway from me about three years and six months.[1]

After his manumission in 1819, Free Frank continued to live in Pulaski County. Many areas of the Pennyroyal remained undeveloped, and the services and commodities that pioneer blacks could provide still proved a necessary and even integral part of that region's developing economy. Throughout the 1820s Free Frank carefully expanded his business activities. Land speculation and the improvement of those holdings for sale to prospective farm settlers were added to his own commercial farming activities. His saltpeter manufactory, too, showed continued growth and became even more profitable. Perhaps it was his business success that prompted the litigation in which he and Lucy were involved from 1820 to 1827. It was common knowledge in Pulaski County that Free Frank had recently paid $1,600 for both his and Lucy's freedom. Obediah Denham, who initiated the suit against them, for $212, obviously considered the former slave solvent. Lucy's former owner, William Denham, had died intestate. His son Obediah, the appointed executor, was at that same time being sued by other heirs to the Denham family estate when he made his claim against this free black couple as a debt encumbered upon his father's estate. As the litigation proceeded, Denham's motive for the suit emerged as increasingly suspect, although when the case was initially heard it was quickly disposed of by the Pulaski County Court in Denham's favor.

When the case was first brought to the court, Lucy and Free Frank stood as co-defendants. As the case developed, two distinct issues emerged, which subsequently would be heard in the Kentucky Court of Appeals. The state's highest court made two separate determinations, the first in 1824, the second in 1827.[2] As the records show, what initially brought the case to the Pulaski County Court was "an action of debt brought by the administrator of William Denham deceased, upon a sealed writing executed by Free Frank and Lucy, stipulating for the payment of two hundred and twelve dollars to the intestate."[3] In their defense, Free Frank and Lucy proffered separate pleas. Lucy's defense was allowed first. This former slave woman held that "at the time of the supposed execution of the note in writing declared on by the plaintiff, she was, and is still married to Frank, a person of color and this she is ready to verify."[4] Lucy based her defense on the rule of law of *femme couverture,* whereby all contracts with married women had to be made by their husbands or they were invalid and not binding upon the wives to fulfill.[5] Free Frank's defense was that even though he was her husband he was not liable: he was a slave at the time the contract was made, and slaves, being legally incapacitated, could not make contracts.[6]

William Denham had died in December 1819. Since Lucy did not plead that she was a slave at the time the alleged debt was made, probably the note was executed sometime during the period between April 1817, when Lucy was manumitted, and September 1819, when Free Frank received his freedom.[7] The Pulaski County Court refused to allow Free Frank's defense to be entered in the record, although there was enough evidence on hand to show that Free Frank had been a slave who hired out his own time to William Denham during that two-year period. The $212, then, must have been the payment Free Frank received for the services he provided Denham, not a debt for an unsecured loan.[8] After quashing Free Frank's defense and disallowing the available evidence, the court quickly overruled Lucy's plea. Strengthening her defense, Lucy proffered what the higher court would subsequently rule as a "demurrer in pleading," which meant that she admitted that the facts of the case were true, but again emphasized that as a married woman she was not liable for the repayment of the debt. When the Pulaski Court considered the issue of the legality of her marriage, it ruled in favor of Denham. His argument was that "the defendants are free persons of color, and therefore, not authorized to unite in bonds of wedlock; and this he is ready to verify."[9] With this decision, Lucy was ordered to repay the $212.

Refusing to accept the verdict of the lower court, Lucy and Free Frank appealed the decision. Because significant issues of Kentucky's civil, common, and organic laws were involved, the case was eventually heard by the Court of Appeals, which surprisingly ruled in Lucy's favor in a landmark decision in 1824 that allowed free blacks in Kentucky to marry. The court ruled that "Whilst in a state of slavery, we admit that persons of color are incapable of contracting marriage, for any legal purpose . . . but immediately upon being emancipated, the restraint which was imposed upon their will and actions, by their bondage, is removed and with that, their competency to contract marriage is restored . . . and whenever in fact contracted by persons able and willing to contract, the femme becomes subject to the disabilities of couverture though in form [the marriage ceremony] the requisitings of the act of this country may not have been pursued."[10] The case was remanded to the lower court because the Court of Appeals also ruled that the

Pulaski County Court had "erred in overruling the demurrer of Lucy, and the judgment must, consequently be reversed with cost."[11] The Pulaski court refused to comply with the ruling, and as the record shows, the case was "continued for several terms."

Free Frank and Lucy were not represented by counsel when the case first went before the Kentucky Court of Appeals, but to force the Pulaski County Court to comply with the 1824 decision, they secured an attorney. Even then they encountered difficulties before the Pulaski Court would hear their case, but the record shows that "after several fruitless attempts on the part of Free Frank by his counsel to file additional pleas, the case came on to trial."[12] Still the lower court refused to find in favor of the two former slaves, and again the record shows that "verdict and judgment were recovered by the Administrator of Denham."[13] Free Frank and Lucy with their attorney appealed the decision, this time on the issue that Free Frank's defense had not been allowed on record in the lower court. The Kentucky Court of Appeals finally agreed to hear the case, and made their decision in January 1827. In this appeal, too, the higher court ruled in favor of Free Frank and Lucy, saying: "In our opinion, the court below should have allowed the plea offered by Frank, in which he alledges that he was a slave when the writing sued on, was delivered by him, to be filed."[14] The case also fell on procedural issues.

The legal decisions in the two cases had turned on the thinking of the court in regard to contractual obligations as expressed by the justices in the controversial 1823 Lapsley case.[15] The Lapsley decision had ruled a Kentucky statute unconstitutional for being in violation of the United States Constitution's provision which prohibited the states from passing any law impairing the obligations of contract. While there were several issues involving contractual obligations in the Lapsley case, the most important with regard to the Free Frank and Lucy cases was the point of law which stated that "whenever the laws of society will not uphold or enforce a contract, that contract possesses no civil obligation." Thus the court, in upholding Free Frank's plea that he had been a slave and therefore not capable of entering into contractual agreements, was in effect only reinforcing the status of a slave as it had evolved in American common law. The legal incapacity of the slave was restated in the 1827 Free Frank decision, which reaffirmed that slaves "possess no freedom of will or of action, and of course, by no contract, can they acquire any additional capacity."[16]

In upholding Lucy's plea under the rule of *femme couverture,* the court also proceeded from the presumption of the law involving civil contractual obligations for those "persons able and willing to contract" marriage. It is evident that with both legal issues in the Free Frank and Free Lucy cases, the court's rulings sustained its principal concern—to preserve the basis on which contractual obligations rested under the American legal system, rather than to assure equity for Free Frank and Lucy. For, as the court emphasized in the Free Frank case, "If there is one thing more than any other which public policy requires, it is that men of full age and competent understanding shall have the utmost liberty of contracting, and that contracts, when entered into freely and voluntarily, shall be held good and shall be enforced by courts of justice."[17] According to the facts stated in the case, William Denham had loaned money under a sealed agreement to a slave and his free wife. It was understood that slaves were legally incapacitated from making contracts. Denham's administrator thus lost the case against Free Frank, notwithstanding the procedural issues involved, because, although William Denham had been of full age and apparently of competent judgment, he had failed to comply with public policy.

Prior to the Free Lucy case in 1824, no precedent had been established that allowed freed blacks a legally constituted marriage. Obediah Denham lost his case against Lucy because the higher court ruled that with slaves, once emancipated, "the restraint which was imposed upon their will and action, by their bondage, is removed, and with that, their competency to contract marriage is restored." Free black married women were now subject to the law of *femme couverture,* a civil obligation on which the court would not infringe. Lucy's case provided the court with another instance whereby the legal inferiority of women could be reinforced. On the other hand, by this decision free blacks were given the legal right to marry in Kentucky, and the significance of this right cannot be underestimated. With the Free Lucy case in 1824, then, Kentucky for the first time gave legal recognition to the existence of the free black family unit, and as a consequence sanctioned the rights and obligations inherent in that union.

The decisions in the Free Frank and Free Lucy cases reflected not only the social order on which slavery rested but also the anomalous position of free blacks in a slave society. Yet neither Free Frank nor Lucy hesitated to use to their advantage those limited rights which the society allowed them as free blacks. While the slave state of Kentucky did allow free blacks their day in court, their judicial rights were nonetheless contingent on the preservation of the social order. Whereas the lower court was prepared to act contrary to both common and civil law, the higher court ruled against its decisions. The Kentucky Court of Appeals was aware that for the cases to be decided in favor of the white litigant would in both instances establish precedents which would impair the contractual obligations on which the whole social structure rested. And this the court would not do. Yet as A.E. Keir Nash found, southern high courts, unlike trial courts, encouraged "a measured insistence on the rule of law as against hysterical protection of the institution of slavery."[18]

Free Frank and Lucy showed great fortitude and courage in contesting

this action, especially under a judicial system in which their rights as free
blacks had really never been clearly defined. That they did so is typical, for
both Free Frank and Lucy were resolute, displaying indomitable nerve and
shrewdness in the face of Denham's claims. Lucy not only supported her
husband, but as a woman in her own right stood her ground. She would not
be intimidated, especially in any issue which denied her status as a married
woman simply because she was black, particularly if her status imposed an
additional burden on her husband.

Free Frank's and Lucy's fortitude was further tested by another event at
this time: their son, Young Frank, at the age of twenty-one, fled as a fugitive slave in December 1826, just before the Court of Appeals made its final
determination in January 1827.[19] It is not too much to suppose that Obediah
Denham, Young Frank's owner, may have threatened to sell the slave as a
means of intimidating his parents. If Denham could force their withdrawal
of the appeal, Free Frank and Lucy would have to comply with the lower
court's ruling and pay the $212. This assumption is of course highly inferen-
tial, but one cannot ignore the coincidence of events. Obviously the family
felt very strongly that Free Frank should not pay Obediah under any circumstances. The immediate consequence of Young Frank's escape was that Obediah was left without the threat he had thought would force Free Frank and
Lucy to withdraw their appeal. Young Frank's escape also made it clear to
Denham that the family would not pay, even if they lost the appeal. Yet
throughout the period of litigation Free Frank was purchasing land. That he
acquired property which could be attached suggests that the former slave
was not only determined in his defense, but also confident that he and Lucy
would win. Perhaps Denham knew it, too, and the threat to sell Young
Frank was made as much from vindictiveness as to force their withdrawal of
the appeal. For free blacks, property ownership not only provided the basis
for acquiring standing before the law and for expanding their economic opportunities, it also "provided them with an independence that translated
into a feisty self-confidence in face to face contact."[20]

Free Frank and Lucy did not have to pay the $212 once Kentucky's high-
est court upheld the appeal in 1827, but their defense in court had resulted
in the temporary separation of the family. Since 1799 Free Frank's whole
motivation had been to keep his family together while he worked to buy
their freedom. The litigation only reinforced his determination that his
slave-born children would be free. Doubtless it also increased his knowledge
of the American legal system. Both the 1820s cases and his experiences with
his former owners when they filed their "agreement to emancipate" document in the Pulaski County Court in 1815 surely impressed upon Free
Frank the powerful impact of the judicial process. A careful study of Free
Frank's land purchasing activities also reveals that the former slave realized

that as long as he was a party in a legally enforceable contract, the rights derived from that contract might be upheld in court, even in the case of a free black man.

From 1821 to 1829 Free Frank acquired land in Kentucky under two different state land-granting systems: the Kentucky Land Treasury Warrant System, initiated in 1815, and the Head Rights Claim System, begun in 1795. Under both systems the cost of the land purchased directly from the state was ten dollars per 100 acres.[21] In addition to that land acquired from the state, Free Frank purchased land from other Pulaski County settlers through private transactions. Pulaski County and Kentucky State Land Office records show that Free Frank acquired altogether 759 acres through ten separate land transactions. Table 3 lists Free Frank's land purchases between 1821 and 1829.[22] A detailed examination of those land records, specifically the graphic and written descriptions of the survey plats and deeds, however, shows that Free Frank shared interests in four of the ten transactions listed. As the table indicates, those joint interests were shared with Free Zibe, Ephraim Farris, James Harris, and Joseph Love.

Interestingly, in only one of these four transactions was Free Frank's name listed on the face of the land warrant—that with Harris and Love for 100 acres under Kentucky Land Office Warrants 16189 and 16190.[23] In the three other joint land transactions, however, only the names of the other patentees were listed on the face of the warrant, although each in turn wrote on the back of those warrants that Free Frank held an equal interest in the land. Two of the transactions were made with Ephraim Farris, who was white, as were Harris and Love.[24] Free Frank's other joint land purchase, and also his first, however, was made with Free Zibe, a former slave in Pulaski County.[25] Free Zibe, who had also purchased his own freedom, was manumitted in 1820.[26] Thus, of the 759 acres acquired through these transactions, Free Frank owned 309 acres as an individual patentee and was a joint owner of 450 acres.[27] If the acreage held in joint tenancy were divided between the patentees, Free Frank would thus own a total of 517 acres.

An examination of the Pulaski County Surveyor's Office Books and Real Estate Conveyances Books suggests the reason why Free Frank did not apply for these warrants himself—he could not write, and signed his name with an "X." While this was not uncommon with whites, the legality of a black man holding land under a warrant signed "X" would have concerned Free Frank. Moreover, the procedure required the signing of unfamiliar forms which he could not read. Each step in the land purchasing process was important if a claimant wanted to be sure he obtained a clear and unclouded title to the land.[28] At the State Land Office a claimant followed several steps before title to the land was secured. First, the purchase price was paid to the treasurer.

Table 3. Free Frank's Land Acquisitions in Kentucky, 1821-1829

Patentee(s)	No. of Acres	Kentucky Land Office Warrant No.	Date	Surveyor's Office Book and Page No.
Free Frank and Free Zibe	100	5805	May 30, 1821	1:524
Free Frank	50	8826	Oct. 19, 1822	1:336
Free Frank	50	8825	June 18, 1823	1:375
Free Frank	50	8825	June 18, 1823	1:449
Free Frank	59	436[1,2]	Jan. 9, 1826	1:551
Free Frank	50	5805[1]	Feb. 18, 1826	1:524
Free Frank and E. Farris	50	16466[1]	Jan. 20, 1827	1:552
Free Frank and E. Farris	200	16468[1] 16470[1]	Jan. 22, 1827	1:553
Free Frank	50	18166[1]	Nov. 2, 1829	2:64
Free Frank, J. Harris, and J. Love	100	16189[1] 16190[1]	Jan. 6, 1829	2:231

SOURCES: Compiled from the following records in the Pulaski County Courthouse, Somerset, Ky.: General Index to the Surveyor's Office Books; Surveyor's Office Books; Real Estate Conveyances Books; and General Index to Real Estate Conveyances: Grantors and Deed Record Books. Also compiled from Kentucky Secretary of State, Land Office, Frankfort.

1. Free Frank was marker and director of survey.
2. Pulaski County Court certificate for land obtained under the Head Right Claims System.

The receipt was then given to the auditor of public accounts, who provided a land certificate that stated the quantity of land to which the purchaser was entitled. The certificate once obtained had to be taken to the Land Office Register. The registrar issued a land warrant that specified the number of acres to be surveyed. He also provided the purchaser with a certificate that authorized the surveyor to survey the land. With the certificate, the land claimant then had to go to the county surveyor's office, where an application for the survey had to be made, and from this application the surveyor's office could authorize the survey. Once the survey was made, the surveyor would enter into his book the date the application for survey was made, the number of the warrant, the number of acres surveyed, and the name of the person or persons for whom the application was made.

In contrast, when Free Frank obtained land through private transactions, he did not have to follow this tedious procedure. Only a change in title was required. Most important, he could be assured that the title was

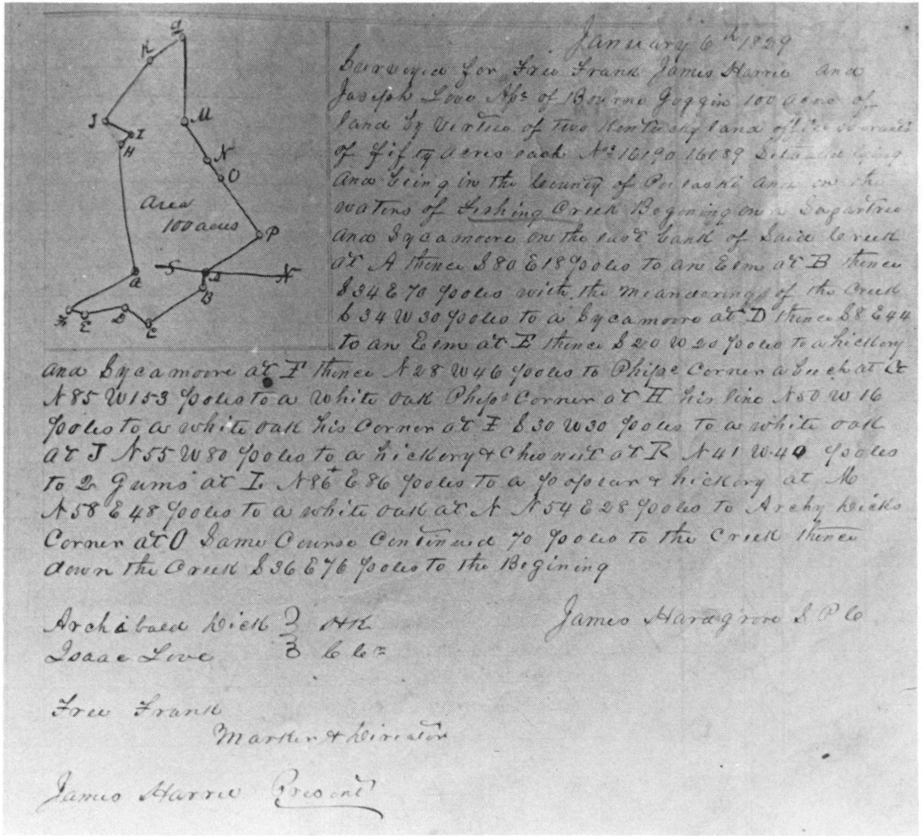

Fig. 2. Surveyor's plat of the Pulaski County land purchased by Free Frank on January 6, 1829. Free Frank was marker and director of the survey. From Pulaski County Surveyor's Office Book 2:231. Photo by Robert Kidd, Jr.

clear and unclouded, since the Kentucky Land Treasury Warrant Law of 1815 stated: "And for quieting litigation, *be it further enacted* that all entries heretofore made, and all titles founded upon surveys heretofore made, which, by the laws at the time being, were authorized to be made, shall be deemed superior to surveys made upon warrants obtained by this act."[29] Since the surveyor was required to record the names of the previous owners of the land on the survey patent, Free Frank's basic legal interest in the title was affirmed by a county official legally certified by the state to perform these duties, an official whom Free Frank knew personally. The surveyor's patent, rather than a land claim in which the primary legal right was derived from a certificate with an "X" signature, thus served to validate his land claims. A similar procedure was also in force when Free Frank claimed land under the Head Rights Claim System.[30]

That Free Frank knew the defense of his title would be more secure if the burden of proof rested on the surveyor's patent can be seen in a review of his land-surveying activities. Other than the land transaction in which he and Free Zibe were involved in 1821, Free Frank from 1822 on is listed as the initial patentee in the Surveyor's Office Books Index.[31] That meant that it was Free Frank who went to the surveyor's office to apply for the patent to have the survey made—application for the patent being the first step in establishing claim to the land. Free Frank was also an active participant in the land surveys. An examination of the survey plats and land deeds shows the former slave listed as the director and marker in six of his land surveys between 1826 and 1829. Again, a review of the land law reveals the significance of his participation in the survey, since the statute explicitly states: "The actual survey shall be considered the commencement of the title; and when perfected by grant, the title shall relate to the time of survey, so as to be available in courts of law against an elder grant found upon a younger survey."[32]

The director of the survey was not only the patentee who applied for the survey, but also the person who indicated which land was to be surveyed. The land surveying procedure under the Kentucky Land Treasury Warrant Act required that "every survey made under warrants obtained by virtue of this law, shall be bounded plainly by marked trees, stones, if to be had, or stakes, except where a water course or ancient marked line shall be the boundary."[33] The law also required that the survey "shall be made in the presence of two housekeepers resident in the county in which the survey may be made, and who are in no respect interested in such survey." The surveyor took notes of the survey, which were witnessed by the two disinterested parties. The surveyor was also required to list the "names of the housekeepers, . . . the chain carriers and marker."

The survey date was also the one used in court when there were disputes over who had first claim to a tract of land. On the frontier, conflicting land claims resulted in numerous legal suits, which explains Free Frank's reluctance to enter any land purchasing venture in which his land title might not be said to be free and unclouded. The legal deficiencies inherent in his status as a free black were an additional liability that might prevent him from successfully defending his land claims. Experience had demonstrated to him the necessity of being circumspect in all of his activities. Like slaves, free blacks were really never quite sure how the law would be applied to them. From the colonial period on, as Berlin notes, "Free Negroes who pressed their legal rights often found themselves confronted with subtle legal constructions or new laws proscribing just what they were doing." On the other hand, "much of the seeming elasticity of the freedmen's status owed simply to the fact that the few free Negroes did not threaten white control."[34] Free Frank's land-claiming activities thus reflect the systematic and thoughtful steps he took to assure that title to his land would not be alienated because of his failure to comply fully with the many qualifying provisions of the land laws.

It is interesting to note, however, that in 1821, when there were only two free black men in Pulaski County, they cooperated in broadening their economic base by using the land laws to purchase property for themselves. With their first land purchase, Zibe, who could write, applied for the grant and indicated on that application that Free Frank held an equal interest in the two fifty-acre surveys. Moreover, both men secured additional land after their initial joint purchase. Obviously they had discussed the likelihood of their ability to purchase land.[35] If it could be secured, the same hard work the two former slaves had put into developing land for others could be directed to developing it for themselves.

Free Frank's land speculations demonstrate white participation in business transactions with blacks, just as his saltpeter marketing activities had. Ephraim Farris, a joint purchaser with Free Frank in two land transactions, and Cyrenius Wait and Bourne Goggin, both of whom sold land to Free Frank at one time or another, were prominent whites, all of whom were elected to the Kentucky General Assembly. Bourne Goggin was elected in 1824, five years before he sold land to Free Frank. At the time of the sale he was a slaveholder. Farris was elected to the Kentucky House of Representatives in 1832. Cyrenius Wait was elected to the Kentucky Senate, although not until 1848-1850, and he too was a slaveholder. At the time he sold his land to Free Frank, Wait was considered one of the richest men in the county.[36]

Free Frank's land-claiming activities were primarily speculative, based on improving the land for future sale. But there was a limit to the amount of money that small landowners could make in Pulaski County. This was the case with Free Frank, as with other settlers who had taken advantage of the liberal land laws. They purchased large tracts of land and then found themselves unable to afford the necessary labor to develop these tracts. Yet one can imagine the impact that Free Frank's and Zibe Harrison's land purchasing activities made on the Pulaski County slaves. Many must have realized that if they were free they too could set up farm homesteads that would profit their own families rather than their slaveholders.

In the 1820s, then, Free Frank was involved in virtually every economic activity in which free blacks could make money on the Pennyroyal frontier. He had established a farm and had purchased land for speculation. He had developed the mineral resources of the area with his saltpeter manufacturing. But the virtual subsistence level of much of the county's population precluded the sale of saltpeter in large quantities. There were few towns in Pulaski County. Somerset, the county seat and largest town, could support only those businesses that provided the most basic goods and services that a rural self-subsistence population could afford.[37] Free Frank obviously needed a substantial sum if he was to purchase his family from slavery, but the continuing rurality of Pulaski County did not permit him to increase his income. Broadening the base of his market was the one way he could earn additional money, but only one of his commercial activities could be expanded and relocated elsewhere—his saltpeter enterprise.

A free black had more than just business considerations to make when moving his business (or even himself) about the countryside. Freedom was always relative: "The liberty of free Negroes while they remained at home among their neighbors, was not questioned; but when they began to move about from place to place, they were usually suspected and often taken up and imprisoned as fugitive slaves." Coleman further emphasizes the precarious limitations that qualified the mobility of free blacks: "All unknown Negroes who could not produce their 'free Papers' were taken up as runaways. Free Negroes thus arrested were occasionally sold secretly and cheaply by unscrupulous patrollers to the despised 'nigger traders.'"[38] Although Free Frank would take all the precautions possible to keep from being reenslaved once he expanded his saltpeter enterprise, the risks were still great. But the desire to do everything possible to free his family from slavery was even greater.

Of the several towns in Kentucky that were centrally located with a population base that could support Free Frank's manufactory, Danville, less than forty miles north of Somerset, was the closest. For several years it was the only town in the area, and had very early become the center for the distribution of goods and services for people in the surrounding frontier areas. In fact, access to Danville was considered so important to Pulaski County that, within four years of the county's organization, a county order in 1802 directed the construction of a road to Lincoln County, and the Pulaski County commissioners then encouraged Lincoln County to continue building the road on to Danville, which was located directly north in Mercer County.[39]

Danville was the one town in south-central Kentucky that could provide Free Frank with a rapid market turnover for his saltpeter. It was located on one branch of the Wilderness Road, which was important because many westward-moving pioneers stopped there to replenish their supplies before they continued their journey. In the mid-1820s Danville took pride in the fact that "emigrants . . . [were] daily passing through our town westward." It was estimated that within one month over fifty families moved through the town.[40] The road was mainly used by migrants from the Southeast— North Carolina, Georgia, and Virginia—moving in caravans that included "families, carriages, wagons, slaves and fine stock," as a Danville resident noted in 1826.[41]

Having lived in Pulaski County since 1798, Free Frank knew that Danville's location on the Wilderness Road would provide him with a more rapid turnover in the sale of his saltpeter than could be found in Pulaski County. Danville's market penetration area, which to some extent can be determined by the distribution of the local newspaper, the *Olive Branch,* was another factor in his decision. Various advertisements informed readers of the goods and services available in Danville. The *Olive Branch* also provided notices of the circuit court sessions for the counties of Wayne, Adair, Lincoln, Pulaski, Knox, Washington, and Rockcastle. *Olive Branch* readers in these counties were thus attracted to Danville, where they purchased those goods which were not available in their own communities.

Danville's trade was perhaps the most important factor in Free Frank's decision to establish a branch of his saltpeter works there in the 1820s. That Danville was relatively close to Pulaski was also important and made the risk of reenslavement less severe than if he relocated in a town with a larger population and more extensive trade area but at a greater distance. Although Danville's population was only 684, which included 220 slaves and 13 free blacks, it was considered the most important trading town in the area. The occupational distribution shows 12 persons engaged in agriculture, 30 in commerce, and 103 in manufacturing.[42] Shakertown, located three miles west of Danville, was the point of entry for goods coming to Danville from Philadelphia and New Orleans, since "most of the goods sold there . . . came up or down the Ohio River to the Kentucky River and by ox-cart from

Shaker Landing to town."[43] Shakertown was the home of a religious sect that practiced celibacy. In 1820 the town's population was 410; there were no slaves, but six free blacks were residents.[44]

Free Frank was able to capitalize on Danville's trade area once a branch of his saltpeter enterprise was established there. Most of the local stores carried this commodity and it was widely advertised. In an 1826 *Olive Branch* advertisement, a newly established Danville grocery store prominently announced that it carried a full stock of "salt, both Common and Table and . . . Salt Peter and Glauber Salts."[45] Free Frank's market area could include not only the local population, the westward migrants passing through, and the eastern market available via the trade at Shaker Landing, but the local merchants, as well. He could sell his product either retail or wholesale and in either case undercut the price of saltpeter in the Danville stores.

Free Frank's illiteracy did not hinder his business transactions, for literacy was not a requisite for conducting business. On the contrary, as H.C. Nixon emphasizes, "inability to read and write was the rule." Nixon's comment applied especially to the white tradesmen and craftsmen, who "developed ingenious makeshifts" to compensate for this deficiency. In weighing goods, for example, "some learned to read the printed figures on hand scales . . . by remembering accurately the amounts," which were then translated into prices per ounce or pound.[46] Free Frank undoubtedly also used this method in the conduct of his business activities.

The Danville saltpeter enterprise was obviously profitable, and in May 1829 Free Frank traded it for his son's freedom. Young Frank, who had fled as a slave to Canada, was now about twenty-five years old and worth at least $1,000 as a slave. Free Frank's business was actually worth more than Young Frank's market value, but his son's freedom was obviously more important to him. Doubtless Free Frank began negotiating with Obediah Denham for his son's purchase from the time the Court of Appeals decided in his favor in 1827. But Obediah, perhaps feeling that close family ties would bring Young Frank home, refused to allow the purchase. After more than three years, however, Obediah was not so obdurate. Young Frank obviously had no intention of returning to Kentucky as a slave, and each year of his absence saw Obediah losing the value of his labor. Even if Young Frank returned, Obediah would never be sure that he could prevent him from running away again. And if Denham sold Young Frank on the slave market, over the long run the monetary compensation would probably be less than the present value of the saltpeter manufactory and its prospective profits. Securing the manufactory would provide more than adequate compensation for the manumission of the slave. At the same time the transaction would assure Denham of additional capital satisfaction, probably securing him the

$212 for which he had sued Free Frank, and which obviously had resulted in a loss of face for the slaveholder in Pulaski County. The terms of the transaction were recorded as follows: "I Obediah Denham of the County of Pulaski have for and and in consideration of two stills—the one got of John Denham and the other got in Danville by Free Frank and 24 Still Tubbs, Two Stake stands two singling and one doubling kegs. I have bargained sold and delivered to said Free Frank and do by these bargain sell and deliver to said Free Frank one mulatto boy named Frank who has runaway from me about three years and six months."[47]

The specific events surrounding Young Frank's escape can only be reconstructed from the circumstances surrounding Free Frank's activities during this period. The John Denham who was involved in Free Frank's saltpeter works in Pulaski was the brother of Obediah, Young Frank's owner. That either Free Frank or John, or both, hired Young Frank from his owner is highly probable. Obediah, involved in the suit against Free Frank and Lucy, obviously wanted money and would not turn down the wages that slaveowners received from hiring out their slaves. While Young Frank's work probably included digging the crude niter from the caves, one can also assume that on occasions he was required to travel back and forth between the Pulaski County saltpeter works and the Danville enterprise. Perhaps a routine was established that attracted little attention. Young Frank could leave Pulaski in the morning, reach Danville in the late afternoon, then spend the night in town and return to Pulaski by the following afternoon. On occasion perhaps he spent two nights in Danville. With a systematic pattern of activity established, once Young Frank escaped he was assured of at least two days' head start before his owner knew he was gone. This reconstruction of his escape is of course only speculative. Even if Young Frank never got to Danville, his father's business activities brought him in contact with townspeople, travelers, and other blacks. Over a period of time Free Frank could have acquired the information needed to facilitate his son's escape, just as he had acquired the means to tap a network that reached Canada informing Young Frank of his manumission. With his freedom papers, Young Frank returned from Canada in time to help his father and mother as they made plans to leave Kentucky.

Trading his saltpeter manufactory for his son's freedom was one of Free Frank's final activities as a freedman in Kentucky. In that same year he revealed his plan to "remove from Pulaski County to a free state."[48] Although his position as a tradesman in Danville over a period of time provided him with numerous advantages, Free Frank was never far removed from antiblack sentiments expressed in that town, and these increased in intensity during the 1820s. The free black population was never welcomed in Kentucky. In an act passed in 1808 that state sought to prohibit their immigration. Although Kentucky did not attempt to remove its own free black population until the 1850s, the state did support the activities of the American Colonization Society, an organization that worked to expedite their removal. The Danville *Olive Branch* was thorough in its coverage of the activities of the society, and especially enthusiastic in reporting the activities of blacks who supported colonization, as one article in 1820 shows: "It is but a few years [1815] since Paul Cuffee [a free black man] carried thirty-eight from Boston to Sierra Leone, chiefly at his own expense; and in a letter, written after this voyage, he declares, that he could have obtained the consent of the great part of the free people of colour in that city and its vicinity to remove to Africa."[49]

Free blacks in Mercer County, where Danville was located, were strongly encouraged to emigrate to Africa, and some seriously considered the possibility. A leader of a settlement of free blacks in the county had asked one of Mercer's leading planters, a man said to be a friend to blacks, for his opinion on the advantages of black settlement in Liberia. The planter's only response was to refer the free black to his slave, tersely announcing, "My Gilbert's a sensible nigger, ask him." The slave, when asked, had only one reply: "Do you reckon there's a place on the face of the yearth where they make two crops in one year and the white folks hain't took it?"[50] For this reason many free blacks, while anxious to leave Kentucky, were cautious about Liberia as the place to settle, as the *Olive Branch* reported: "Some of the free Blacks in America who had been consulted on this subject, have, it is true not consented to the choice of country [Liberia] made for them by the society."[51]

While blacks viewed the American Colonization Society's aims with suspicion, the organization nonetheless won support for its activities from some of the leading institutions and citizens of Kentucky. Some religious organizations gave enthusiastic support to the society's aims. John Robinson noted that in 1823 the Presbyterian Synod "approved the work of the American Colonization Society and appointed a special committee to further its objects of the state." Asa Martin, in his detailed discussion of colonization, adds that even Kentucky's abolition societies adopted colonization as one of their objectives in 1823, "gradually giving it increasing prominence until in the late twenties they had become in reality colonization societies."[52] Danville's Centre College also encouraged the activities of the society, and in the 1820s, notes Daviess, "was the favorite and frequent meeting place of the Synod of Kentucky."[53] The scurrilous attack on free blacks made by Henry Clay in an address to the American Colonization Society in 1829, then, reflected the attitudes of many Kentuckians: "Of all the descriptions of our population, and of either portion of the African race, the free people of

color are by far, as a class, the most corrupt, depraved and abandoned. . . .
They are not slaves, and yet they are not free. The laws, it is true, proclaim
them free; but prejudices, more powerful than any law, deny them the privileges of freemen. They occupy a middle station between the free white population and the slaves of the United States, and the tendency of their habits
is to corrupt both."[54] The American Colonization Society, encouraged by
Clay's support, intensified its commitment. In its 1829 constitution the organization took a firm stand in favor of expediting the removal of free blacks
for the announced purpose of ending "the serious inconvenience resulting
from the existence among us, of a rapidly increasing number of free persons
of color who are not subject to the restraints of slavery."[55] Increasingly Kentuckians began to act on the position that blacks were slaves—or ought to
be.

Another factor may have influenced Free Frank's decision to leave Kentucky. The frontier period in the Pennyroyal was coming to a close in the late
1820s, and as the white population increased the economic climate became
increasingly competitive for free blacks.[56] By 1829 he no longer had his saltpeter works; any money earned came primarily from his land speculation
and farming activities. Though his primary purpose was to earn money to
buy his children from slavery, if his economic situation continued to deteri-
orate he would in addition have to be concerned about the future status of
his freeborn children, who by 1830 were thirteen, seven, and five years of
age. In 1825 an act was passed that gave the state the power to apprentice
free black children "whose parents are incapable of bringing them up in
honest courses." The statute emphasized, however, that "no distinction is
made between white children and children of color," and also required that
children who were apprenticed out were to be given training in a skill or
trade, as well as food, clothing, shelter, and a small salary, and they were to
be taught to read and spell.[57] Although Free Frank could support his children with his farm, the state always had the power to determine their economic status. Although free, they could be forced to work under conditions
that differed little from slavery. Even legal remedies offered little that could
offset the precarious conditions of freedom for Free Frank and his family in
Kentucky by 1830.

Free Frank's tenuous economic situation was indeed dangerous. Pressed
by a feeling of tremendous urgency, the former slave made no secret of his
desire to leave Kentucky. His preparations were known to many people in
the Pulaski County community. The clearest available evidence of his systematic steps to leave the South and buy land in a free state is found in a
deposition taken from Joseph Porter in 1856. The deposition concerned Porter's testimony in a suit brought before the Circuit Court of Pike County, Il-

linois, in which Free Frank's wife Lucy and his son Solomon were the plaintiffs. Porter was a justice of the peace in Pulaski at the time Free Frank was making preparations to leave the county, and during the first decade of the nineteenth century was the surveyor for George McWhorter's land. In 1817 he was elected to the general assembly. Porter's was also the first name on the character reference Free Frank obtained when he began preparations to leave Pulaski County.

There is some discrepancy (such as the order in which Free Frank and Lucy were freed) in the information provided by Joseph Porter, who in 1856 was 85 years old. But the deposition is important, for it also provides a summation of most of Free Frank's life in Pulaski County. The process whereby he secured his first land in Illinois is specifically indicated. Much of this information is found in the answers to two of the questions put to Porter:

Question: Were you or not acquainted with Frank McWorter a Free Colored Man generally known by the name of Free Frank. If so where did said McWorter reside when you were acquainted with him, and when did he remove from his said place of residence and where did he remove to?

Answer: I was well acquainted with Free Frank or Frank McWorter from the year 1804 until he removed to Illinois in the year 1831. Where I first knew him he was a slave belonging to George McWhorter of Pulaski County. William Denham who lived in the same neighborhood owned Frank's wife Lucy a slave. Denham purchased Frank from McWhorter and sometime after Frank bought his freedom from his master Denham and afterwards purchased Lucy his wife from Denham and then they set up housekeeping for themselves and assumed the Sir names McWorter, he Frank sum time after purchased a tract of land in Pulaski County, and resided on the same until he removed to Illinois. I suppose he lived in Pulaski County about Thirty years.

Question: Did or did not said McWorter or Free Frank as called purchase of Dr. Elliot one of the tracts of land formerly owned by Oldham in the State of Illinois—If so what time said purchase was made, was it before or after said McWorter had removed to Illinois. State also in what County in Illinois the land so purchased by McWorter lay; were you or not ever in Pike Co. Illinois in the neighborhood of said land, if so when and state whether or not it was on your recommendation that said McWorter bought the same.

Answer: Frank became desirous to remove from Pulaski County to a free state. Dr. Elliot hearing this made a proposition that he would take Frank's land in Pulaski for one of the tracts he got from Oldham in Illinois, at first Frank was unwilling to take Either of the tracts, no persons here knowing anything about the quality of the land nor where it lay in Illinois. It so happened that I had business at that time that made it necessary to go to Illinois in Pike County and I did go in the Spring of 1830. Dr. Elliot requested me to make some inquiry when I got there whose land lay on the . . . the location quality and get a memorandum of no of township section of his patent for the tract he got of Oldham. When I arrived in Illinois I stayed with Cap.

Ross (who resided in Atlas Pike County). I stayed there some days he has been spec-
ulating in Soldiers claims extensively and gave me the information I desired where
the lands of Doctor Elliot lay and the tract that Frank McWorter afterwards purchased of Elliot I found a few miles Westwardly of where Pittsfield now stands the
Patentee of that quarter section was I think by the name of [indecipherable]. When I
returned home to Pulaski I gave both Elliot and Frank the information I had received
and advised Frank to close the trade [with Elliot] without delay. Frank done so forthwith he gave his tract on which he lived to Elliot for his Elliot's tract in Pike County
the following Spring moved to Illinois and settled in at the same.

In another question closely related to the preceding one, Porter was asked
"whether it was known that he [Free Frank] was removing to Illinois to go
into the possession of said land." Porter's reply was: "I think it was well
known to Frank's neighbors and all concerned in Pulaski County that Frank
had bought said tract of land from Dr. Elliot with the intention of removing
to it and did remove to and take possession in the year 1831."[58] Apparently
Free Frank revealed his plans to leave Kentucky either late in 1829 or early in
1830. Porter left for Illinois sometime after hearing of the proposed transaction between Free Frank and Dr. Elliot, probably delaying his trip until
spring because of the weather. Many travelers going west left in the spring in
order to avoid the additional rigors and hardships caused by the severe winter weather.

Porter's testimony also suggests that initially, before anyone knew the
quality of Elliot's tract in Illinois, Elliot was going to trade it for Free Frank's
land in Pulaski County. Porter's testimony was contradictory, however, since
he also said that Free Frank purchased Elliot's land. Perhaps when Porter returned and gave them both the information on what was obviously a valuable tract of land, Elliot decided to sell rather than make a trade. The deed
of sale, which was recorded, shows that Free Frank paid Elliot $200 for the
160-acre tract:

This indenture was made the thirteenth day of September in the year of Our Lord
one Thousand Eight Hundred and thirty between Galen R. Elliot of Somerset Kentucky of the one part and Free Frank of the County of Pulaski and State aforesaid of
the other part Witnessedth that for the consideration of the sum of two hundred
Dollars in hand paid the receipt whereof is hereby acknowledged the said Galen R.
Elliot both this day bargained and sold and doth by these presents bargain sell . . .
and convey to the said Free Frank a certain tract of land containing one Hundred and
sixty acres being the South East quarter of section twenty two of Township four
South in Range five west in the tract a named by . . . acts of Congress for Military
found in the Territory . . . (Now the State) of Illinois and patented in the name of
Martin Turner on the 16th day of March 1818.[59]

Free Frank willingly paid the $200. One year earlier Illinois had passed a law requiring that any free black moving to the state pay a $1,000 security bond to guarantee that he (or she) would not become a public charge.[60] By owning a valuable tract of land, Free Frank demonstrated that he was self-supporting and unlikely to become dependent on the state.

Free Frank's careful preparations had another purpose. The slaveholders who owned his children and grandchildren had to be convinced that he intended to continue the tradition he had established of working conscientiously and diligently to buy his family from slavery. His purpose obviously was to reinforce their confidence in him, to persuade them that even on the Illinois frontier he would still earn enough money to purchase his children's freedom. The very real possibility existed that they might be sold before he could return. As he prepared to leave Kentucky, Free Frank had every reason to be concerned. By the late 1820s antislavery thought increasingly indicted the border states, a region where tobacco or grain were the staple crops, as "nurseries which support the cotton grounds with human flesh. In consequence of this there is nearly as great a slave trade floating annually on the Mississippi or its branches as ever wafted across the Atlantic. The raising and transporting of slaves to perish on the cotton and sugar land is what keeps up the value in Kentucky."[61] Free Frank's son Solomon was fifteen in 1830 and, since the demand for male slaves in the Deep South had escalated, a high price could be commanded if he were put up for sale. Free Frank was also deeply concerned about slavery's dehumanizing effect on the lives of his daughters. In 1830 Juda was thirty and Sally was twenty. Coleman explains that "by degrees, as the importance of slave labor increased in the Deep South, the trade grew; men took up slave trading as business, and slave owners in the border states began to breed slaves for the southern markets."[62]

In his preparations to leave Kentucky, Free Frank acted with the same kind of deliberate thoughtfulness and systematic planning that had characterized his life on the Pennyroyal frontier. Notwithstanding the urgency of his desire to leave Kentucky as expeditiously as possible, as a black he could not proceed as casually as the white southerner, described by William Pooley as one "who packed up his household goods, faced the West and traveled by the most convenient road."[63] His Illinois land purchase was only one of the special preparations he had to make before migrating. He would need capital to begin commercial farming immediately when he got to Illinois, since he could not wait a dozen years to move beyond self-sufficiency, so two days after Free Frank purchased the Illinois land he sold his Pulaski County farm. He had already sold one of his tracts of land in December 1828, fifty-nine acres "for and in Consideration of One hundred and five dollars and fifty cents."[64] The original purchase price had been a little more than five dollars. While the land was improved, it did not have the farm buildings that Free Frank included in the sale made on September 15, 1830, which was for a 50-acre tract that he had purchased, also for five dollars. The deed of sale reads in part: "The said Free Frank for and in consideration of the sum of two hundred and fifty dollars to me in hand paid have this day granted bargained and sold unto Hiram Smith one certain parcel of land. . . . It is understood that the said Free Frank only conveys one equal undivided third part of the foregoing boundary containing 50 acres in all with its appertainances and premises above mentioned."[65] By the time Free Frank was ready to leave for Illinois, he had secured $355.50 from his land sales, certainly a remarkable return for an investment of little more than ten dollars. The remainder of his land eventually reverted to the state. As late as 1833, however, surveys made on land adjacent to his used his property as a mark to indicate boundary lines.

It was characteristic of Free Frank that he secured his character reference before he made his final land transactions. Illinois law required, in addition to the security bond, that free blacks have a certificate of good character which they were to register with the clerk in the county in which they intended to reside.[66] Free Frank's character reference demonstrates that he did all he could, as a black man in a slave society, to survive. It is a testament to his endurance and points also to one aspect of black survival. Despite his free status, a black man had to function in a capacity far beyond that of other free men to survive, and even then would not be allowed to "enjoy his full freedom as if [he] had been born free." Free Frank's character reference was signed by nineteen Pulaski County citizens. It, too, documents his life in Kentucky:

State of Kentucky, Pulaski County

Whereas Free Frank a man of colour intends leaving this state and removing to the state of Illinois and requests the undersigned to give a statement of what we know concerning his character, we therefore state that we have known Frank for many years some of us upwards of twenty years and that he has always been an honest industrious man punctual to his word in all of his dealings. Frank was formerly a Slave of George McWhorter and served him faithful as such until he purchased his Freedom from his master and both before and since his emancipation he has demeaned himself morally and honestly. Frank by his industry purchased his wife Lucy formerly a slave of William Denham and for which he has paid a valuable consideration by her he has three children born since her Emancipation to wit, Squire, Commodore & Lucy Ann.

Lucy also has always sustained a good character as a virtuous industrious woman.

September 7th 1830[67]

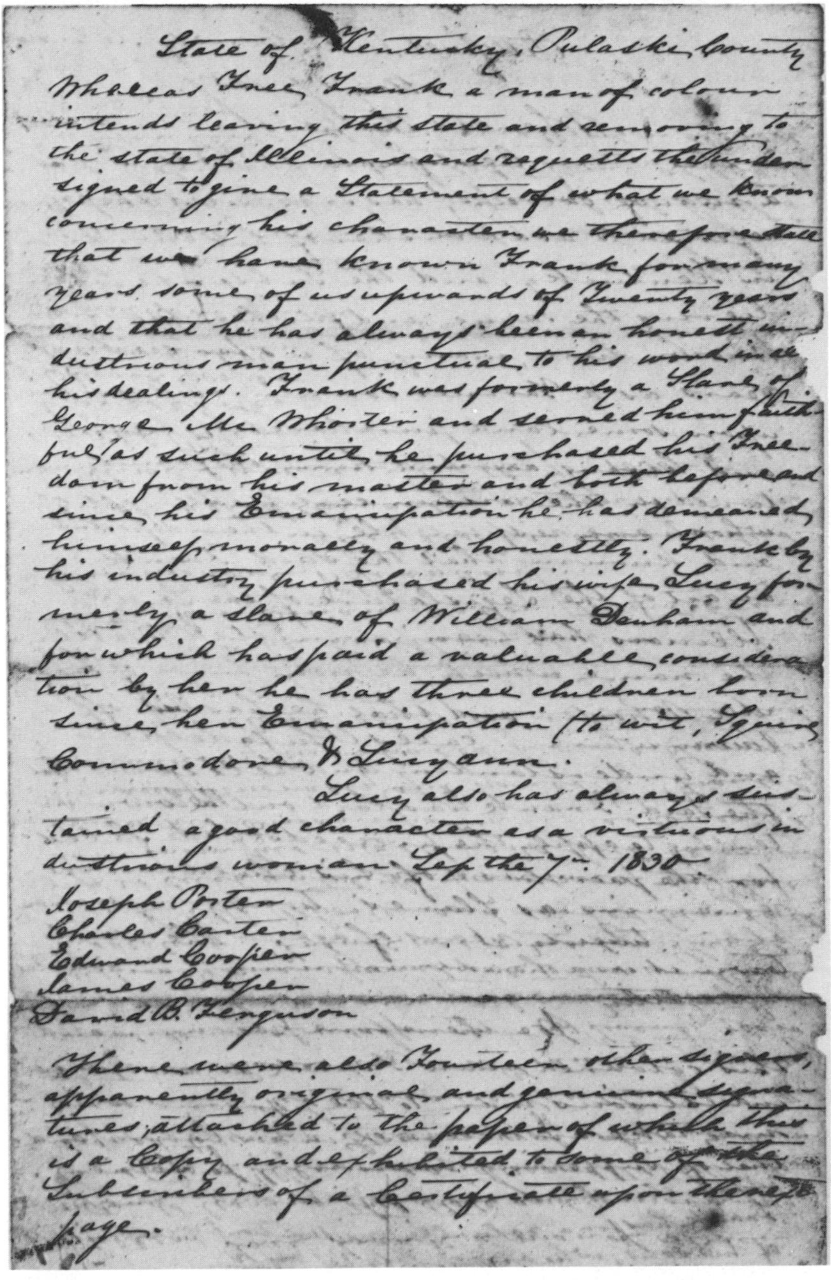

State of Kentucky, Pulaski County

Whereas Free Frank a man of colour intends leaving this state and removing to the state of Illinois and requests the undersigned to give a Statement of what we know concerning his character we therefore state that we have known Frank for many years, some of us upwards of twenty years and that he has always been an honest industrious man punctual to his work in all his dealings. Frank was formerly a Slave of George McWhorter and served him faithful as such until he purchased his Freedom from his master and both before and since his Emancipation he has demeaned himself morally and honestly. Frank by his industry purchased his wife Lucy formerly a slave of William Denham and for which has paid a valuable consideration by her he has three children born since her Emancipation (to wit, Squire Commodore & Lucyann.

Lucy also has always sustained a good character as a virtuous industrious woman Sep the 7 — 1830

Joseph Porter
Charles Carter
Edward Cooper
James Cooper
David B. Ferguson

There were also Fourteen other signers, apparently original and genuine Signatures, attached to the paper of which this is a Copy and exhibited to some of the Subscribers of a Certificate upon the next page.

Fig. 3. Certificate of Good Character obtained by Free Frank before leaving Kentucky in 1830. Illinois law required such a character reference of free blacks who wished to settle in the state. Photo by University of Illinois Photographic Services.

When Free Frank left Kentucky he was fifty-three years old. It had taken him the first twenty years of his adult life—that time which is ordinarily considered to be the prime years of a man's life—to purchase one member of his family, his wife, from slavery, and two more years to purchase himself. He passed an additional ten years as a free man before circumstances allowed him to purchase one of his children, his firstborn son Frank. Few men successfully begin a new life after fifty. Considering also the constraints imposed on free blacks, especially in a racially biased state such as Illinois, the possibility of success for Free Frank must have seemed virtually nil. His past experiences had shown him that he would have to use all his resources— mental, physical, and financial—if he was to succeed in securing the survival of his free family and the purchase of those remaining in slavery. Yet when Free Frank left Kentucky, he probably had no idea that it would take him the rest of his life to achieve his goal.

CHAPTER FIVE

Black Pathfinders on the Illinois Frontier

> The first settler in this township [Hadley] after the Indians
> had been driven westward, was not a white man, but a col-
> ored man. He was known as "Free Frank," and came with
> his wife and three children to this township, . . . He was
> from Kentucky, and had spent the previous winter in
> Greene county, Ill. He had purchased his freedom and
> that of his family.[1]

After spending more than a year in careful preparation for the move north, Free Frank sold his farm homestead in September 1830 as his final step before leaving Kentucky to settle a new frontier. The family left in the fall of that year: Lucy, now approaching her sixtieth birthday; their three freeborn children, Squire, Commodore, and Lucy Ann; and their slave-born son Young Frank, whose manumission had been secured the previous year. Free Frank was intent on making the westward trek before winter set in. Adequate food provisions to sustain the family during the cold and barren season had been carefully prepared, and for Free Frank, as for most farmers, the autumn months afforded favorable conditions for travel: "The weather was mild, the roads dry and hard and the rivers fordable . . . the crops of the year had been gathered and sold, and . . . the cattle were fat and in good traveling condition."[2] Free Frank's farm wagon with its heavy tarpaulin cover, contemporaneously called a "steamboat wagon" and pulled by an ox-team, provided transportation for the family's journey to their new home in Illinois. These covered wagons were large—numerous pioneers who settled the early Pike County frontier recalled that enormous quantities of freight could be stored in the hold: "beds, baskets, tubs, old-fashioned chairs, including all the household furniture usually used by our log-cabin ancestors."[3]

The most important and valuable possessions that a prospective pioneer farmer could take west were his farm tools and equipment. Without a pick-ax, plow, or sickle, several years could pass before a cash crop could be put in that would earn him the cost of these implements. Because of their scarcity on the frontier, the prices for agricultural tools were almost prohibitive. Ox-teams used for plowing were also invaluable and sold for prices ranging from $5 to $55. Ox-wagons of the Conestoga type which Free Frank owned, and which were used to haul farm produce to market, could only be purchased for prices ranging from $50 to $64 or more. Thus in the move west the covered wagon was especially valued, since it carried most of the provisions needed by the family to survive the winter, to set up a homestead in the spring, and to market the crops in the fall.

Free Frank's careful preparations to leave Kentucky also required thoughtful deliberation to determine the route that the family would take in their move northwest. From Pulaski County, the Cumberland-Ohio river route was the quickest to Shawneetown in southern Illinois. The Cumberland, a tributary of the Ohio River, however, flowed south through Tennessee before turning northward through Kentucky again before joining the Ohio. However anxious Free Frank was to expedite his move north, to travel south first would not seem the most practical nor the safest way to reach his destination. Nor was the more direct route west to the Ohio River through southern Kentucky, using a road which ran through Christian, Caldwell, and Livingston counties, without its limitations. This land route was also twice the distance of roads to Louisville, the nearest point from Pulaski County where Free Frank could cross the Ohio. For most Kentuckians in their move to settle the Old Northwest, "as a general rule where there was a tendency to follow a beaten line of travel it was towards some point on the Ohio between Cincinnati and Louisville."[4] While Free Frank wanted to get out of Kentucky and into Illinois as rapidly as possible, and a direct river route would have been the quickest way, it was not necessarily the safest. Slave catchers operated much more effectively on the rivers than on land. Free Frank was aware that his family's freedom papers could be stolen and destroyed by "nigger stealers," who, as Coleman says, "secretly seized and sold back into slavery many free persons of color." The particular tragedy was that "when thus reduced to slavery, the once free Negroes had little or no recourse through the courts of the land."[5] For a black man moving west, then, Free Frank's choices in the routes he could take, unlike those available to white pioneers, were limited.

With these considerations in mind, the family began the westward move. They first traveled the familiar roads that ran from Pulaski County to Danville in Mercer County. From there they continued on the Wilderness Road to Louisville, a distance of only about seventy-five miles, but still a slow and tedious journey. "A yoke of oxen hauling a heavy load generally lounged onward at the rate of one and one-half miles an hour." As the family headed northwest through Kentucky, they would be stopped innumerable times. All whites had the authority, if not the responsibility, to check the papers of any black person and to ascertain his status. In 1830 the uncommon sight of a free black family traveling northwest in a covered wagon pulled by a team of oxen and with cattle trailing behind must have raised more interest and curiosity than the more common sight of their slave brothers on the roads, sometimes chained in gangs, being moved southwestward. As a precaution, Free Frank and Young Frank were not hesitant about taking their rifles. Their determination to use them offered much more protection for the family than their free papers ever could if they should encounter kidnappers, since this free black family represented a potential value of at least $4,000. As an added precaution, Young Frank trailed the family, a tactic which afforded greater opportunity for their escape if they should be seized or kidnapped as a group.

Once Free Frank reached Louisville, he had to make arrangements to cross the Ohio by flatboat. Again caution was needed. Few riverboatmen could be trusted to take them across the Ohio into Indiana, rather than downriver into the hands of kidnappers. The family reached the Indiana shores safely, however, and continued their journey westward to Illinois, traveling on territorial roads built between 1817 and 1822. These roads were really so bad that some early Illinois settlers, faced with inclement weather, traveled less than a mile a day. The Indiana-Illinois border at the Wabash River would present another kind of danger, but for the family's safety it was better that they cross the Wabash into Illinois rather than the Ohio. Had the family traveled down the Ohio River from Louisville or taken the southern route through Christian, Caldwell, and Livingston counties, there was little chance they could avoid Ford's Ferry, "the chief point of egress from Kentucky into Illinois," and also the point "over which most of the migration from Kentucky, Tennessee and the Carolinas passed into Illinois."[6] Ford, the owner of the Illinois-based ferry operation, constituted as much of a threat as the obviously feared "nigger stealers." His mode of operation, although much more subtle, was equally dangerous, for Ford had devised an almost foolproof scheme to rob pioneers: "His ferry catered to the travelers on the trace, his bandits robbed them, his court listened to their complaints."[7] Ford was just one of many outlaws and river pirates who attacked and robbed pioneers as they crossed the Ohio and Wabash rivers into Illinois, although he carried out his operations with greater sophistication than most. Even some blacks operated as river pirates at this time. One example of their activities is provided in an advertisement for two runaway slaves owned by a man in Livingston, Kentucky, one of whom was said to have had "both his ears off close to his head, which he lost for robbing a boat on the Ohio River."[8] John Murrell, another pirate as creative as Ford, also established a successful career robbing westward-moving pioneers. He pretended to be a frontier preacher, attracting many lonely pioneers to his camp meetings. Pike County settlers who came in the late 1820s and early 1830s claimed that, with this captive audience, Murrell would then "lay down counterfeit currency, . . . run off niggers [free blacks] and unload stolen slaves, and rob travelers of their gold unsuspected, in the frenzied atmosphere of the camp meeting."[9]

Even when they reached Illinois, the Free Frank family was not safe. In addition to "land pirates" like Murrell, Illinois's roads encouraged all kinds of delay. Most were merely forest trails, beaten down paths covered with brush and fallen branches, and full of potholes, always potentially hazardous, causing wagon wheels to break, sometimes beyond repair. For a free black family, any delay increased their susceptibility to kidnapping. Moving northwestward through Illinois, the family passed through Equality, Mount Vernon, and Carlyle, early frontier towns. From Carlyle they continued northwestward on the road to Edwardsville and Alton, and then turned northward to Greene County, just south of Pike and east of the Illinois River. Here they would spend the winter. Although the family thought they had left Kentucky in time to reach their new home before winter, they had come at the worst possible time in Illinois history for settlers new to that state. As the Chapman history of Pike County notes, old Illinois settlers, even after fifty years recalled that time as "the winter of the deep snow, 1830-1831," which they said "commenced falling Nov. 10, and did not all go away until the following April, yet the largest fall of snow did not begin until the 29th of December."[10] Blizzard conditions only intensified sub-zero temperatures that lasted throughout the winter, and even huddled in a hastily constructed hut that provided the family shelter, it was extremely cold. The family also barely escaped starvation. While they had left Kentucky with food and provisions to last the winter, Free Frank had also planned to supplement their supplies by hunting wild game, now frozen because of the severe weather.

The worst of the winter was over by early April, when the family left Greene County. Although snow still covered the ground, Free Frank and his family had scarcely survived "the winter of the deep snow," and with their food supplies exhausted they had no alternative but to leave. Over a half-year had passed since they left Kentucky and the family was now even more anxious to reach their new home and begin their new life. Leaving Greene County, they proceeded north through what is now Scott County to the Phillips Ferry Road, which would take them to the Illinois River. This road, like most of the early forest trails, was barely there. Similarly obscure was the landing where the ferry was located which would carry them across the river to Pike County. At the time of Free Frank's initial crossing, "Phillips Ferry, so long a port of entry for Pike County settlers, was merely a landing on the wild Illinois shore. There was nothing there save the rude ferry and the Phillips cabin."[11] But Free Frank and his family, having lived on the frontier all of their lives, were neither shocked or astonished by what they saw. Their arrival in Pike County can be contrasted with that of an English family, the Burlends, who came that same year with their three children. Mrs. Burlend said that when her family saw Phillips Ferry they were "utterly confounded" because "there was no appearance of a landing place, no luggage yard nor even a building of any kind within sight." The Phillips cabin was totally ignored. The Burlends could not imagine that it could be used for anything at all, much less a home. Rebecca Burlend found the experience terrifying: "My husband and I looked at each other till we burst into tears, and our children observing our disquietude began to cry bitterly."[12]

Rebecca Burlend's account is important, since it provides the only contemporary published record of the severe hardships encountered by an early settler on the Pike County frontier. Her intimate accounts of the activities and experiences of pioneer families, specifically of pioneer women and the special demands put on them as they coped with the wilderness environment, also provide some insight on Lucy's experiences. In his introduction to Burlend's book, Milo Quaife emphasizes that "one cannot read this simple story without realizing that these pioneer women did their full share in conquering the new world." While Lucy and Rebecca would share similar experiences in the Pike County wilderness, Rebecca's perceptions in 1831 were also influenced by her English background and her total unfamiliarity with frontier life.

While the Burlend family would make the adjustment to frontier life, eventually developing their holdings into a prosperous farm settlement, Free Frank and Lucy encountered more than the usual rigors and hardships developing their wilderness land. Their settlement on the Kentucky frontier in the late 1790s had prepared them for the challenges they would face in the northern wilderness, but they were also a black family attempting to survive in a racially hostile society. The tenacity of strong family ties provided a source of strength, although, with three children and now new grandchildren still remaining slaves, their personal hardships more than severely tested the limits of this black family's endurance. Lucy, the center of her family, a woman of tremendous courage, intelligence, and fortitude, was tenacious, however, as she concentrated her energies on the survival of her family. Remembering the incredible obstacles and hardships they had encountered when they were slaves only strengthened her determination that her family would succeed in the new land and that her slave children would be free. By contrast, then, if Lucy and her family cried when they saw Phillips Ferry, it was with relief. As a black family with only a tenuous hold on freedom, they had succeeded in completing a long, dangerous, and harrowing journey.

Yet for Free Frank and his family, migration from Kentucky to Illinois was not simply a matter of moving from a slave state to a free state. Racism was just as pervasive in Illinois, and the threat of reenslavement was just as persistent. Both were constant factors that would determine and circumscribe the nature and extent of Free Frank's experiences and activities on the Pike County frontier. In any business enterprise that he would develop, Free Frank would have to contend with the broader social and economic conditions in Illinois. In 1831 that state was only nominally free for blacks. The location of Free Frank's land, less than fifteen miles from the Mississippi River and just across from the slave state of Missouri, served as a constant reminder—even more than Illinois black codes—that less than a half day's journey separated the family from slavery. Free Frank did not even have to cross the Mississippi River to find slavery, which existed in Illinois under the unique guise of indentured servitude.[13] Blacks could also be held outright as slaves in the state. Illinois law allowed slaveholders to travel through the state with their slaves, and although it was illegal for them to remain longer than thirty days, this law was easily circumvented. In Pike County, a settler who lived in Montezuma township on the Illinois River, just fifteen miles from Hadley township, held a black woman in bondage, "and not wishing to remove for the time, kept her until the expiration of the 30 days and took her to Missouri for a few days, and brought her back again, and so continued to do, thus evading the law for nearly a year."[14]

While their free papers might serve to protect Free Frank and his family from this kind of sequential slavery in Illinois, they were never really free from the threat of being reenslaved if they were kidnapped by slave catchers or "nigger stealers" and sold south. Even though there was a law that made the kidnapping of free blacks illegal, its interpretation by unsympathetic judges made punishment for this crime virtually impossible. Slave catching was a lucrative business that was difficult to suppress. The ease with which free blacks could be seized, the money kidnappers received for selling them as slaves, and the limitations the law placed on blacks in defending their freedom certainly did not discourage this practice. Randall Parrish emphasizes the vulnerability of free blacks in Illinois during its frontier stage of development: "In so new a country, overrun with desperate men, many of them criminally inclined[,] such kidnapping of free negroes and indentured servants [was] a regular and profitable business. The rough hill country between the Ohio and the Mississippi witnessed in those days much of crime and sorrow never to be recorded."[15]

Settlement in Illinois, moreover, did not provide free blacks with any more rights than their free brothers had in the slave states. Under the 1818 Illinois constitution, it was against the law for blacks to vote, to be jurors, to be witnesses in any court case against a white person, or to serve in the state militia.[16] Perhaps most disastrously, blacks were excluded from the benefits of a free public school education.[17] In 1828, in fact, the Illinois Senate called for an inquiry into the expediency and practicality of preventing free blacks from settling in Illinois. In their report, the special committee strongly recommended the passage of "some law to prevent further emigration of that class of people into the state."[18] As a result of the committee's report, four new provisions were added to the Illinois Black Code that went into effect in 1829, including the proviso that "no black or mulatto person, not being a citizen of some one of the United States, shall be permitted to reside in this state, until such person shall produce to the county commissioners' court where he or she is desirous of settling, a certificate of his or her freedom, which certificate shall be duly authenticated." Under the new act, the state also tried to discourage black settlement by closing avenues to employment. Certificates of freedom were required to secure a job, and rewards were offered for information leading to the apprehending of blacks who lacked certificates.[19]

Although there were blacks with freedom papers who qualified to settle in Illinois, the infamous security bond, included in the 1829 Black Code, still helped to check black migration into the state. Without certified means of support and financial stability, free blacks were required to post a $1,000 bond before entering the state. The extent to which the new provision was effective in discouraging the settlement of free blacks is not known. Evading the law is somewhat easier in a frontier society than in an established one, and free blacks did manage to settle in Illinois. But although their total numbers increased, proportionately the free black population showed a precipitous decline in the total Illinois population in the period between 1830 and 1860, as indicated by Table 4.

Blacks who could not prove their freedom, or fugitives who went unclaimed, were held in custody for a year and were hired out by the county in which they were apprehended.[20] On his family's arrival in Pike County, therefore, it was imperative that Free Frank first report to the county seat at Atlas, register the family's free papers, and, as an added measure, present the family's Kentucky Certificate of Good Character so as to establish immediately their status as free blacks. Atlas, some thirteen miles west of Free Frank's farm and located on the Sny Cartee, an inland channel flowing five miles to the Mississippi River, had been the seat of Pike County since the early 1820s. William Ross, the county clerk, and his brothers from Pittsfield,

Table 4:   Illinois and Pike County Population, 1810-1860

	Population of Pike County[1]		Population of Illinois[2]				
Year	Whites	Free Blacks	Free Blacks	Slave Blacks	Total Blacks	Whites	Proportion of Total Blacks to Whites
1810	. . .	. . .	613	168	781	11,501	6.36%
1820	. . .	. . .	457	917	1,374	53,788	2.49
1830	2,396	0	1,637	747	2,384	155,061	1.51
1840	11,716	12	3,598	331	3,929	472,254	0.83
1850	18,819	43	5,436	0	5,436	846,034	0.64
1860	27,182	67	7,628	0	7,628	1,704,291	0.41

SOURCE: U.S., Bureau of the Census, *Population of the United States in 1860: The Eighth Census* (Washington, D.C.: Government Printing Office, 1864).

1. Present boundaries established in 1825.

2. Attained statehood in 1818.

Massachusetts, had been in Pike County since 1820. They were the Rosses who had provided Kentuckian Joseph Porter with information on the location and quality of land that Free Frank subsequently purchased. Free Frank's arrival in Pike County, then, was not totally unexpected. More important, the Rosses, who later became one of the most influential families in Pike, were not unnecessarily alarmed that a black family was settling in the county. They were speculators in military bounty patents, and new pioneers who set up productive farm homesteads only served to demonstrate to prospective settlers that the land was fertile and could be profitably cultivated. Later, in the mid-1830s, William Ross would use his influence to help Free Frank acquire legal rights to protect his property.

Aside from the Atlas community, Pike County during this period was largely settled by families from Kentucky who had originally come from Virginia or North Carolina, though some had come from Pennsylvania. Their racial attitudes were more a matter of their own biases or prejudices than of their place of origin. Abraham Scholl, for example, was from Kentucky but was known to have "loathed slavery," and perhaps for this reason, when Free Frank settled in Pike County, Scholl was remembered as one person who "took a kindly interest in the old man [Free Frank] and his struggle to free the family from the galling yoke of southern slavery."[21] That there were some whites in Pike who were not hostile to Free Frank's settlement was important once he began to expand his farm activities in the mid-1830s.

Free Frank's farming activities during his first year of settlement were similar to those of the other Pike County pioneers. Hadley township is in the central part of the county. Early settlers in their reminiscences described it as "a magnificent township and for agricultural purposes is surpassed by few in the Military Tract. It is what may be properly termed a prairie township."[22] Moreover, Free Frank's arrival was significant, for Chapman's history of Pike County reported that "this family were the first settlers in that township and none others arrived for two years."[23] Illinois was not a populous state, and the Military Tract where Free Frank settled was a wilderness area when he arrived. The entire 1830 population of the Tract was some 13,000 out of Illinois's total white population of 155,061. Pike County's population in 1830 was 2,396.[24] Few people new to Illinois had settled in the Military Tract, and until 1831 the only legal land titles available to settlers were those under cover of the military bounty land warrants. Most of the soldiers who had received these 160-acre grants had not migrated to the state. Despite information on its arable and fertile land, which was widely circulated after completion of the 1816-1817 surveys, many prospective settlers considered the Tract a prairie wasteland until the 1830s.[25]

Increasingly in the 1820s much of the bounty land came into the hands

of speculators through tax sales. The prices asked were sometimes less than
the fair market value of the land, but many prospective settlers, hesitant
about buying property covered by tax titles, purchased land elsewhere.
Nevertheless, there were many squatters who preempted land. Having a
military bounty therefore put Free Frank in a virtually indisputable legal position, quieting any litigation involving his possessory rights. But on his arrival in Pike County, his military bounty title would not help him if he was
unable to find his land and so settled on land belonging to someone else. It
was important that every settler have some knowledge of the federal land
surveying system in order to identify his land.[26]

For Free Frank, whose recorded land-surveying and land-claiming activities dated back to 1821, identifying his land was perhaps the least of his
concerns. Other settlers could obtain information on the system from the
traveler guides and gazetteers as well as the government field notes of the
survey, which were available in the surveyor general's office in St. Louis.
Moreover, as Carlson states, field notes were not only valuable for locating
claims but also "reduced to a minimum later disputes over location."[27] For
those unfamiliar with the system, the information must have seemed extremely complex, but E. Dana told his readers that his "descriptions of the
land was the most simple we could devise, and is believed to be intelligible
to every man of good common sense who can read."[28] Since a great many of
the early pioneers in the Old Northwest could not read, practical knowledge
of land surveys was even more important in land-claiming activities.

The federal surveyor's 1816 description of Free Frank's land provides
specific information on the potential productiveness of the tract that the
black pioneer purchased sight unseen in 1830. The surveyor recorded in his
field notes that he "set post for corner of Sec. 22 . . . 23 . . . 26 . . . 27 for
T4SR5W from which a Brook . . . runs . . . over Broken Bushy Barrons Timber oak undergrowth and Hazle."[29] "Barrens" was a "term in the western
dialect [which] does not indicate poor land, but a species of a mixed character, uniting forest and prairie."[30] A surveyor's map of 1830 shows section 22,
Free Frank's property, as being half prairie and half timber.[31] The timberlands covered virtually the entire western part of the tract. The land was extremely fertile, according to Dana's description, which shows section 22 as
first rate, but this was also true of most sections in the township. Several sections, however, were described as second rate, consisting of "mostly much
broken growth, oak, hickory, ash, lynn, grape and pea vines."[32] In addition,
Free Frank's land was on Hadley Creek, which Pike County settlers described
as "a valuable stream, watering by its numerous branches, the northern-
middle portion of the county."[33] Peck in his travels through the county recorded that "the land through which the creek ran was undulating but
good."[34]

Free Frank and his family settled on their Hadley township land in the early spring of 1831.[35] Their initial efforts to establish a farm demanded a great deal of work, but during their first year there Free Frank "built a house and made a farm."[36] According to an 1869 map of Hadley township (see p. 129), he established his farm dwellings near the timberlands, where he would have access to building materials as well as fuel.[37] The forest acted to break the force of the chilling winter winds and also provided some respite from the summer heat, as well as shelter for stock until pens could be built. The remaining prairie land was used for farming.

Free Frank's farm was typical of the early pioneer settlements, which Captain Melville Massie, a Pike County resident, said "were invariably made near the edge of a piece of timber and within easy reach of a spring, many of which were found in the townships."[38] While the remainder of the land would be used for farming, only a few of Free Frank's 160 acres were put under cultivation that first year. In his study of the initial activities of the early settlers in the Military Tract, Carlson found that the pioneer farmer, who usually arrived in the spring, first "plowed a few acres in the rudely prepared soil [and] planted his 'sod corn.'" During the summer a few additional acres would be broken for the wheat crop, and "in the late summer or early fall he sowed his wheat and then harvested his sod corn."[39]

Cash farming was out of the question during that first year of settlement. The pioneer farmer's primary concern during the spring and summer months was to make provisions to survive the following winter. Fences had to be built to protect the crops from livestock, and a more substantial cabin had to be constructed to house the family. These first log cabins were nearly all constructed by the same method. Burlend notes that "the walls of the house consisted of layers of strong blocks of timber, roughly squared and matched into each other at the corners: the joints filled up with clay." Usually there were two rooms on the ground floor, from thirty to forty square yards each. Beneath one of the rooms was a cellar, the floor and walls made of mud and clay. Usually the cabin had two doors to allow a breeze through in the summer, and some had lofts, windows, and a fireplace. Other cabins, however, were quite primitive and were built with only one room, no windows, and a dugout in which a fire was built at one end of the building.[40]

Free Frank's first Pike County home differed little in outward appearance from the others; however, the cherry cupboards, Lucy's beautiful hand-sewn quilts, her spinning wheel, cast iron kettles, and the other kitchen utensils that the family brought with them from Kentucky gave the cabin warmth and familiarity, and added to the family's determination that they would succeed.[41] Yet, unlike the white settlers' homes, Free Frank's offered only limited security for his family. They were never above the suspicion that they were using their home as a refuge for fugitive slaves.[42] Nor were they

ever free from the fear of being kidnapped and returned to slavery themselves. Yet by making careful preparations during the first months of settlement, Free Frank and his family were able to make it safely through the following winter. While other Pike County settlers were aware that Free Frank
and his family had settled in, at first they were not particularly concerned
with the family's activities. One black family living in virtual isolation in the
desolate Illinois wilderness and attempting to farm was not considered as
great a threat at this time as the Indians to the north, led by Black Hawk,
chief of the Sacs.[43]

The Indian threat was quite real in the Military Tract in 1831. Some Illinois settlers had attacked Black Hawk, and the other settlers feared retalia-
tion. Pike County was not at first in any direct line of attack from the Sacs,
but throughout the Tract the fear expressed was that once "the U.S. troops
expelled the Indians from the villages that they would, instead of crossing
the Mississippi, fall back on the frontier settlements, and destroy the inhabitants."[44] If this should occur, then Pike and the other counties from the
Mississippi River to the Illinois Rapids, a distance of one hundred miles,
were in direct danger. Those pioneers who had lived through other Indian
attacks took no chances. Carlson, in reviewing the early settlement of the
Tract, says that for this reason "the Indian scare attending Blackhawk's war
caused the evacuation of this region [settlements in Mercer, Henderson,
Bureau, Marshall, and most of Stark County] as well as others in the northern counties of the Military Tract."[45] After his defeat in 1831, however,
Black Hawk was not in a position to retaliate. Many of his warriors had been
killed and his people were starving. In violation of the treaty, he recrossed
the Mississippi to Illinois in the early spring of 1832 to begin cultivating the
land. He brought the women and children with him, convinced that "so
long as he showed no warlike inclination and was not entering his old village, the government would not molest him."[46]

Black Hawk's return was viewed as a threat to the safety of the white pioneers, and Illinois men were again called to arms. In Pike County a frontier
Paul Revere—this time a blacksmith—rode through the county to notify the
settlers of the planned attack on Black Hawk and his people. The men, "almost without exception, dropped their work, mounted their horses and set
out for Atlas," the Pike County militia headquarters. Illinois law forbade
blacks to participate in the militia, but America's frontier history shows that
when it came to fighting the Indians, whites did not hesitate to encourage
blacks to join them. Over one hundred men eventually left Pike County to
fight the Sacs. They were gone almost two months but most returned before
any confrontation took place. The Illinois pioneers were prepared to fight,
however, and their military leaders included Zachary Taylor, Abraham Lin-

coln, Winfield Scott, Jefferson Davis, and Joseph E. Johnston.[47] Once hostilities broke out, Black Hawk was quickly defeated at the Massacre of Bad Axe. Over 700 Indian children, women, and men were slaughtered, out of the nearly 1,000 who had returned to Illinois.[48] The justification for the massacre, as reported in the Illinois press, not surprisingly was that "the Indians forcibly took possession of lands occupied and owned by citizens of the State."[49] Certainly the Indian threat on the Pike County frontier offered no new challenges to Free Frank. He had lived the first years of his adult life on the Kentucky frontier, where as a slave he was armed to join the white settlers in defending the new lands from the Indians. Doubtless the family was even better prepared now if forced to join in the defense of the Pike County frontier—this time it would be their own home that they defended.

The war ended in the spring of 1832, as Free Frank began his second year on the Illinois frontier. By now he was prepared to do some cash farming. Wheat cultivation was especially profitable for pioneer farmers since, as Carlson noted, "it stands transportation well, and [possesses] considerable value in relatively small bulk."[50] Mitchell, in his promotion of the Illinois Military Tract in the 1830s, pointed out to prospective migrants that wheat cultivation was especially profitable. In some cases farmers were able to produce from 75 to 100 bushels of wheat per acre. In fact, one good crop could pay not only for their land but also for "fencing, break up, cultivation, harvesting, threshing, and taking to market." This would certainly amount to a staggering sum for the early 1830s. At that time, the estimated average cost for establishing a 160-acre farm was $945, which included $200 for the purchase price of the land (at $1.25 per acre), $320 for breaking up the prairie (at $2.00 per acre), $175 for fencing in four fields with a Kentucky fence eight rails high, and $250 for cabins, corncribs, and stables.[51] But that sort of profit could be realized only under the most ideal conditions, and very seldom in the first years of settlement.

The number of bushels of wheat that could be obtained per acre was important; one acre usually yielded from twenty to thirty bushels, which sold in the market for prices ranging from $.50 to $1.50 per bushel. Most farmers attempted to plant some wheat the first year. Even the Burlends, who cultivated their land under the most primitive conditions, lacking the proper agricultural implements, were able to secure eighty bushels of wheat from three acres their first year.[52] While their profits were limited, they earned enough money to pay for the rental of their tools and to buy the provisions they were unable to produce on their farm. That the Burlends cultivated only three acres of wheat that first year was not simply because of inexperience. The method of farming used at the time, known as grubbing, required only six days to prepare an acre. What worked against the early farmers, as Pooley explains, was their belief that when plowing up the land "the sod when turned over must have time to rot or it would remain heavy and unproductive for two or three years."[53]

Maize, or Indian corn, the other main crop cultivated by farmers on the Illinois frontier, was also a prairie staple, providing food for both the farmer and his stock, in addition to what could be marketed for cash. With a limited amount of labor, the pioneers found that a farmer with one or two helpers and several plow animals could easily raise 100 acres of corn. Particularly appealing to the pioneer farmer who planted corn, as Carlson explains, was that "there was no haste in harvesting, and no injury was suffered by allowing the crop to stand either uncut or in the shook for many weeks." Farmers found, moreover, that "in good years, sixty bushels of corn could be grown on the same land which would yield only twenty bushels of wheat."[54]

Free Frank had brought his agricultural equipment with him, and he also had a team of oxen to help in the plowing. According to Massie, an ox-team hitched to a pair of cart wheels, attached to a plow with a 14-foot beam and a share weighing from 60 to 125 pounds, allowed a farmer to plow a little over two acres a day, as compared with one acre for a team of horses.[55] Free Frank also had the assistance of his three sons: Squire, who was by now fifteen years old; Commodore, who was nine; and Young Frank, who was twenty-seven. In their second year of farming they were quite able to put almost 80 acres under cultivation, and by 1833, their third year, they were prepared to cultivate almost all of their full quarter section.

In that same year a second settler, Joshua Woosley, came to Hadley township and settled in section 19. The Pike County history recorded that Woosley was "the first white settler to locate in Hadley . . . [that he] cut logs, and built the second house in the township, the first being erected by [Free Frank] McWorter." Woosley brought a grain cradle that was used to cut wheat, and charged the settlers a bushel of wheat per acre for doing their cutting. "This new method of cutting wheat was a great curiosity to the settlers, many . . . came from far and near to see it."[56] Many Pike County farmers no longer had to rely on the sickle for wheat harvesting. Woosley lived to provide his own oral history, and his reminiscences of the early Pike County frontier are important because they suggest much about the early years of Free Frank's settlement. The 1872 *Atlas* recorded that during his first years of settlement

Mr. Woosley has had many hardships to endure in his pioneer life. Where he first settled in Pike County, the inhabitants were few and far between. He frequently found it difficult to procure breadstuff for himself and his family, as there was but one mill within twenty miles of him, and that was run by horse power. He has had to remain at the mill for five days at a time, awaiting his turn to grind. The prices of groceries were so high that it was almost impossible for a poor man to obtain them. Produce was very low, wheat of the best quality bringing only twenty-five to forty cents per bushel. The best of pork was worth from $1.25 to $1.50 per hundred. . . . Clothing was rather hard to obtain, and in lieu of the broadcloth, fine cassimeres, and patent-leather boots of the present day, they then used buckskin for coats, pants, and moccasins.[57]

Despite the isolation of the early Pike County pioneers, there were social activities. By 1833 Free Frank and Lucy had begun to take an active part in Pike County religious life. They were Baptists and attended meetings held at the home of one of the settlers in Pleasant Vale township, which was southwest of Hadley. The church group was part of the Salt River Association, which in 1833 changed its name to the Blue River Association. When the association met in 1834, Free Frank was one of the delegates.[58] That he was allowed to participate again provides insight into the attitudes of some whites in Illinois who tolerated the settlement of free blacks in the state.

This insight is important when one considers that many whites in Illinois, including some members of the state General Assembly, shared the sentiments of the American Colonization Society.[59] Numerous articles were published in the *Illinois Advocate* supporting the society's promotion of Liberia as a haven for free blacks. The articles highlighted the opportunities available for trade, education, and religious activities, and especially agricultural productivity. Even the military strength of Liberia was reported. Typical of the articles was one which asserted that "the population is 2,000; they have six militia companies, a fort, 20 pieces of cannon, and arms enough to arm 1000 men."[60] The *Illinois Advocate* was widely circulated in Pike County; with so little news from the outside, settlers there eagerly awaited each issue.

The Illinois branch of the American Colonization Society began an active push for the removal of its free black population in the summer of 1833. In its annual report of the previous January, however, the society announced: "Happily for us . . . our civil institutions coinciding with public sentiments, have in great measure, excluded from our country, that class of population, who form the immediate objects of this branch of christian benevolence—the free people of color." The society recommended that Illinois's black population be left undisturbed, for "the free blacks are not so numerous as to become burthens to us—nor considered of sufficient importance to be made special objects of oppression. Few in number, and harmless in character, their situation attracts, in our happy and plentiful country, but little notice, and, less sympathy."[61]

By July, the society's position had changed remarkably. It now advocated almost vehemently an entirely new policy: "It should be the constant aim of the friends of this society to disseminate a perfect knowledge of its designs and operations." The society particularly urged its members to take an active part in working to "convince the colored friends in this section many of whom are able of themselves to remove to this Heaven [Liberia] for the oppressed."[62] This particular commentary is of unusual interest, since the principal stated reason for excluding blacks from Illinois was that they would become economic liabilities. The position of the society confirms in part what Harris found as he examined the conditions of racial hostility under which free blacks lived on the Illinois frontier. Regardless of their financial circumstances, as settlement advanced, many whites "tolerated their presence on the soil of Illinois merely as an unavoidable evil."[63]

In spite of these hostile racial conditions, Free Frank intensified his economic activities. His efforts to earn money were made especially difficult by the low prices paid for farm produce in the early 1830s. To provide food and other necessities for his family, Free Frank, like other Pike County farmers, cultivated oats, flax, barley, and potatoes. Many pioneer farmers also raised sheep for wool, which along with flax provided material for clothing and other household needs. The first two years were the hardest, but as the Pike County history explained, Free Frank "then went to work in good earnest at farming and raising stock, at which he was quite successful."[64]

Mitchell underscored the extensive stock raising activities on the Illinois frontier during the 1830s, where he found that "the Wild Prairie everywhere covered with grass, invited the raising of cattle. Many of the farmers possess large droves and they may be multiplied to an almost indefinite extent."[65] There was always a ready market for cattle. From the early 1830s on, drovers from Ohio purchased steers from three years of age and up in great numbers in Illinois, buying them at a market price of twelve to twenty dollars a head. Then, too, as Peck notes, the cattle were "sometimes sent on flat boats down the Mississippi and Ohio for the New Orleans market."[66] Free Frank, like many other pioneers, brought his cattle with him, and it was generally understood that unenclosed lands, whether purchased or otherwise, were common pasturage.

Rebecca Burlend wrote that there were thousands of acres of unsettled land which allowed any person to keep as many cattle during the summer as he chose.[67] Pike County's terrain encouraged cattle raising because "about two-thirds of the county" consisted of prairie.[68] All a farmer needed for stock raising was to provide salt for the cattle and keep them from straying. Altogether, during the period from May to October when the cattle were on the open range, the cost of pasturage was usually no more than a dollar per head. At the end of this period, when the corn had been harvested, the cattle were turned into the corn fields to feed. This procedure amounted to a cost of some 10 cents an acre. The total cost per head was between two and three dollars for winter feeding. "Under these conditions, cattle were made ready for the market in from three to five years at a cost of from $6.00 to $12.00 a head."[69] Peck said that a pioneer farmer who raised a hundred head of cattle or more might still call himself poor.[70]

Hog raising provided Free Frank additional farm income. The new settlers discovered quite early that hogs could be raised without any expense except for a few breeders with which to start. Hogs weighing from 60 to 100 pounds usually sold for $1.00 to $1.50 per head, and a farmer who fattened his hogs on corn could get "from three to four dollars [per hog], according to his size, quality and the time it was delivered." That a farmer could increase his income by raising hogs, said Peck, was seen in the case of a man in 1829 who "drove forty-two fat hogs to market, which he sold for one hundred and thirty-five dollars. [With this money he was able to pay $100 for his land, and] the remainder served to pay some small debts, and purchase his salt, iron and groceries for the ensuing year."[71]

Horse raising was also profitable on the Pike County frontier, where a good farm horse usually sold for $50. By 1834 Free Frank "took up" keeping stray horses. In the January 1835 special term of the Pike County Commissioners' meeting, it was "ordered that the treasurer pay Free Frank fourteen dollars eighty-seven cents for charges in taking up and keeping estray mares."[72] Under the law, the "taker-up" could acquire ownership of the property if its assessed value was under ten dollars and if, after a year had elapsed, there was no claim made on the property. Otherwise there would have to be an auction, with the property going to the highest bidder, "deducting the costs and charges paid by the taker-up, and reasonable expenses for keeping the same."[73] If the auction failed to secure enough money to pay the various expenses, the county could allow the taker-up to retain possession. One particular advantage for the taker-up was that within a year's time the mares could have foaled, and the taker-up could also maintain possession of the foals. Consequently, horse raising offered Free Frank another way to make money during his first years on the Illinois frontier.

Free Frank and his sons were not the only ones engaged in agricultural activities to secure money for the family enterprise. Lucy, like the wives of other frontier farmers, had several money-making activities. Butter- and cheese-making offered pioneer women in the Military Tract, especially in the counties bordering the Illinois River, a chance to contribute to the family income. Good cheese sold for eight cents and sometimes ten cents a pound, and could be easily sold. Collecting honey and wax was also profitable, and Mitchell reported that in the 1830s, "many of the frontier people make it a prominent business after the frost has killed the vegetation, to hunt [bees]

Table 5. Average Market Commodity Prices in Pike County,
1833-1835

Commodity	Price	Unit
Spring cows	$12.00 - $20.00 and higher	per head
Hogs, wild	3.00	per 100 lbs.
Hogs, domestic	4.00-5.00	per 100 lbs.
Hogs, stock	2.00-2.50	per head
Hams	.12- .35	each
Bacon	.10- .12	per slab
Wheat	.50-1.25	per bu.
Corn	.30	per bu.
Eggs	.10- .12	per doz.
Cheese	.08	per lb.
Butter (out-of-state market)	.20	per lb.
Butter (intrastate market)	.12	per lb.

SOURCES: *Atlas Map of Pike County, Illinois* (Davenport, Iowa, 1872); Samuel
Augustus Mitchell, *Illinois in 1837: A Sketch . . . of the State of Illinois* (Philadelphia:
S. A. Mitchell, 1837); John M. Peck, *A Gazetteer of Illinois: In Three Parts* (Jackson-
ville, Ill.: R. Goudy, 1834); Captain Melville D. Massie, *Past and Present of Pike
County, Illinois* (Chicago: S.J. Clarke, 1906); Chas. C. Chapman, *History of Pike
County, Illinois* (Chicago: C.C. Chapman, 1880); and Jess M. Thompson, *Pike County
History* (Racine, Wis.: Preston Miller, 1967).

for the honey and wax, both of which find a ready market." He emphasized,
too, that "bees are profitable stock for the farmer, and are kept to a considerable extent." Beeswax was even used sometimes as a medium of exchange.

Poultry raising also brought in money for pioneer farm women, and
Mitchell observed that in the Military Tract "poultry are raised in great pro-
fusion." It was not uncommon for farmers' wives to "raise three or four hundred fowls, besides geese, ducks, and turkeys, in a season." Settlement in
the Illinois Military Tract thus afforded pioneer farm women a chance to develop their own home enterprises, for Mitchell noted that "young fowls,
butter, and eggs, were the three articles usually mastered from every farm in
the counties adjacent to St. Louis for that market."[74] Most farm families
used this money to buy coffee, sugar, tea, and various articles of clothing.
But Free Frank's family could not afford these luxuries, for every cent was
needed as they saved for the freedom of the family.

By 1835, with the family now involved in cash farming, Free Frank's immediate concern was to find some means to locate a road to Atlas, the ship-

ping point for the family's farm produce and livestock. There were no roads in the wilderness area where he lived, but sometime before 1834 Free Frank began to clear the land to build his own road. The Pike County commissioners gave notice of the existence of this black pioneer's road in an 1834 report. After indicating that a new road would run to Pittsfield, the county seat established in 1833, the commissioners said that it would continue "thence north 47° W or nearly on a trail made by Free Frank to his house on Sec. 22—Town 4S Range 5W 11½ miles thence north 48° deg. W. or nearly to the north west corner of Section 2 in Town 4S Range 6W [Barry Township] to Adams County line 8 miles making 33 miles designated by stakes in the Prairie to Hacks & Blazes in the timber."[75]

Free Frank's road became the major trail that he and other Pike County settlers in adjacent areas, including county officials, took to Quincy when going there on federal land business. It was not until 1836, however, that an act was passed by the Illinois General Assembly to complete the road, thus making Free Frank's trail a public highway.[76]

Road building in Pike County would be carried out on a much larger scale once the population in the county began to increase after 1835.[77] Until then, Free Frank made his way to Atlas on paths and trails made by other farmers like himself.[78] But in 1834 the county commissioners also ordered that a new road be built from Atlas to Phillips Ferry. This road was less than six miles from Free Frank's farm. By 1835, then, Free Frank was able to move his produce to the Mississippi River with much greater ease, and, more important, he would be able to get the full market value for his agricultural commodities since he now had access to the eastern and southern markets. Table 5 lists the average prices paid for commodities produced on Pike County pioneer farms between 1833 and 1835.

In 1835, four years after his initial settlement in Illinois, with the money earned from the sale of his agricultural products, Free Frank was able to purchase his son Solomon from slavery for $550. The purchase required that he return to Kentucky. Anxiously he made the trip south, using the same route he had taken when he came to Illinois five years earlier. And what Free Frank had feared when he left Pulaski County in 1830 had happened: Solomon had been sold. Fortunately the new owner lived in Pulaski County and was willing to sell the young slave to his father. The purchase was made and the emancipation deed was recorded in the Pulaski County records. The deed, written by the clerk and given to Solomon by Free Frank, read:

Be it known to all whom it may concern, that whereas the undersigned Free Frank of Pike County of the state of Illinois have purchased a mulatto boy named Solomon aged about twenty-one years (a slave) from John Eastham Senr of the county of

Fig. 4. Solomon McWorter (1815-1879), slave-born son of Free Frank whose freedom was purchased by his father in 1835. Photographed about 1860. Courtesy of Thelma McWorter Kirkpatrick Wheaton.

Pulaski and state of Kentucky for the sum of five hundred and fiftey dollars, and for divers consideration have determined to emancipate and set free the said Solomon. Therefore, I [Free Frank] do by these presents emancipate and set free the said Solomon, and hereby release him from all obligation to me or my heirs as a slave. And to go hence, and henceforth enjoy all the rights privileges and immunities of a free man agreeable to the laws and constitution of the United States.

In testimony thereof I the said Free Frank have hereunto set my hand and seal this 17th day of August 1835.

his
Free X Frank
mark

At a county court held for Pulaski County at the courthouse thereof in the Town of Somerset on Monday the 17th day of August AD 1835. This Deed of Emancipation from Free Frank to Solomon, a slave, was acknowledged in open court to be his act and deed, and ordered to be recorded and the same is done accordingly.

Aft Will Fox Clark[79]

By purchasing and emancipating Solomon, his second son, Free Frank had accomplished part of his goal. Yet there still remained as slaves in Kentucky his two daughters and their children. While he was in Pulaski County, Free Frank doubtless again reassured the owners that he would return and purchase them, too. But another eight years would pass before that would occur. Yet that Free Frank was able to earn $550 from his agricultural activities in four years and to purchase Solomon points to the indomitable will and perseverance of this black frontiersman during his pioneer years in the Illinois wilderness.

From all indications, especially from the promotional literature, it appears that conditions for settlement in Illinois, particularly in the Military Tract, were never more favorable for the pioneer farmer than in the early 1830s. John M. Peck, an itinerant Baptist, in his travels through the Illinois Military Tract observed that any prospective migrant could "have a large farm under cultivation in a short time."[80] But for a black family, establishing a farm on the Illinois frontier involved more than just settling on good land in a favorable location and breaking the prairie sod. For a free black family, it also involved more than just moving from a slave state to a free state. Racism was just as pervasive on the new frontier, and the threat of reenslavement was just as persistent. Both were constant factors that the black pioneer could not ignore while working to make a success of his farming operations.

One particular advantage Free Frank found when he settled in Pike County was that its sparse population of diverse origin encouraged organized community efforts to develop the county. Government land disposal policies made it difficult for prospective settlers to purchase Military Tract land until 1835. Moreover, the few white pioneers who settled Pike County in the early 1830s were more concerned with Indian threats and the desire to move beyond self-sufficiency than with interfering with the activities of a free black farmer. Even with prejudiced Illinois lawmakers, "nigger stealers," and the American Colonization society working to effect the removal of free blacks, Free Frank was able to develop his Hadley township land. Having arrived prepared to cope with agricultural conditions on the Illinois frontier, Free Frank used his entrepreneurial ability as well as his skills as a farmer to make his pioneer farm homestead pay.

CHAPTER SIX

Land Acquisitions and
New Philadelphia's Origin

Be it Remembered that before me Jonathan Piper a justice
of the peace within and for said county and State Free
Frank a collered man the proprietor of a new Town named
Philadelphia . . . in the County of Pike and State of Illinois and who is personally Known to me to be the identi-
cal person who Claims the same as proprietor and acknowledged the within and foregoing to be a true and perfect plat of said Town delivered hand and seal of Pittsfield
the 16th day of September in the year 1836.[1]

The town of New Philadelphia was platted on an eighty-acre tract that Free
Frank had purchased from the federal government for $100 in 1835.[2] While
this tract was the first of eight that Free Frank and his sons would buy within
the next four years, the town's site was the only land purchase made that
year. Solomon's manumission from slavery had been Free Frank's paramount objective. With that accomplished, and with both Young Frank and
Solomon working the family's farm, Free Frank intensified the cultivation of
their 160-acre farm holdings. In the following year, with money earned from
the sale of farm produce and livestock, he acquired five additional tracts
amounting to 280 acres. Four of those tracts were purchased from the federal
government, a total of 200 acres for $250. The other tract involved a private
land purchase of 80 acres for $112, twelve dollars more than what the land
would have cost at a minimum if purchased from the federal government. In
this instance the site's location, adjacent to the tract purchased in 1835, was
important to Free Frank. Its acquisition allowed him to consolidate his holdings. The last two tracts, a total of 280 acres purchased during a depression
also involved private transactions. One of these was a 120-acre tract purchased by Free Frank's son Commodore in 1839 for $900. Over a decade
passed before final payment was made, in 1852.

Federal lands laws controlled the purchase of those tracts that Free Frank
acquired from the federal government.[3] Under the Land Act of 1820, the
federal government had for the first time allowed a minimum eighty-acre
acquisition but also required full payment at the time of purchase. After

Table 6. Real Property Purchased by Free Frank and His Sons in Pike County, 1830-1839

Tract[1]	Location of Land	No. of Acres	Date of Purchase	Purchase Price	Grantor	Grantee
A	SE 1/4 sec. 22	160	Sept. 13, 1830	$200	G. Elliot	Free Frank
B	N 1/2 of N 1/4 sec. 27	80	June 11, 1835	100	U.S. Govt.	Free Frank
C	W 1/2 of SW 1/4 sec. 26	80	Feb. 12, 1836	100	U.S. Govt.	Free Frank
D	NE of SW 1/4 sec. 26	40	Apr. 23, 1836	50	U.S. Govt.	Free Frank
E	SE of SE 1/4 sec. 27	40	May 13, 1836	50	U.S. Govt.	Squire Frank
F	NW of SE 1/4 sec. 26	40	June 10, 1836	50	U.S. Govt.	Commodore Frank
G	W 1/2 of NW 1/4 sec. 26	80	June 10, 1836	112	Higbee	Frank McWorter
H	NE 1/4 sec. 28	160	Nov. 13, 1839	480	Lamb & Dunlop	Frank McWorter
I	SW 1/4 sec. 22 (part)[2]	120	Sept. 29, 1839	900	Adams	Commodore McWorter
	Total	800		$2,042		

SOURCE: Pike County Tract Index, Hadley-Berry (T4SR5, 6W), Pike County Courthouse, Pittsfield, Ill.

1. See Fig. 5 for location of these tracts.
2. Final payment for this tract was made in 1852.

1835 Free Frank's land was purchased under the 1832 Land Act, made effective in the Illinois Military Tract when public land in this area was put on sale in 1834. While this act allowed a minimum purchase of forty-acre tracts, under the 1836 Land Act the federal government required full payment in specie for public land. Private land offices, quickly established in frontier areas, provided loans, but interest rates, which ran as high as 37 percent, discouraged some prospective buyers. Until the full amount was paid, the office controlled title to the land, and payment default often resulted in the farmer's loss of property and any improvements, as well. Table 6 shows a total of 800 acres in Hadley township purchased by Free Frank and his sons from 1830 through 1839. The location of each tract is shown in Figure 5, a federal surveyor's map of Hadley township.

Those acquisitions would comprise the family's only land purchases in Illinois before the Civil War. As Paul W. Gates emphasizes, "Immigrants newly arriving in the West soon learned that unless they quickly established a claim to land, their chances of making good selections would be minimized, perhaps lost to other more foresighted settlers or to speculators."[4] From his experiences on the Kentucky frontier, Free Frank had found that in wilderness areas with sparse populations, few pioneer whites interfered directly with the economic activities of blacks. Doubtless he realized that while land was available, especially in an area of demonstrated productivity, and while he was not barred from buying it, he should purchase as much as he possibly could. That decision was not made lightly. The money paid for the land could instead be added to the savings to purchase an additional family member. At the same time, if he waited, his options for future land purchases would be considerably diminished, thus limiting the expansion of his farm holdings. By increasing the acreage under cultivation, over the long run his earnings would put Free Frank in a better financial position, which would expedite the purchase of his family in slavery. Not only would those new holdings provide him with a broader economic basis, but the land could be developed and sold. Expanding his holdings would also provide an economic base for his children, once they were free.

The government surveyor who drew the map of Hadley township gave the following description of the land purchased by Free Frank and his sons: "Between Sections 26 and 27 T4SR5W there was a creek. Sections 22, 23, 26, and 27, brook running through over Broken Bushy Barrons. Timber oak, undergrowth oak and hazel." E. Dana, a private citizen who traveled through the Military Tract in 1819 to secure information for distribution to prospective settlers, also described Hadley township: "Range 5—secs. 16, 17, 18, 19, 20, 21, 22, 28, 29, 30, 31, 32, 33, 34, west half of 15, 2, 3, 36, first rate; secs. 24, 10, 5, 6, 7, north half of 8, 9, second rate; remainder

mostly much broken: growth oak, hickory, ash, lynn, grape and pea vines."[5]
Thus, government surveys and contemporary private descriptions show that
the land purchased by Free Frank and his sons was all first rate. The government descriptions provided the basis for the tax rates assessed on their holdings.

The federal records also indicate that two other blacks purchased land in
Pike County in 1835 and 1836 adjacent to Free Frank's.[6] Whether this was
by choice or because frontier land-claiming activities in Pike made it difficult for blacks to buy land in other areas of the county is open to speculation. In either case, that there were so few black landowners in Pike County
demonstrates again that free blacks were frequently excluded from access to
America's vast land resources on the new nation's frontiers. Federal and
state laws covering the sale and distribution of public land in Illinois did not
preclude its sale to blacks, but Illinois Black Codes and frontier land-claiming activities were as effective as any exclusionary land laws in discouraging
land acquisitions by blacks. All of Free Frank's land purchases were in the
Military Tract. The history of the disposal of Military Tract land provides an
example not only of how blacks were denied access to the public domain,
but of how various proposals offered for the distribution of public land before Free Frank's settlement sought to reinforce prevailing social policies relating to blacks. It provides a historical context to examine the implications
of land acquisitions by black pioneers during this period.

When the United States Congress first debated the issue of Military
Tract land distribution in 1816, Free Frank was still a slave. At that time the
Kentucky Abolition Society had proposed that Congress set aside part of the
1,860,000 acres of this land, contemporaneously referred to as "Congress
land," for free blacks. The basis for the society's proposal was the government's policy of granting land to soldiers as payment for military service:
"Your petitioners are well aware that the Government has not been in the
habit of giving away lands without a suitable remuneration except to the officers and soldiers who have served in the Armies of the United States." The
society pointed, however, to the noncombatant military services provided by
slaves during the War of 1812, forcefully arguing "that although the negroes have not rendered service to our country in that way, they were toiling
in the field and without any compensation, furnishing by their labour and
means of support to those who were conflicting with the enemies of our
Country."[7]

While the federal government might reluctantly concede the home-
front contributions of slaves during the War of 1812, a policy supporting
land grants for free blacks was not to be its form of acknowledgment. Even
when the question arose as to whether black veterans of the War of 1812

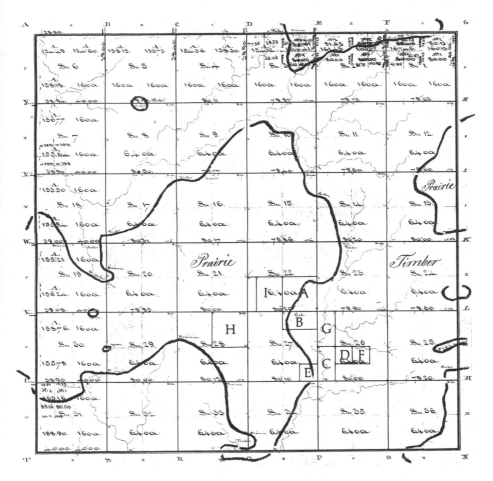

Fig. 5. Federal surveyor's map showing the land purchased by Free Frank and his sons in Hadley township, 1830-1839. New Philadelphia was platted on tract B. From Federal Field Notes, vol. 263, Illinois State Archives, Springfield. Courtesy of Wayne C. Temple. See Table 6 for explanation of letters.

were entitled to military land bounties, there was a general reluctance by the federal government to grant them this free land.[8] Under these circumstances, Congress's rejection of the Abolition Society's proposal was not surprising, particularly since federal policy decisions would in this instance, according to the Abolition Society, serve as a "preparatory measure which may pave the way to a total emancipation of the unhappy negroes in the United States." The society felt its petition merited serious consideration, since its recommendation was based on the response of "a great number of slave-holders [who] have declared their willingness and desire to liberate their slaves if the General Government would make provisions for colonizing them."[9] No action was taken by the federal government, since the proposal was also predicated on moving former slaves out of the states into the federal territories. The Abolition Society had apparently disregarded Illinois's rapid advance to statehood. Even if Congress had seriously considered the desirability of such a proposal, once Illinois became a state in 1818 the federal government would exercise judicious restraint before reserving public land for black colonization or using its power of eminent domain to appropriate state land for this purpose.

Illinois, with its 1819 Black Code, enacted one year after statehood, attempted to discourage the settlement of free blacks. Finding the code ineffective in restricting black emigration, more stringent legislation was proposed, and in the General Assembly hearings of 1828 the state was urged to support the program of the American Colonization Society to resettle free blacks in Africa. In 1829 the General Assembly announced the state's position in regard to free blacks when it stated that "the colony of free blacks now settling in Africa, under the paternal care of the Colonization society, it is thought will go far to effect this desirable object."[10]

Not surprisingly, when the federal government announced in 1830 that the "Congress land" in the Illinois Military Tract would be put on sale, the American Colonization Society presented a proposal to Congress urging that funds from the sale of the land be used to colonize free blacks in Liberia.[11] The reponse of the federal government, however, was that such funds could not be used for this purpose since this was too "delicate [a] question for Congress to touch." The primary concern of Congress was to assure the slave states that the federal government would not provide support for any program that was even remotely related to slavery. In this report of 1831, Congress emphasized that the general consensus of the federal government precluded their support of the Colonization Society's proposals: "The harmony of the States and the durability of this confederacy, interdict the legislation of the Federal legislature upon this subject." While not addressing itself directly to the issue of the colonization of free blacks from free states, the federal government's categorical response, for states that looked to Washington for directives, was that "instead of assuming the business of colonization, leave it to the slave holding states to do as they please; and leave them their resources to carry into effect their resolves."[12] By this statement, the Illinois legislature was given tacit approval to enact any legislation or to pursue any policy it chose relating to the disposition of its black population.

Restrictive legislation that discouraged black settlement in Illinois was one response of the state legislators. The law that required blacks to post a $1,000 admission bond to enter the state, however, actually served a dual purpose. While designed to exclude free blacks, the astronomically high security bond would at the same time provide a unique source of revenue. Illinois during the early period of statehood was a poor state. The majority of whites who settled there were poor and contributed very little to the state's support. Illinois's principal source of revenue was the land tax, but, as Carlson shows in his review of land taxes paid in the period 1821-1832, nonresidents' taxes accounted for most of the state's income. The tax was based on the quality of the land. The tax was one-half of 1 percent of the total land value for Military Tract lands which were assessed as second-rate. Thus the tax on a quarter section, 160 acres, would have been $2.40. If this was considered an oppressive burden for whites, one can only speculate on the nature of the security bond of $1,000 for blacks.

The fiscal period for state tax collection on real property was two years. In the 1830-1832 period, when Free Frank first paid his property taxes in Illinois, only 7.1 percent of Illinois residents paid property taxes. The total tax receipts in that year amounted to only $95,001.[13] LuDuc in his study of federal land policies underlines Illinois's dire financial straits during the early years of statehood: "the interior of the United States between 1815 and the Civil War furnished a prime instance of the underdeveloped area." LeDuc emphasizes the state's potential, but adds that even with its vast "resources of soil, climate, vegetation, energy, and metals, its greatest need was a tremendous dose of capital."[14] The security bond was high and was designed to keep out blacks, but Illinois needed money from any source during this period, and if blacks could pay the bond, the state would not hesitate to take it.

Requiring blacks to post a security bond on the basis that they might become financial burdens to the state rested on a somewhat specious policy basis. Agriculture paced the state's economy, and most blacks had experience in farm labor. During the early years of settlement in Illinois, especially in the 1820s and 1830s, the state's potential for agricultural development, as Peck observed, pointed to the success of pioneer farmers: "Any laboring man, with reasonable industry and economy, with a family, may arrive here without any capital, and in half a dozen years be the owner of a good farm, with stock in abundance."[15] This is exactly what many whites did. They arrived by the tens of thousands and, without funds, preempted the land and set up pioneer farm homesteads.[16] LeDuc's study reveals that preemption was not an unusual practice, although it was in violation of federal policy. "Squatting became universal [even though] Congress had forbidden occupancy of the public land in 1807, and had authorized the President to use the Army to eject intruders. . . . With the tide of migration after 1815, enforcement became politically inexpedient and collapsed."[17]

Tax receipts during the 1820s and early 1830s indicate that most of the settlers in Illinois were squatters. The irony is that those squatters were ultimately rewarded for their defiance of the government's attempts to restrict their settlement. In 1828 the federal government for the first time endorsed a policy of preemption. Those who had preempted land by 1829, and who had settled and cultivated their holdings, were allowed first chance to buy that land before sales opened to the public. The basis for this action, as announced in the Preemption Act, was the need to provide some form of compensation for those early pioneers who had contributed to the initial development of the state. "It is right and proper that the first settlers, who have made roads and bridges over the public lands at their expense and with great labor and toil should be allowed a greater privilege than other purchasers."[18]

Access to land ownership in Illinois by free blacks under the Preemption Act, however, was difficult if not impossible. The state's Black Codes had discouraged their emigration and settlement, so that few free blacks were in the state to take advantage of this radical new policy. Having only limited means to protect themselves, few blacks dared to settle the Illinois wilderness in the 1830s. Any white squatter could easily run them off the land and would be happy to do so, especially if improvements had been made. Few blacks could even find employment as farm laborers, since most white landowners in this period lived at a virtual subsistence level. As LeDuc explains, "If they [the white settlers] had no liquid capital with which to buy land, neither did they have it to hire labor to develop the land."[19] Most of the state's free black population therefore lived in towns as much for their own protection as to find employment to support themselves.

Even blacks who could afford to buy land under federal land acts encountered difficulty. On the Illinois frontier, land-purchasing involved more than just going to the land office and buying a tract sight unseen.[20] While many people used federal land maps or travel gazetteers, such as Dana's *Descriptions of the Bounty Lands,* to get some indication of the quality of the land and its site and situation prior to purchase, many attempted to see the land first-hand by riding out to view it. Considering that free blacks were constantly being kidnapped or detained as fugitive slaves in Illinois, it is unlikely that many traveled about searching for good land to claim.

For those few blacks who threw all caution to the wind and decided to take advantage of the Preemption Act, frontier land-claiming practices made this a very difficult and dangerous process. Land claiming was serious business. Even white prospective land purchasers encountered difficulty. Before 1835 Pike County land-claiming practices acted to discourage the settlement of newcomers, especially squatters. According to Chapman, "the new settlers had an agreement among themselves by which they allowed a man to 'claim about as much timber land as he might need, generally not over 160 acres, . . . and woe unto the speculator or newcomer who should attempt to 'claim' land already occupied by a bonafide settler."[21] That Free Frank was in the Military Tract during this period can be attributed in part to the fact that his Hadley township land was purchased before he settled there. That his land was under cover of Military Tract bounty warrant provided an added advantage. This black pioneer was at least afforded legal protection from any squatter, and also from any legitimate Pike County landholder who might want to preempt his holdings.

Thus, when the Quincy federal land office put large tracts of "Congress land" on sale after 1834, Free Frank was in a position to make his claim for additional Hadley township land. A bona fide settler, he also knew what land was available for sale. Furthermore, with Illinois's exclusionary Black Code, there was little fear among Pike County whites that they would soon be inundated by waves of black settlers because of Free Frank's precedent-setting 1830 land purchase. When the land did go on sale, Free Frank's first land purchase was the 80-acre tract directly south of his Pike County farm, the site on which the former slave subsequently platted New Philadelphia. The deed of purchase was recorded in part as follows:

The United States of America to all to whom these presents shall come Greetings. Whereas Free Frank of Pike County Illinois has deposited in the General Land Office of the United States a certificate of the Register of the Land Office at Quincy whereby it appears that full payment has been made by the said Free Frank according to the provisions of the act of Congress of the 24th April 1820 entitled an act making further provision for the sale of the Public land for the North half of the North East quarter of Section twenty seven in Township four South of the base line of Range Five West of the fourth principal Meridian in the District of land subject to sale at Quincy Illinois Containing Eighty acres according to an official plat of the survey of the said Land returned to the General Land Office by the surveyor General, which said tract has been purchased by the said Free Frank. Now know ye that the United States of America in consideration of the promise and in conforming with the several acts of Congress in such case made and provided Have Given and Granted, and by these presents do Give and Grant unto the said Free Frank and to his heirs the said tract above described. To Have and To hold the same together with all the rights privileges immunities and appurtances of what ever nature thereunto belonging, unto the said Free Frank and to his heirs and assignes forever.[22]

Table 7. Hadley Township Public Land Sales, 1833-1850

Section	No. of Acres	Date of Sale	Section	No. of Acres	Date of Sale
18	77	May 1833	26 (cont'd)	80	June 1836
	40	Nov. 1833		80	Oct. 1836[4]
	38	Apr. 1834		40	Oct. 1838
	38	Sept. 1835		80	Nov. 1838
	38	Dec. 1835			
	38	Dec. 1835	27	80	Nov. 1834
	40	Dec. 1835		40	Nov. 1834
	76	Feb. 1836		80	June 1835[5]
	40	Apr. 1836		40	May 1836[3]
	40	Apr. 1837		40	Oct. 1837
				40	June 1841
23	80	Jan. 1836			
	40	Oct. 1836	28	40	Mar. 1834
	40	May 1837		40	Apr. 1836
	40	Oct. 1837		160	July 1836
	40	July 1837[1]		80	Oct. 1836
	40	Aug. 1847[2]			
	40	Sept. 1850	31	81	
				40	
25	160	Nov. 1840		40	
	80	Nov. 1840			
	80	Nov. 1840	32	40	Sept. 1835
	160	Nov. 1840		40	Aug. 1836
	160	Mar. 1843		80	Nov. 1836
26	80	Oct. 1833	33	80	Oct. 1833
	40	Nov. 1834			
	40	Mar. 1835	35	80	Oct. 1833
	80	Feb. 1836[3]		80	Feb. 1834
	40	Apr. 1836[3]		80	Nov. 1835
	40	May 1836		80	Aug. 1836
	40	June 1836[3]		80	Oct. 1836

SOURCE: Federal Tract Book S: Quincy, Township 4S Range 5 West, 701: 17-22, Illinois State Archives, Springfield. The average price of the land was $1.25 per acre.

1. Land purchased by a black man; federal tract records have written beside his name "man of color."

2. Land purchased by another black man; federal tract records have written beside his name "col man."

3. Land purchased by Free Frank and his sons.

4. Land purchased by a black man; federal tract records do not indicate he was black, but the federal manuscript census for Pike County in 1840 lists him under the "Free Colored" column along with Free Frank and his family.

5. Land on which New Philadelphia was sited.

The minimum subdivision allowed for sale after 1834 was a forty-acre parcel, and in the following year Pike County experienced a precipitous population increase. With the settlement of small landholders, the county's population almost doubled within the year, from 3,570 in 1834 to 6,037 by 1835.[23] The reduced acreage allowed per purchase was one factor that contributed to the county's growth, but the proposed construction of the Illinois-Michigan canal was even more important. After construction began in 1836, over 500 towns were platted in the state. Although not all of the sites developed into towns, as John Reps shows, "hundreds of paper towns, did gradually become actual settlements."[24]

New Philadelphia was one of these towns, and one of twenty-three founded in Pike County between 1834 and 1837.[25] As Chapman says, "Towns were laid out on every hand, and a majority of the villages of Pike County were platted, christened and started upon their way during this eventful period."[26] Until 1833 the only town in the county was Atlas, the county seat, platted in 1823. The founding of Pike County's new towns reflected liberal public land policies and deferential land-claiming practices, as well as the town-building mania precipitated by the construction of the canal. Most Pike County town founders anticipated the future expansion of Illinois River trade with the completion of the canal. Only three towns founded during this period were located near the Mississippi River, while almost half were on the Illinois River side, with the others in the central part of the county. Commercial agriculture in the Illinois-Mississippi Valley had begun in the early 1830s, and with the advent of the steamboat as the principal common carrier, the Illinois River became, as Carlson says, "a great avenue of trade for goods pouring into and out of the western regions of the Military Tract." The building of the canal thus increased Pike's trade advantages, since "10 to 20 miles was as far as grain or bulky products could be hauled profitably," and no site in the county was more than twenty miles from either river.[27]

In the interior of the county most Pike town founders selected sites already established as central places, either where frontier businesses—distilleries, mills, blacksmithies, and groceries—were located, or where a school or church was established, with a surrounding agricultural population. New Philadelphia fits this pattern with respect to the population of Hadley township. It was centrally located in an area of increasing population. Table 7 shows the public land transactions in sections 18-35, the area surrounding section 27, where New Philadelphia was located. Those sections not included were under cover of Military Tract bounty land warrants. As New Philadelphia developed, it would service farmers in other sections of the township, as well, but federal tract records show that population settlement in some sections of Hadley township proceeded at a much slower rate. For

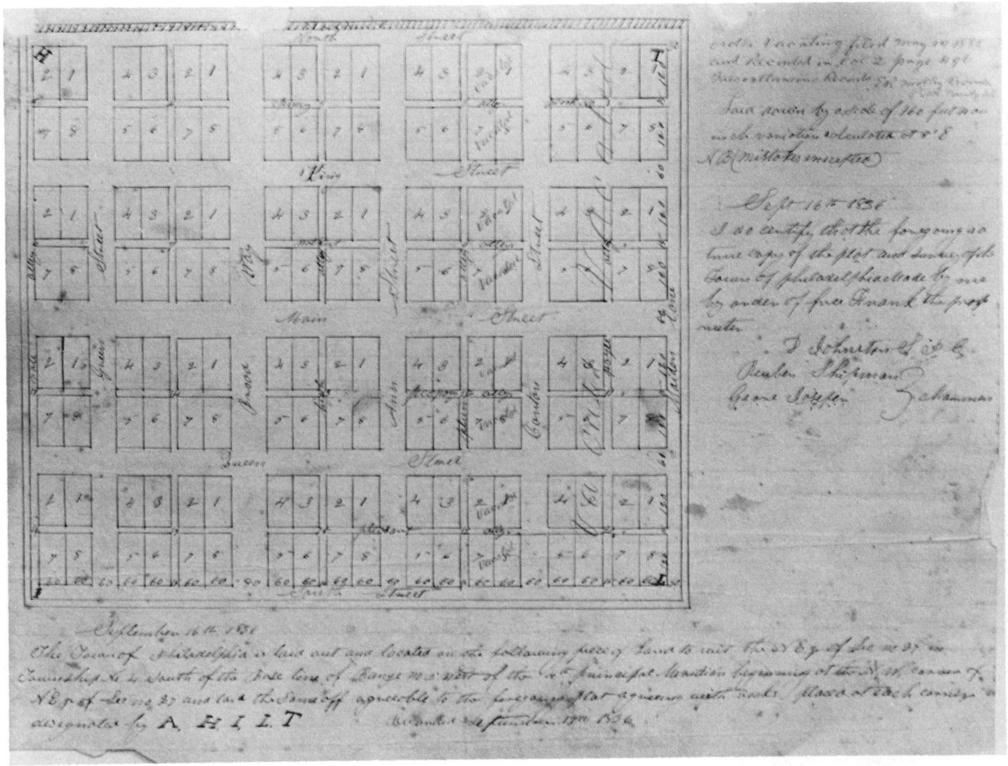

Fig. 6. Town plat of New Philadelphia, drawn up and recorded in 1836, with later notations of lots vacated. From the Pike County Deed Record Book, 9:183, Pike County Courthouse, Pittsfield, Illinois. Photo by Sandidge Studio.

sections 1-6, twenty-seven purchases are shown, but only six were made before 1836, seven in the period 1837-1839, and the remaining fourteen in the years 1842-1861. In sections 7-15 there were forty-three purchases, seventeen in 1836, fourteen in 1837-1839, and twelve in 1840-1855. Military bounty land sales and county tax sales are recorded in Pike County Deed Record Books, which, with the listings obtained from federal tract records, are important sources on the sale of small land tracts in the area where Free Frank platted New Philadelphia.

The Illinois Town Plat Act, which regulated the activity of town founding, included no provision which would prevent blacks from platting a town. Free Frank, for one, never hesitated to take advantage of state and federal laws, especially when the possibility existed that additional money could be earned to buy his family from slavery. Platting a town was one way to generate income. All that was necessary initially was to own the land, since the act stipulated only "that whenever any county commissioners or other person or persons wish to lay out a town in this state, or an addition or subdivision of outlots, said commissioners or other person or persons shall cause the same to be surveyed, and a plat or map thereof made by the county surveyor." [28]

A plat of New Philadelphia is shown in Figure 6. It was made in conformance to the Town Plat Act, which required that the "plat or map shall particularly describe and set forth all the streets, alleys, commons, or public grounds, and all in and out-lots, or fractional lots, within, adjoining, or adjacent to said town, giving the names, widths, corners, boundaries, and extent of all such streets and alleys." Following the gridiron or checkerboard pattern characteristic of American towns, New Philadelphia was platted with 144 lots, each 60 by 120 feet. [29] Main Street and Broad Way, the two principal streets, were 80 feet wide; the others were 60 feet wide, with alleys 19 feet wide. Although there is no indication of a town square on the plat, one was located at the intersection of Main Street and Broad Way. The names of the streets and alleys, their length and width, and the number and size of the lots were all determined by Free Frank, according to the Pike County surveyors, who entered the following statement in the plat book:

Sept. 16th 1836

I do certify that the foregoing is a true copy of the plat and survey of the Town of Philadelphia Made by me by order of Free Frank the proprietor

P. Johnston SPC

Reuben Shipman   chairmen

Geane Joseph

Free Frank also had to pay the fees stipulated by the Town Plat Act for the survey and the recording of the plat. The surveyor was paid twenty-five cents for each lot surveyed, and the county clerk was paid four cents per lot, making Free Frank's total payment $41.76. This was not a trifling sum. Only three years earlier, in 1833, the Pike County commissioners had to borrow $200 just to buy the land where the new county seat, Pittsfield, was sited.[30] Land ownership, then, was only an initial precondition to platting a town. It was a speculative venture, and because of the risks that their investment might fail, many prospective proprietors arranged for a survey of less than twenty lots.

By 1836, in addition to platting a town, Free Frank owned 600 acres of land. As a free black his right to the ownership of his property under Illinois law was somewhat limited. It was at best a specious right emanating from property rights granted blacks who had been indentured servants.[31] But Free Frank's land-purchasing activities in Kentucky and the court cases in which he had been involved in that state had demonstrated to him that in some instances American law could be used to the advantage of blacks. In 1836, using as a precedent the Illinois law that permitted manumitted blacks to own property, Free Frank petitioned the Illinois General Assembly for the right to take a legal surname so that title to his property would not be alienated. The surname requested in the petition was McWorter.[32]

In 1820, when he was first listed in the federal manuscript census, the newly manumitted slave did not assume a surname but had his name recorded as Free Frank. In the 1830 federal manuscript census, Free Frank used Denham, the surname of Lucy's former owner, as his own surname. Gutman, in his study of the black family, found evidence that "slaves over the entire South in the century and a half preceding the general emancipation had surnames different from their owners'."[33] Several factors may account for Free Frank's use of Denham in 1830. At that time he and Lucy were preparing to leave Pulaski County. Obediah Denham still owned Lucy's and Free Frank's slave-born children. Doubtless the litigation in which the three had been involved for several years had not improved their relationship. Using his surname may have been Free Frank's way of ingratiating himself with Denham, showing the slaveholder that he harbored no ill will, and perhaps offsetting any further hostility which might result in the sale of the children before Free Frank could return to purchase them. It might also provide him one way of tracing his children if Denham should sell them. After the Civil War, as the tragic consequences showed, many black families separated during the antebellum period were never reunited. Without a surname, former slaves sometimes encountered great difficulty in tracing family members sold during slavery.[34] Free Frank never used the surname Denham in his business transactions, and land records in both Kentucky and Illinois show that until 1836 he and his sons used Frank as their surname.

When Free Frank moved to assume a legally authorized surname in

1836, he chose one of the variant spellings of McWhorter, the name of his former master, even though it appears that he had severed any connections with the McWhorter family in 1819, when he purchased his freedom. The available record of his forty-two years as a slave does not suggest that George McWhorter had ever shown any paternal interest in him. Even McWhorter's sons always referred to Free Frank as a Negro, rather than a mulatto, possibly to obviate any legal record that Free Frank's father was perhaps their own. The use of McWorter as a surname, then, may have been Free Frank's way of announcing this relationship. Under the law of slavery the father of a slave child had no legal existence, and Free Frank may have wished to establish his paternity legally, even though his father was a slaveholder. That he chose McWorter as a surname provides no validation of George McWhorter's paternity, of course, but the family's oral tradition recognizes the relationship.

Free Frank's petition was approved by the General Assembly, but he quickly petitioned that body again, asking that the act be amended to grant him further legal powers. In its entirety, the amended act stated:

Sec. 1. *Be it enacted by the people of the State of Illinois represented in the General Assembly,* That the name of Free Frank, of the county of Pike and State of Illinois, be and is hereby changed to that of Frank McWorter, by which latter name he shall hereafter be called and known, and sue and be sued, plead and be impleaded, purchase and convey both real and personal property in said last mentioned name, and the children of said Free Frank shall hereafter take the name of their father, as changed and provided for by this act.
Sec. 2. This act to be in force from and after its passage.
APPROVED 19th January, 1837.[35]

Significantly, this was perhaps the first time in all his years as a land-owner that Free Frank acquired some degree of security in the ownership of his property. It was particularly crucial at this stage of his life that there be no question regarding the legality of his holdings, either of his town lots or his farm land. His purpose was clear: the money obtained from the sale of town lots would be used to buy his family from slavery. Within a year after Free Frank founded New Philadelphia, a group of prominent Pike County residents made note of his purpose. In his Illinois Certificate of Good Character, dated May 17, 1837, they said that Free Frank "has laid off a town which he calls Philadelphia, and understanding and believing that the said Frank has laid out the town intending to apply the proceeds of the sales for the purchase of his family yet remaining as slaves . . . the said town is in a handsome country, undoubtedly healthy."[36]

Location was an important factor in the establishment of frontier towns, determining to a great extent their potential for future growth and development. At the time New Philadelphia was platted there were no other towns or even settlements of concentrated population within a reasonable market-journey. In frontier areas with undeveloped roads, travel was obviously difficult and time consuming. Improved dirt and gravel roads appear to have made little difference. Even into the early twentieth century, as a former Pike County resident has noted, "On good days when the roads were dry, wagons carrying a heavy load could go only four miles an hour."[37] Barry, platted in 1836 and only four miles from New Philadelphia's site, was the closest place to the west. The town of Washington (now El Dara), also platted in 1836, was seven miles south of New Philadelphia. Until New Salem was founded in 1847, the nearest town directly to the east was Griggsville.[38]

New Philadelphia's site was not only central in respect to the north central part of Pike County, but also in respect to Hadley township's settlement pattern. Readville and Bloomfield, for example, were platted in Hadley township at the same time as New Philadelphia. Readville's site, like New Philadelphia's, was central to an area of increasing population, but its proprietor had made a serious error—perhaps one he could not have anticipated. The town's site was within a mile of Barry in the adjacent township. Even before Barry was platted, it was a central place—a store and a mill had been located there since the early 1830s. Furthermore, in the competition for town development, Barry's proprietors, members of the established St. Louis firm of Stone, Field and Marks, were certainly in a much better position to promote the development of their town.

The people within New Philadelphia's hinterland, in contrast to those in Readville's, being located some distance by wagon road from Barry, would find it much easier to go to New Philadelphia for their trade, except for their milling. In addition, settlers in the eastern part of Readville's hinterland could as easily go to New Philadelphia for provisions as to Readville or Barry. Readville did not survive, nor did Bloomfield; their plats were vacated in 1843.[39] Readville's brief history, however, is interesting as it relates to New Philadelphia. The town's proprietor had platted Readville three months before Free Frank platted New Philadelphia, initially with only eight blocks of 64 lots. Then, ten days after Free Frank platted New Philadelphia with its 144 lots, Readville's proprietor platted an addition to his town whereby it too had 144 lots.

From the beginning, town proprietors competed in promoting the development of their towns. Agriculture was the state's principal economic activity, and most new settlers looked to purchase farmland. Pike County's favorable location in the Illinois-Mississippi River Valley promised prospective farmers almost immediate profitable development. And, as Pooley explains, "Wherever a prosperous agricultural community was found, a town of some importance was close by since the latter must look to the former for support."[40] Even after he founded New Philadelphia, Free Frank remained outside the town, living on his farm. He was shrewd enough to realize that if New Philadelphia was to grow, he must attract farmers as well as townspeople. His own success as a farmer and stockraiser was thus part of his strategy to promote New Philadelphia's development. Farm settlers would help provide the necessary population threshold which would encourage prospective town settlers to purchase lots and establish businesses to provide goods and services for the farmers in the town's hinterland.

In addition to its fortuitous location in a demonstrably rich agricultural region, New Philadelphia was fortunate in being situated at the intersection of several important cross-county roads that offered access to markets. The town was on the route of a major highway proposed for construction from Pittsfield, the county seat, to Quincy, the location of the federal land office.[41] In addition, a petition presented to the county commissioners in 1837 to build the Barry-Griggsville road shows that it was planned to run through New Philadelphia. The petition was approved, as stated in the commissioners' records: "On reading and filing the petition of a competent number of signers praying the location of a Road from Griggsville to the S.E. Corner of Section 16-4-S-4W thence to Philadelphia to Worchester [Barry] then to New Canton thence to Piketon on the Mississippi. . . . [the viewers] presented their report which being examined and approved It is order[ed] that said road be made and kept in repair by the supervisor of said district."[42] In March 1837 another petition was presented "praying the location of a County road beginning at Rockport thence through Philadelphia to intersect the road from Pittsfield."[43] One section of the road from New Philadelphia was to run in a northeasterly direction to Schuyler County. A year elapsed before any action was taken, since the viewers appointed to plan the route did not follow through on the county's directives. New viewers were appointed in March 1838, and their report, submitted three months later, was accepted at the June term of the county commissioners' court.[44] The New Philadelphia-Rockport road became one of two important state roads that by 1838 ran to New Philadelphia.[45] The Pike County commissioners' records provide a detailed history of road buiding in the New Philadelphia area, and show that as other new roads were planned they were located to feed into the important Barry-Griggsville and New Philadelphia-Rockport roads. The proposed road from Pittsfield to Washington, for example, was slated to intersect the latter.[46]

Free Frank's farm, located just north of New Philadelphia's site, also figured in Pike County's road-building plans. In 1837 a petition was presented to the county commissioners proposing the construction of a road leading up to "the Lane near Frank McWorters."[47] For some reason, when the viewers presented their report to the county commissioners they rejected this petition, explaining that in their opinion it was better "to have so much of said Road as lies between the before mention[ed] point and Lane Rendered null and void." The commissioners disagreed, however, emphasizing that it would "be to the interest of the Public to disanull said petition," and they ordered the road built. Indirectly, this action suggests that Free Frank's agricultural activities were recognized as contributing to the growth and development of the county. It also confirms the importance of New Philadelphia's location and its potential for successful development.

The speculative boom period precipitated by Illinois's internal improvement program came to an end with the building of the Illinois-Michigan Canal, which left the state's credit overextended. The resulting panic of 1837 seriously affected the state's economy: "The state banks failed, specie was scarce . . . people were disappointed in the accumulation of wealth, and real estate was worthless."[48] Yet even the depression which followed the town-lot boom did not initially impede New Philadelphia's growth. Free Frank sold two lots for $59 each in 1837, and four more for $60 each the following year.[49] And in 1839, because of the road-building activity and the town's potential trade advantages, the first business in New Philadelphia, a grocery, was established.

The proprietor, a white businessman named Chester Churchill, was granted a permit to sell goods in New Philadelphia on January 24.[50] The commissioners' records show that Churchill had received a permit to sell retail liquor and other goods in Pike County as early as 1834, and another in 1836.[51] He was also one of two proprietors who in 1836 founded the town of Kinderhook, opened the first store there, and applied for a writ to build a dam in order to construct a mill outside Kinderhook.[52] In June 1838 he was granted a license to sell goods and keep a tavern.[53] Churchill's interest in establishing a store in New Philadelphia, especially during a period of economic depression, underscores the importance of Free Frank's town and its market potential.

It is quite possible, however, that Free Frank's early success as a commercial farmer and what appeared to be his prospects for becoming a successful town proprietor seemed threatening to some whites. He had found support among some Pike County white settlers—William Ross, a state senator, had presented Free Frank's name-changing petition to the Illinois General Assembly, and fourteen Pike County whites had signed his certificate of good character. But the county was not free from racial hostility. From the beginning, Free Frank's activities in promoting New Philadelphia were carried out in an atmosphere of antagonism and racial conflict. From the 1830s on, the entire western Illinois frontier was an arena of bitter racial hostility which kept the settlers in a state of tension. In 1835 the notorious river pirate John Murrell escaped imprisonment and, with a desire for revenge, or perhaps reform, moved to organize what he called a "Mystic Confederacy" which would have its basis in a "negro rebellion." Two Pike County men joined Murrell and were said to be part of this conspiracy.[54] Quincy in Adams County, directly north of Pike, was also considered a hotbed of antislavery radicalism. Abolitionist sentiments were openly expressed in that community, which also served as an active station in the underground railroad.[55] But while the antislavery proponents were persistent in their activities, the proslavery forces more than countered them.

Just a little south of Pike County was Alton, a known station in the underground railroad network. It was also the town where Elijah Lovejoy, the abolitionist newspaper editor and one of the founders of the Illinois Anti-Slavery Society, was killed in 1837 while trying to defend his paper from a mob attack. State and municipal authorities had made little effort to protect Lovejoy, explains Berry, who points out that the Illinois Attorney General had, in fact, "called public meetings in an effort to find a way to shut down Lovejoy's press." Government responses were not encouraging to the expression of antislavery sentiment in Illinois. In a comparison of that incident with the responses of Virginia's local authorities to the Nat Turner Revolt only six years earlier, Berry notes, "The absence of military protection for the abolitionists in Alton lends credence to legal indifference that bound the country at this time. In the aftermath of the Turner Revolt, the mayor of Norfolk had called for military assistance and received it; the mayor of Alton could have asked for the dispatch of federal troops to keep order. He did not; in fact, he incorrectly claimed that Lovejoy and his associates, in asserting their civil rights, had created the disorder."[56] Few antislavery activities found government support in Illinois during this period, nor was this support expected. Yet these activities did not stop. Just two years after New Philadelphia was platted, violence almost broke out in Pike County after an antislavery meeting was held in Griggsville, thirteen miles east of New Philadelphia. At that meeting, a petition was presented calling for the abolition of slavery in Washington, D.C., and for rejection of the admission of Texas into the Union as a slave state. While many of the people at the meeting signed the petition, dissatisfaction was expressed by others, including people described in Chapman's county history as belonging to "the more ignorant class." In a vivid description of the events that followed, Chapman reported that after the meeting this group of proslavery Pike County men

met in a saloon, known then as a "grocery" where liquor was sold, and passed resolutions that the parties who had signed the obnoxious petition should be compelled to erase their signatures from it. To carry out this design, on the morning following the last anti-slavery meeting they pursued the gentleman who held the petition, overtaking him, . . . and compelled him to produce the document. They then waited upon those parties and demanded of them that they should immediately erase their names, and accordingly appointed an evening to "finish up the business," . . . The good people of the county being afraid of their manoeuvers, came pouring into town about twilight, well armed and equipped, to act on the defensive. . . . the committee from the citizens informed the disturbers that they must immediately disband, or else they would be dealt with harshly, and that the first man who dared to intimidate another petitioner would receive a "fresh supply of ammunition."[57]

The intensity of the conflict is surprising, since Pike.County had never had a black population of any numerical significance. The six members of Free Frank's family were the only blacks in the county until 1835. Two other black families came in 1836, settling near Free Frank's farm. By 1840, however, only two families remained, leaving a total of twelve black people in the entire county.[58]

The only indication of how Free Frank regarded the conditions of freedom for blacks in this period can be found in his son Solomon's 1835 emancipation paper. In this document, as recorded by the clerk of Pulaski County, Kentucky, Free Frank declared: "I do by these presents emancipate and set free the said Solomon. . . . to go hence, and henceforth enjoy all the rights, privileges and immunities of a free man agreeable to the laws and constitution of the United States."[59] Of the eighteen emancipation deeds recorded in Pulaski County in this period, this is the only one that refers to the federal government as the guarantor of the former slave's freedom. The others stipulate that the freed slave could now "enjoy the privileges of freedom as though [he or she] had been born free" or "do and act for himself as a person hereby freed agreeable to the laws of the Commonwealth of Kentucky," or the deed says nothing at all about rights.[60] Clearly, Free Frank had learned from experience that emancipating his son from slavery in Kentucky was by no means a guarantee of his freedom in Illinois.

That Free Frank was the only black town founder in Illinois during this period of speculative town founding represents a remarkable achievement. Certainly the sale of town lots would provide additional money to purchase his family's freedom, but he never depended solely on such sales for the obviously substantial sum needed for that purpose. Rather, the black town founder had a driving determination that his town should succeed. Records show that the price of lots was never high enough to prohibit black settlement in the town. Doubtless Free Frank believed that New Philadelphia's development into a thriving market town would offer his family and other blacks an alternative existence to that found by settlement in an isolated agricultural community or in a depressingly hostile urban environment.

Prospective settlers, both black and white, were indeed attracted to Hadley township. Some purchased town lots, and an even greater number settled on farm land outside the town. But few purchasers were black. Illinois's exclusionary Black Codes and frontier land-claiming practices effectively denied access to land to most free blacks.

Significantly, Free Frank's move west and the founding of New Philadelphia reflect in part sentiments expressed during the 1830s by spokesmen who articulated serious concerns over the deteriorating economic and social status of free blacks. Most free blacks lived in urban places. In a discussion of the quality of their lives from 1800 through 1850, Leonard Curry explains that "urban blacks were extensively restricted to low opportunity and other irregular occupations, had a low incidence of property ownership in most cities, and were universally described by contemporary observers as in large part poverty stricken."[61] In response to these conditions, an intense controversy developed in the 1830s which centered on two major reforms. The first was the idea of separate agricultural settlements established for free blacks in undeveloped rural areas, especially in response to what William and Jane Pease have described as the Organized Negro Communities Movement; it had both strong proponents and opponents.[62] The second major proposal centered on the migration of Afro-Americans to settle America's western frontiers. This proposal was largely a response to the American Colonization Society's activities to promote the settlement of blacks in Africa. Both proposals involved the establishment of either individual pioneer farm homesteads or agricultural colonies of black farmers which would provide free blacks with opportunities to develop new economic livelihoods. Throughout the 1830s, as Free Frank expanded his farm production and promoted New Philadelphia's growth, the controversy over the efficacy of these two proposals generated much written and verbal debate, especially among black leaders in urban areas.

Beginning in the late 1820s, the proposals for reform emanating from blacks reflected their heightened opposition to the American Colonization Society's increasingly aggressive promotion of the relocation of newly manumitted slaves and free blacks in Liberia. From 1830 through 1835, black representatives from several states along the east coast met annually in Philadelphia in what Howard Bell has called the National Negro Convention Movement.[63] At the initial meeting, their major proposals for reform were expressed in the name given to the organization: "The American Society of Free Persons of Colour, For Improving Their Condition in the United States; For Purchasing Land; and For the Establishment of a Settlement in Canada."[64] The proposal to settle in Canada was a direct response to racial hostilities that took place in Cincinnati, Ohio, which forced over 1,000 of the city's blacks to leave in 1829. Several hundred settled in Canada, including those who established Wilberforce, a "white philanthropic settlement," located near London, Ontario.[65]

The continued opposition of blacks to the American Colonization Society was given even stronger expression in 1833 at the organization's third annual convention. A resolution was proposed which emphasized that it made as much sense to challenge the wilderness in America as anywhere else. The measure was a response to blacks who were considering colonization in Africa. Participants strongly asserted that, "for those who may be obliged to exchange a cultivated region for a howling wilderness, we would recommend, to retire back into the western wilds, and fell the *native forests of America,* where the *plough-share* of prejudice has as yet been unable to penetrate the soil."[66]

The Old Northwest Frontier provided the major challenge for blacks who looked to settle the American West. A group of blacks who settled the Illinois frontier in 1818, perhaps as their ultimate attempt to live as free men in the United States, were quickly disillusioned and finally more than willing to leave the country. In a letter to the American Colonization Society, Abraham Camp, an early Illinois black pioneer, wrote: "I am a free man of colour, have a family and a large connection of free people of colour residing on the Wabash who are all willing to leave America whenever the way shall be opened." Camp emphasized that the denial of rights and restrictions on their liberties forced them to make this decision, for he added; "We love this country and its liberties, if we could share an equal right in them; but our freedom is partial and we have no hope that it will ever be otherwise here."[67]

Illinois was also the location of the first manumission settlement, the Edwardsville colony, established in 1819, which stood in the forefront of settlements in the Organized Negro Communities Movement. Most of these settlements were founded by whites who acted in a supervisory capacity, overseeing what they considered appropriate for the "freedom training" of blacks. The Edwardsville Settlement, established by Edward Coles, partially reflected this philosophy. Coles freed seventeen slaves, purchased land for them to develop into farms, and "encouraged them to be frugal and industrious, hoping that eventually they would all settle on their own farms as free and independent citizens."[68] Yet, as the Peases explain, most manumission settlements, including Edwardsville, failed. Planned as agricultural communities, they usually consisted of farms too small to sustain even self-sufficiency. Generally blacks in these settlements appear to have subsisted in a limited economic environment, and in Edwardsville, "with a minimum of planning, with no community structure, Coles' venture was the simplest form of paternalism."[69] Finding their affairs mediated by whites, many blacks in such settlements encountered difficulties as they attempted to compete in a profit-oriented market economy.

The white Philanthropic Robert Rose Silver Lake Settlement in Susquehanna, Pennsylvania, established in 1836, the same year that Free Frank founded New Philadelphia, also failed, although it was "rigorously planned and carefully organized." The settlers included nine free black families and five or six single men. Rose allotted land that the blacks worked as tenant farmers, dividing their crops equally with him. While Rose saw communal efforts as the basis for the economic success of free blacks, this early experiment in sharecropping offered little opportunity for any significant economic advancement for black farmers, who preferred to work their own individual holdings. Within two years the Silver Lake Settlement passed out of existence. After 1836 even Wilberforce failed and from this point on "was hardly an organized Negro community." [70]

Because of the black community's interest in such organized communities, the progress of these settlements was followed with eager interest, but more often than not with a critical eye by opponents. The failure of the Silver Lake Settlement gave the editor of New York's *Colored American*, Samuel Cornish, also a minister and a leading antislavery spokesman, a chance to express his opposition. Objecting particularly to the communitarian tendencies sometimes encouraged in the organized Negro communities, Cornish said that he had always felt that "Dr. Rose's colonization plan was defective in its essentials, and never could succeed. The result has proved the accuracy of our views. . . . We really do think it time that our brethren had ceased being carried away by visionary schemes." [71]

Some black spokesmen also objected to the separatist tendencies that these settlements encouraged. Strongly in favor of blacks establishing farms, these spokesmen believed that individual enterprise should provide the impetus, and particularly that these farms should be established on the frontiers of the American West. They advanced the position that blacks, rather than separating from whites, should participate with whites in the joint development of the new wilderness communities. Cornish particularly emphasized the importance of individual enterprise, as he deplored the depressing economic predicament of blacks who lived in these settlements: "Nothing short of prudence, economy, and enterprise in the good old fashioned way, will ever elevate them, and render their situation comfortable and happy in this or any other country." [72] Charles Ray, also a leading black antislavery spokesman who provided editorial assistance to Cornish at the *Colored American*, suggested that settlement of the Wisconsin Territory would be particularly advantageous for free blacks at that time. As in Illinois, public land could be purchased at a minimum of $1.25 an acre. [73]

A few black spokesmen, including the Reverend Lewis Woodson, "the

father of black nationalism," opposed the idea of diffusive population settlement of blacks.[74] Woodson advocated that free blacks establish separate
settlements rather than disperse themselves among white pioneers in the
frontier West. Woodson, like Cornish, stressed the importance of hard
work, thrift, and enterprise, and advocated that blacks invest their money,
principally in banking institutions.[75] Woodson's economic philosophy,
however, did not preclude his constant emphasis that blacks should establish
separate communities, separate businesses, and separate churches. His father's settlement in Jackson County, Ohio, served as his model that separate
black communities could survive and prosper. The Thomas Woodson all-
black settlement was established around 1830, and by 1838 "was socially independent—with a separate church, day and Sunday schools—and econom-
ically prosperous."[76]

Thus, Free Frank's move west to settle the Illinois frontier reflected in
part the social and economic reform ideology expressed by many black leaders in the 1830s. Settlement on America's western frontiers was considered
the most feasible plan by which blacks could develop new economic opportunities. Free Frank's activities in Pike Conty—the establishment of his own
farm and his participation with whites in the joint development of that
western community—were in line with the thinking of Cornish and Ray.
But his development of his farm and his founding of New Philadelphia reflected neither Woodson's separatist philosophy for the organization of all-
black agricultural settlements, nor the separatist tendencies encouraged by
many leaders of those settlements included in the Organized Negro Communities Movement. With the founding of New Philadelphia, Free Frank
went beyond the social and economic reform thinking of that period. Rather
than organizing or promoting the development of an agricultural settlement
for blacks, he established a town. More important, not only from the perspective of nineteenth-century reform thought, but also from the perspective of historic patterns of black land occupancy, New Philadelphia represents the first recorded instance of a self-determined, spatially distinct place
founded by a black in antebellum America specifically for development into a town.[77] As a town founder, Free Frank purchased land, designated the
site for the location of a town, arranged for the survey of the site, and then
directed the platting of New Philadelphia, staking out the site into streets,
alleys, blocks, and town lots.

Even into the 1840s, when the National Negro Convention resumed,
Free Frank's activities in promoting New Philadelphia's development as a
town would stand in direct contrast to the position of many leading black
spokesmen, who continued to encourage the settlement of blacks in the
West, but only as independent farmers. Nor had the promoters of the Organized Negro Communities Movement changed their philosophy that sep-

arate agricultural settlements provided the most viable way for free blacks to improve their social and economic condition. The proponents of these settlements intensified their promotional efforts in the 1840s, especially as new settlements were organized in Canada. By the 1850s, Woodson's philosophy would find increasing expression in black emigrationist ideology, particularly that of Martin Delany, Woodson's student in the 1830s.[78] Yet, throughout this period, of those blacks who had committed themselves to the continued struggle against slavery and the racial constraints that severely proscribed their liberties, but who remained in the United States, most took the position advocated by Frederick Douglass: "You must be a man here, and force your way to intelligence, wealth, and respectability. If you can't do that here, you can't do it there."[79] Thus, while black social reform thought in general emphasized the desperate need to formulate plans that would promote the economic uplift of free blacks, there was more diversity than unanimity in determining which program would best achieve that goal.

Although Free Frank lived on the Old Northwest Frontier at the time he founded New Philadelphia, the black pioneer was never far removed from the social and economic reform thinking of black spokesmen in the East. From 1829 on, several black newspapers existed, and their circulation extended far beyond the cities in which they were published.[80] Abolitionist newspapers also included information not only on the fight against slavery but also on the reform thought of black spokesmen. While Free Frank could not read, his sons Young Frank and Solomon, who had learned while slaves,[81] could be expected to read with avid interest any information on black activities whenever those newspapers were available. With the antislavery controversy growing more intense by the mid-1830s, for their own safety, if for nothing else, few if any blacks failed to make some attempt to keep informed. In Western Illinois, as Elijah Lovejoy's murder shows, opposition to expressions of militant abolitionism often erupted into violence. Nor was the American Colonization Society, as its activities escalated in Illinois, any less than candid in its belief that free blacks should be encouraged to leave that state. While only four Illinois towns outside Chicago had black populations that even approached 100 by 1840 (Springfield, Alton, Jacksonville, and Quincy), those towns were all located in western Illinois within a seventy-mile radius of Hadley township.[82] Although small in size, the black community in that region was especially active in its efforts to mitigate the hostility generated by their presence. At the same time, every effort was made to improve their social and economic condition, as the leaders of those communities intensified their efforts to promote the institutional development of the black community. Illinois's first black churches were organized in western Illinois—the Zion Baptist Church in Springfield in 1838, and the Methodist Church in Alton in 1839. Western Illinois was also the location of the second association of Black Baptists in the Old Northwest, the Wood River Baptist Association in Alton, also organized in 1839.[83] Those religious leaders, too, served as sources of information on black reform thought in the 1830s.

Even earlier, when Free Frank lived on the Kentucky Pennyroyal frontier, his experiences in Danville had sensitized him to the impact of anti-black expressions, and he must have been aware of the activities of the American Colonization Society. Then, from the mid-1820s on, with Young Frank's flight to Canada and their settlement in Illinois, the family was active in the underground railroad.[84] Free Frank thus had some awareness of black settlement activities in Canada. Several of his grandchildren were born in Canada, including Squire, who was born in 1846 in Chatham, Ontario.[85] Blacks had settled in this area since the War of 1812. In the 1830s the new settlements in that area placed special emphasis on encouraging black self-sufficiency in a controlled and isolated setting. Presumably, these settlements would serve as a training ground for blacks to develop skills that would enable them to succeed in the broader community, once they left. In commenting on the success of his father's settlement, Woodson said that once a settler left, "no colored people . . . are more respected, or treated with greater deference than they are."[86]

Doubtless Free Frank's plans for New Philadelphia did not include its development as a transit point for blacks who, having achieved economic success, would subsequently leave to settle in other communities. As the town developed, Free Frank actively promoted its growth so that blacks new to Pike County would be encouraged to settle not only in the town as business proprietors, craftsmen, and professionals, but also in the outlying area as independent farmers. As both a farmer and a town proprietor, Free Frank reflected an awareness that a community in which blacks lived together in relative proximity would allow for mutual assistance and would provide for the development of an even greater sense of self-worth in a racially hostile society. In this respect his activities represented the persistence of two centuries of historic tradition pervasive in Afro-American thought.[87] Thus, while direct evidence indicates that New Philadelphia originated as a response to the internal improvement boom accompanying the construction of the Illinois-Michigan Canal, at the same time its founding reflected Free Frank's response to the oppressive social and economic conditions that confronted free blacks at that time. His entrepreneurial activities as a town proprietor were in line with prevailing black economic thought, particularly Woodson's, for as Floyd J. Miller notes, Woodson believed that "commercial success was essential for the elevation of the race."[88]

The Peases, too, explain that the communal efforts underlying black settlements reflected not only the humanitarian reform impulse of that period, seen in "the rage for utopian settlements," but also "as experiments in free labor and self-dependency, they reflect the American concern with practicality and a growing business ethic."[89] In the founding of New Philadelphia, Free Frank had humanitarian as well as business concerns. But in an area that demonstrated even greater antipathy to utopian communities than to the settlement of free blacks,[90] doubtless the achievement of those humanitarian concerns would be tolerated only within the American tradition. As Sam Bass Warner explains, urban America took "privatism," the private search for wealth, as its basis: "The goal of a city is to be a community of private money makers." This goal was perhaps best exemplified by the economic activities that distinguished the growth and development of Philadelphia, Pennsylvania.[91] That Free Frank named his town Philadelphia may have reflected the business ethos of this black entrepreneur as he envisioned the development of his town.

By the nineteenth century, William Penn's Philadelphia was not only the "City of Brotherly Love," but the nation's model symbolizing the achievement of American urban life. As John Reps observes, "By 1800 Philadelphia had become an imposing city with many fine town houses, elegant public buildings, and numerous churches. It was also a busy industrial and mercantile city, and the waterfront bustled with activity connected with the port. . . . By the standards of any society, Philadelphia had become a great city, and its influence on the life of the country was far-reaching." Philadelphia was the first major American city platted on the gridiron plan, and, with the initial development of its waterworks in the late eighteenth century, it pioneered in municipal technology.[92] Until 1800 it was the nation's capital. While its leadership role in the nation's economic life would be eclipsed by New York City in response to changing transportation patterns, in the expansion of the nation's urban network in the early nineteenth century Philadelphia's image as a model city remained dominant. New towns as they developed on the frontier attempted to emulate its achievements. Richard Wade notes that "part of Philadelphia's appeal to town dwellers was its leadership among the nation's cities, for nearly every young metropolis in the valley coveted a similar primacy in the West."[93]

Philadelphia was also the leading urban place for free blacks, who from the late eighteenth century on assumed a leadership role in the institutional development of the black community and in the organization of benevolent associations, churches, and schools. The Free African Society was founded in Philadelphia in 1787 by Richard Allen and Absolom Jones. Allen also established the Bethel African Methodist Church in 1794. By 1797 there were at least seven schools in that city for black children. Some of the most financially successful blacks, who were represented among the nation's antebellum business leaders, lived in Philadelphia, including James Forten, whose sailmaking enterprise earned him over $100,000. By the early nineteenth century, black Philadelphians not only had become the leading black spokesmen, articulating the grievances of free blacks, but also were among the leading activists in antislavery protest. Black literary and intellectual societies, black freemasonry, and abolitionist societies also paced the continued development of Philadelphia as the nation's leading black community at the time Free Frank founded his town.[94] For blacks at that time, Philadelphia demonstrated the diversity of black urban life and also the strength that black unity in an urban place afforded in the open opposition to slavery.

Free Frank's awareness of Philadelphia may have stemmed from his years as a pioneer businessman on the Pennyroyal frontier, when much of Kentucky's saltpeter was shipped to Wilmington, across the river from Philadelphia. Although indirectly, this market for Free Frank's product doubtless expanded his consciousness of industrial activities in urban centers. But another explanation can be advanced as to why he chose Philadelphia as the name of his town. He was a deeply religious man, and while he could not read, through his active church participation he must have heard enough sermons to become somewhat familiar with the Bible. One passage in particular perhaps held special significance for him. Certainly it provides what could be interpreted as a cornerstone for Free Frank's life, the theological or philosophical basis that sustained his indomitable will and his continued belief that he would succeed not only in promoting the development of his town, but also in freeing his family. That passage, found in Revelation (3:7, 8), says, "To the Church in Philadelphia. . . . I know your deeds; that is why I have left before you an open door which no one can close."

In an era distinguished by wildcat financial speculation and severe racial oppression, Free Frank's platting of a town which he named Philadelphia was a speculation in faith for the freedom and survival of both his own family and other blacks. But the realization of this intent was contingent on the town's ability to survive on a frontier where other towns were located, whose proprietors were as intent as this black pioneer that their towns should also survive. When New Philadelphia was founded in 1836, Pike County was a wilderness area that would remain relatively undeveloped until the mid-1840s. The early growth of the town was crucial to Free Frank. His experiences on the Kentucky Pennyroyal had demonstrated that as a frontier area developed, an increased white population acted to limit economic opportunities for blacks. In their efforts to develop their own enterprises, some whites were not reluctant to move in and take over the business activities of blacks or to develop competitive enterprises. Most blacks, with limited access to resources, found it increasingly difficult to compete with their white business rivals.

For New Philadelphia to succeed as it competed with other towns would require Free Frank to use his leadership ability with tact, diplomacy, and political finesse. As a strategy to offset opposition from antiblack forces in Pike County, he also found it important to win the confidence of the more prominent whites in Pike County, as indicated by the certificate of good character which he obtained one year after he founded New Philadelphia:

> Pittsfield, Pike County Illinois
> May 17, 1837

Whereas the person designated in the within certificate as Free Frank a man of color, has presented the paper referred to as a voucher of his character in Kentucky, and the Subscribers believing the same, and further having known him, many of us, for several years as a Farmer, owning and residing upon some land purchased by himself, and having around him the family mentioned in the within certificate, all of whom are respectable in their deportment, and knowing that the said Frank, by an act of the Legislature of the State of Illinois has been permitted to take the name which he now bears of Frank McWorter . . . and that he has laid off a town which he calls Philadelphia, and understanding and believing that the said Frank has laid out the town intending to apply the proceeds of the Sales for the purchase of his family yet remaining as Slaves, two young women about twenty years of age—the said town is in a handsome country, undoubtedly healthy.

We therefore recommend this coloured man Frank as an honest industrious man to all persons who may take an interest in his behalf, and that of suffering humanity for Slavery. And further that we are informed and believe that Frank has for a valuable consideration purchased two of his sons, who are now free men.[95]

Free Frank's activities as a town proprietor suggest that he had not changed his strategies for black survival on the frontier. From its origin, and with consumate skill, he capitalized on New Philadelphia's site and location in promoting the initial development of the town. The sale of town lots in 1837 and 1838, the establishment of a store in 1839, and the building of cross-county roads that ran near or through the site, all suggested that New Philadelphia might survive the depression. At least by 1837, Free Frank must have felt some degree of security in the ownership of his property. It was also important to him that Lucy's dower rights in their property be protected. In 1839, therefore, he and Lucy were remarried under the law of Illinois, reaffirming his desire to provide for her as he had done since the two first became man and wife in 1799.[96] And as the 1830s drew to a close, despite the depression, Free Frank must have been somewhat assured that although good land remained available in Pike County, his town would be among those that would develop beyond the paper state of town platting.

CHAPTER SEVEN

The Development of New Philadelphia

Free Frank . . . laid out the town of New Philadelphia
which once had great promise of making a good town.[1]

By 1840 the financial crisis had depressed property values throughout Illinois, but the effects on town development were catastrophic. At the height of the depression, especially from 1840 to 1843, as Pooley shows, "the little towns suffered. Land and town lots became almost worthless; improved lands could be bought for a dollar and a quarter an acre." Perhaps the most tragic consequence was that "much property was forfeited because of the inability of the owners to pay taxes." Only two of the six Pike County towns founded by single proprietors during the speculative period of town platting would survive; New Philadelphia was one of these. Free Frank was never solely dependent on the sale of town lots for his livelihood, and he did not have to vacate New Philadelphia's plat. Despite depressed farm prices, he managed to pay his property taxes, even in 1840 and 1841, when "farm produce was well-nigh worthless."[2]

Free Frank's tax receipts for 1840 and 1841 provide information on the assessed valuation of both his real and his personal property during those two years. In 1840 he paid $18.60 in taxes for property valued at $2,694; his real property, 560 acres, was valued at $2,320, and his personal property at $374. In 1841 his property taxes totalled $24.92 for property valued at $2,817; his real property, 560 acres, was valued at $2,400, and his personal property at $417. Certainly the appreciation of the assessed value of his property was more real than apparent, perhaps revealing the monumental effort by Free Frank and his sons to increase farm production during this period to offset low commodity prices. In 1843, even before the depression's end, Free Frank was able to purchase his daughter Sally, age thirty-two, from slavery for $500.[3]

Significantly, a substantial part of Sally's purchase price came from the sale of New Philadelphia lots and property adjacent to the town site. Even during the depths of the depression Free Frank continued his efforts to promote New Philadelphia's development, emphasizing the site's potential for future growth. In 1840 and 1842 he succeeded in selling four town lots. The most spectacular sale, however, was made in 1841, when a ten-acre section of the eighty-acre tract was sold for $200,[4] a substantial amount at that time for any property, especially town lots. With public land and even improved farmland averaging $1.25 an acre, 160 acres of good farmland could have been purchased for that amount. Obviously confident that New Philadelphia would succeed, the buyer perhaps anticipated that he would capitalize on the town's growth by dividing his ten-acre tract into lots which he would subsequently sell. Perhaps the buyer even planned to have his section annexed to New Philadelphia. Town additions were common during the frontier period, but in 1841, when the tract was purchased, the effects of the depression had impeded the development of the county, and town growth was literally brought to a standstill, including that of New Philadelphia.

A revealing description of the impact of the depression on New Philadelphia's development in 1841, and of the relatively undeveloped character of Pike County during its late frontier period, is provided in Thompson's collection of the oral reminiscences of early Pike County settlers. The discussion of New Philadelphia was provided by the family of the mail carrier, a Mr. Wilson, who rode through Free Frank's town in the early 1840s. Wilson's mail route covered the main east-west road that ran from Griggsville to Kinderhook. The town of Barry, also founded in 1836, is included in this account. Although the mail carrier shows that Barry's development was even more limited than New Philadelphia's, the former town, founded by representatives of a prominent St. Louis business firm, would also survive the depression and by 1850 would be one of the three largest towns in the county.[5] Yet in 1841, as Wilson shows, neither New Philadelphia nor Barry gave any indication that it would survive:

There were only six houses on the mail route from Griggsville to Kinderhook when he carried the mail. One of these was Joab Shinn's east of present New Salem. The site of modern New salem was still wild land on which the prairie grass interspersed with hazel thickets grew to an immense height. It was six years later, December 2, 1847, that William Hooper and Joab Shinn laid out the town of New Salem. Shinn told of having once seen 40 deer feeding at one time on the site of modern New Salem.

The next settlement after Shinn's was at Philadelphia (known also as New Philadelphia), bustling metropolis of the early days and the largest town on Wilson's mail route. There were three houses in Philadelphia. The celebrated "Free Frank" was proprietor of this early Pike county town, which at one time was a place of great promise. . . . He platted the town into 144 town lots, 141 of them still unsettled when Wilson carried the mail [1841]. Main Street, over which went the mail, divided the town into equal parts, north and south. . . . The center of the budding metropolis was at the intersection of Main and Broad Streets.

West from Free Frank's settlement, Wilson, the early mail carrier, touched next at the present site of Barry, where a town named Worcester had been laid out on July 4, 1836 by George Bartlett and John E. Birdsong, agents for Calvin R. Stone, of the firm of Stone, Field & Marks of St. Louis. There was a log house just east and north of present Barry and another on the site of the modern town; also a sawmill . . . located northeast of the present public square in Barry.

Young Wilson was seldom burdened with mail, which consisted mostly of a few letters, folded and sealed, on which the postage was "two bits." No newspaper was yet printed in Pike county and few came in from the outside. News a month old was read eagerly.

John Wilson says his father told of frequently encountering deer, sometimes in considerable droves, along the mail route. Sometimes wolves followed him on the trail, on which occasions Mr. Wilson remembers his father saying that he made his "old hoss rack awful fast."

The mail went three times a week. Wilson, leaving Griggsville, after the arrival of the stage from Meredosia, went to Kinderhook, stayed all night there, and returned to Griggsville the following day.[6]

Although Free Frank had sold eight town lots by 1841 in addition to a ten-acre section, Wilson's description of New Philadelphia points to the existence of only three houses, indicating that it was not much of a town during the early years of the depression. But for a place to be recognized as a town at that time, little was required. Peck, in his traveler's directory for Illinois in 1839, gave the following criteria: "In placing town sites on the map, the compilers desired to be impartial. . . . Hence they adopted a general principle, to place no town on the map unless it actually contained six dwelling houses including stores, and as many facilities."[7] The town of Perry had been singled out in Mitchell's 1837 traveler's guide, and was said to have "two or three stores, several families and is a pleasant village."[8] Most frontier villages and towns, including New Philadelphia, were simply collections of small log cabins that served as homes, though usually a store or two—also log—would be found there, as well. Initially, few towns had schools or churches, and any educational or religious activity took place in one of the cabins. Thus Perry, to judge by Mitchell's description, was a typical frontier town in the late 1830s and early 1840s. In essence, these early settlements represented town life reduced to its simplest elements.

Travelers' guides are important sources that suggest the existence of early Illinois frontier towns which might otherwise be identified only by the nonagricultural activities of their inhabitants. Prior to the 1850 federal manuscript census, which provides information on a town's occupational distribution, the only contemporary sources from which one could obtain information on the existence of a town and its businesses or social institutions were newspapers, business gazetteers, personal papers, and state, county, or local records. The federal census of 1840, taken four years after New Philadelphia was platted, provides little specific information on frontier towns.

It does, however, show a population of 11,720 people in Pike County in 1840, of whom 3,454 worked in agriculture, 68 in commerce, 385 in manufactures and trades, and 61 in the learned professions and engineering.[9] The page containing information on Free Frank, which presumably would include information on people who lived in New Philadelphia, lists 30 heads of household with a total of 162 people: 64 occupations are listed under agriculture and one person is listed under manufactures and trades. This evidence, then, does not at all suggest the existence of a town. Seven people are listed in the Free Frank household, four under occupational classification of agriculture and one under manufactures and trades. The Free Frank Papers show that Solomon was involved in a cabinet-making business, so quite possibly he is the one listed under manufactures and trades. Solomon did not live in New Philadelphia, however, but on his father's farm. Thus the federal manuscript census of 1840 provides very little precise information on New Philadelphia's development

The county deed records on town-lot sales, however, are invaluable sources on the growth of New Philadelphia. With the depression coming to an end after 1843, migration to Illinois, including Pike County, steadily increased and was reflected in new sales of New Philadelphia town lots beginning in the mid-1840s (see Tables 8 and 9). In addition to those Free Frank sold, other New Philadelphia lots were sold by former purchasers, although some grantors are listed whose names are not found in the records of Free Frank's sales, suggesting that the transfer of town lots was through means other than sale. The sale price of town lots varied, as Tables 8 and 9 show. In 1837, for example, two lots sold for $59, while in the depression year of 1840 two lots went for $5. In 1845, with the improved economic outlook, one lot sold for $80. Yet prices remained variable, for in 1848 two quarter-lots sold together for only $15.[10]

The somewhat precipitous increase in town-lot sales and transfers in New Philadelphia in the mid-1840s was a reflection of the increased prosperity of the county. With the end of the depression, as Pooley points out, "came a new era in the settlement of the state." The new settlers located in areas that offered the best prospects for economic development. In Pike during the mid-1840s, the interior of the county, where the population was scarce and where good farmland remained available for a reasonable purchase price, was the best place for settlement. The river landings that came into existence during this decade, especially on the western side of Pike, also reflected the increased trade and marked the county's economic recovery. Of the eight major river towns on both sides of the county, Cincinnati Landing on the Mississippi was the most important. It was also the shipping point for Free Frank, for other farmers in Hadley township, and for the townspeople

Table 8. New Philadelphia Town Lots Sold by Free Frank, 1837-1854

Date Sold	Block	Lots	Grantee
Apr. 28, 1837	4	6, 8	James Ray
Apr. 28, 1838	3	4	Henry Brown
July 5, 1838	4	4, 5, 7	Henry Brown
Aug. 8, 1840	8	1, 2	Christopher Luce
May 27, 1841		SW / NE of NE 1/4 sec. 27 (10 acres)	James Robinson
May 30, 1842	11	1, 2	William Bennet
Nov. 26, 1845	3	6	John Bixler
May 16, 1846	4	S 1/2 of 1	Spaulding Burdick
Feb. 1, 1848	5	1, 2, 7, 8	James Pottle
Feb. 1, 1848	7	1-8	James Pottle
Aug. 13, 1848	3	7, 8	Adam Hadsell
Sept. 4, 1848	4	N 1/2 of 1	D. A. Kittle
Sept. 11, 1848	4	N 1/2 of 7, 8	Spaulding Burdick
Mar. 27, 1850	15	7, 8	Alvah Wilson
Mar. 27, 1850	18	1-8	Alvah Wilson
Sept. 27, 1850	16	1, 2	Alvah Wilson
Sept. 15, 1852	2	2	
Sept. 15, 1852	3	2, 3	Spaulding Burdick
Sept. 15, 1852	4	4, 6, 7, 8	Spaulding Burdick
Sept. 6, 1854	7	5-8	Squire McWorter
Sept. 6, 1854	9	5	Kizie McWorter Clark
Sept. 6, 1854	12	5	Squire McWorter
Sept. 6, 1854	13	1-8	Squire McWorter
Sept. 6, 1854	3	4	E. Clark

SOURCE: Pike County Deed Record Book, Town Lot Index, "Philadelphia," pp. 46-61, 269-71, Pike County Courthouse, Pittsfield, Ill.

in New Philadelphia.[11] Conger, in his study of the Illinois River Valley, reported that "Cincinnati Landing on the Mississippi is a good illustration of a Pike county steamboat town. In 1848 it did the biggest river business of all the towns in the county on either river. Up-river and down-river packets brought cargoes of freight and deck loads of passengers to its wharf." To emphasize Cincinnati Landing's importance as a river town, Conger noted that "the largest of the big white New Orleans steamers served Cincinnati Landing."[12]

The increased agricultural prosperity within the New Philadelphia area is also evident in the Pike County commissioners' records, which detail road-building activity during the 1840s. Several petitions, road-building orders, and maps or plats mention Free Frank's town, which figured prominently in

Table 9. New Philadelphia Town Lots Sold by Others, 1844-1854

Date Sold	Grantor	Grantee	Block	Lots
July 5, 1844	W. Bennet	E. Franklin	11	1, 2
Mar. 29, 1849	E. Thomas	E. Clark	11	1, 2
Aug. 10, 1849	A. Stone	I. Ware	12	1, 2
Apr. 8, 1850	C. Luce	G.W. Berriam	6	N 1/2 of 1, 2
Sept. 8, 1850	C. Luce	G.W. Berriam	7	1-4
Nov. 6, 1850	N. Smith	S. Wesmith	3	1, 2
Aug. 9, 1851	J. Wilson	P. Hadsell	11	1, 2
Oct. 5, 1851	E. Franklin	E. Thomas	11	2
Nov. 20, 1851	A. Wilson	C. Luce	15	7, 8
Nov. 20, 1851	A. Wilson	C. Luce	17	1, 2
Nov. 20, 1851	A. Wilson	C. Luce	18	1-8
Feb. 3, 1852	B. D. Brown	J. Roberts	7	3, 4
Mar. 8, 1852	J. Pottle	C. Luce	7	1-4
Mar. 10, 1852	Sheriff of Pike Co.	Frank McWorter	7	3, 5, 6
Mar. 18, 1852	J. Pottle	C. Luce	6	1, 2
Apr. 8, 1852	C. Luce	W. LaSalle	6	S 1/2 of 1, 2, 3, 4
Sept. 8, 1852	C. Luce	W. LaSalle	7	S 1/2 of 1, 2, 3, 4
Jan. 7, 1853	S. Hull	D. Green	8	8
Mar. 24, 1853	C. Luce	S. Clark	15	7, 8
Mar. 24, 1853	C. Luce	S. Clark	16	1, 6
Mar. 24, 1853	C. Luce	S. Clark	18	1-8
Mar. 24, 1853	C. Luce	Calvin Arnold	8	1, 2
Apr. 5, 1854	D. Kittle	J. Taylor	3	5
Apr. 5, 1854	D. Kittle	J. Taylor	4	N 1/2 of 1
Nov. 20, 1854	S. Hall	J. Roberts	6	Part of 6

SOURCE: Pike County Deed Record Book Town Lot Index, "Philadelphia," pp. 46-61, Pike County Courthouse, Pittsfield, Ill.

Pike's road development program. Unlike the 1830s, however, the county's road-building plans in the 1840s were not encouraging to New Philadelphia's growth. In May 1840 the commissioners ordered the relocation of the important east-west road that initially ran through New Philadelphia's main street from Griggsville on the Illinois River to Kinderhook on the Mississippi. The 1840 petition called for relocating this road to the outskirts of Free Frank's town. After relocation the road would run through Barry's main street, rather than on the outside of that town, as it had previously. Since this was a state road, permission to relocate it had to be obtained from the Illinois General Assembly, and Barry's proprietors were in a more favorable position to secure the approval of the state legislature. The law was in force as of February 1, 1840, and required that several people be appointed "to review and relocate so much of the State road, leading from Griggsville in Pike county to Kinderhook as is situated between New Philadelphia and Kinderhook." [13] Thus, within four years after Free Frank founded his town, some Pike County residents on two occasions urged the approval of road-building plans that would prove detrimental to New Philadelphia's growth. In 1837 Free Frank had been able to convince the county commissioners of the importance of county roads intersecting his farm and town. Three years later the black town proprietor, lacking the right to vote, had little real influence on the state legislature. On the other hand, in 1837 the Illinois General Assembly had supported Free Frank's petition for a name change, and more important, contrary to the Black Code and even the Illinois Civil Code, it had also granted him full property rights. But by 1840 the state legislature was not prepared to give a black town proprietor an economic edge, however indirect, over white town proprietors.

In 1840, neither the state nor the county could pay the manpower required for relocating the road, but with the end of the depression, the new road was finally built. The impact of the road's relocation on New Philadelphia's development was felt by 1850. By that time Barry had developed into one of Pike's most important towns. In 1845 a new town, St. Louis, was founded only three miles west of New Philadelphia but also only one mile east of Barry. It did not survive, its plat being vacated in the 1850s, but its founding points to the importance of the cross-country roads in encouraging town development. A comparison of Barry's and New Philadelphia's town lot sales in the 1840s shows that the road's relocation was an important factor in Barry's growth and New Philadelphia's eventual decline.

Yet the county's continued development and expansion of the New Philadelphia-Rockport road indicates the significance of New Philadelphia as a trading area in Pike. By 1844, as it ran north, this road was intersected by the Pleasant Vale-Pittsfield road, the Barry-Pittsfield road, the Barry-Griggsville road, the Barry-Perry road, and the Quincy-Griggsville road. The importance of the New Philadelphia-Rockport road is also indicated by the decision of the county commissioners in 1844 to widen the road by two rods. [14] Then in 1846 they ordered that the road "be opened three rods wide." The surveyor's 1846 plat also shows the road with two lanes, as compared to the usual one lane, suggesting its already heavy use. But as the road-building order indicates, even then two lanes were insufficient for the increasing traffic.

Apart from the site advantages described in Free Frank's Pike County certificate of good character, the topography shown in the surveyor's records, the mail carrier's description of three houses in the town in 1841 (in-

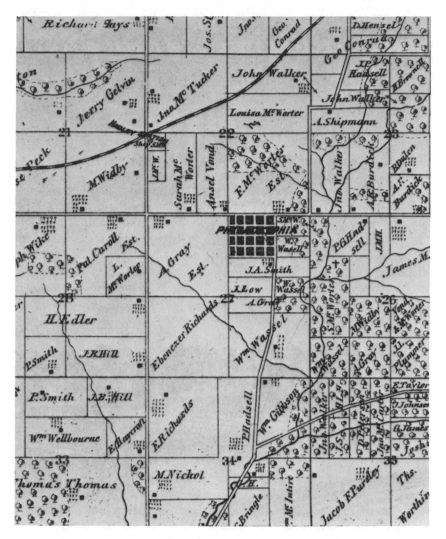

Fig. 7. Map of a portion of Hadley township, showing New Philadelphia and the farm holdings of Free Frank's family and their neighbors. From *Atlas Map of Pike County, Illinois* (1872). Photo by University of Illinois Photographic Services.

cluding the place where the merchant Churchill sold his goods), and the
county commissioners' records on road building in or near the town, precise
physical descriptions of New Philadelphia in the 1840s are just not available.
But a general description of the physical structure of the town and some information on the occupational activities of New Philadelphians in the late
1840s and early 1850s can be deduced from two sources which are available—the 1850 federal manuscript census for Pike County and the New
Philadelphia town-lot records. The manuscript census provides information
on the occupational distribution of New Philadelphia's inhabitants. When
correlated with the names of town-lot purchasers, this information can be
charted on the town plat to show the location not only of the town's residents but also of their business enterprises. Census information also suggests the kinds of activities in the town. These sources, then, when used in
conjunction with other material available on Illinois frontier towns, permit a
general reconstruction of Free Frank's New Philadelphia as it developed
from a wilderness hamlet of three houses in 1841 to an important agricultural service center by 1850.

The federal manuscript census of 1850, unlike that of 1840, lists occupational information according to county subdivisions, such as townships
and towns. For the larger towns, listings were made according to wards, districts, or precincts. The published census of 1850 provides information only
on large or important towns; for Pike County it shows the existence of only
three towns: Griggsville, population 585; Perry, population 402; and Pittsfield, population 637.[15] The manuscript census, however, provides information that indicates the existence of other towns. Some census-takers, before
recording any information on a town, made notations such as "The beginning of the town of . . ." or, at the end of the listing, "The end of the town
of. . . ." Rarely were both statements given to mark the distinction between
the town population and the rural population, and for some towns no statements were given at all. In these instances the existence of a town is suggested only by the listings of nonagricultural occupations in sequential
order, but these indicators are never really satisfactory as a method of ascer-
taining the exact occupational distribution of the people in a town or even
the town's population. Moreover, it is difficult to distinguish between a
town and its hinterland, since some people with nonagricultural occupations
lived outside towns, and some farmers lived in towns. In contrast, the Illinois State Census for 1855 lists the names of places referred to as "villages,"
along with their population, and includes New Philadelphia.[16]

Hadley township is found in the 1850 federal manuscript census under
"Township Four South Five West." Two pages of the manuscript census indirectly indicate the existence of the town of New Philadelphia through the

following occupational listings: two shoemakers, one merchant, one cab-inet-maker, one wheelwright, and one Baptist teacher. Moreover, since Free Frank lived directly outside the town, it is possible that the town population began with the people listed after his name. Included in this listing is Free Frank's son Squire McWorter. Although he is shown as a farmer, he is known to have lived in the town. Two tax receipts, one for 1855 and the other for 1856, show him as owning one block in New Philadelphia valued at $266 in 1855 and at $335 in 1856.[17] The assessed valuation of the lots sug-gests that they included a home and/or other buildings. Following Squire McWorter's listing is that of the Clarks, another black family. Table 9 shows that one member of this family, Simon Clark, purchased twelve lots in 1853. Adam Hadsell, listed as a farmer in the 1850 census, is shown in Table 8 to have purchased two town lots in 1848. Hadsell too may have lived in New Philadelphia, as indicated by the value of the real estate owned, which is listed in the federal manuscript census as $50. Thus it appears that in 1850 there were at least eleven residences in New Philadelphia with a population of fifty-eight people. Eight of the dwellings were occupied by whites, with a total of thirty-four persons. There were also three black families with twenty-two members. Two of these black families had one white person residing in the household.

The federal census manuscript, however, was not always inclusive or cor-rect. Solomon McWorter is recorded as living with his father but is not listed as having any occupation. Solomon was not only a farmer and his father's business partner, but was also involved in a cabinet-making firm, as is indi-cated by two receipts concerning business transactions.[18] One reads:

$30. On or before the first day of August next, We or either of us, promise to pay James M. Wilson, or bearer the sum of thirty dollars for valued received of him.
February 1st 1850

James M. Pottle
Solomon McWorter

Pottle, who was Solomon's business partner, was white and is listed in the manuscript census as a cabinet-maker. The second receipt reads:

Received of Solomon McWorter Sixty two and 1/2 cents as part pay for halling a load of BedSteads to Grigsville for the firm of Pottle & McWorter and also twenty five cents as a part of my witness fees for attending court before Esq Hayse. . . . Wm Brown was plaintiff and said firm Defnt.
New Philadelphia
Pike Co Ill 13th Aug 1850

D.A. Kittle

Kittle, who was also white, is listed as a merchant. Table 8 shows that both Pottle and Kittle purchased lots in New Philadelphia in 1848.

Another omission of an occupation is that of Alexander Clark, a black man whose occupation as a blacksmith does not appear until the 1860 census.[19] And Christopher Luce, a white who is listed as the Baptist teacher, was also the postmaster of the town between 1849 and 1853. Thus, in its occupational distribution, New Philadelphia in 1850 had, besides those occupations previously mentioned, a blacksmith, a postmaster, and a second cabinet-maker. A comparison with the occupational distribution of other towns reveals that New Philadelphia was a typical agricultural service center. Interestingly, New Philadelphia had a greater occupational distribution than did the next three larger towns: Martinsburg, with one carpenter, one cooper, and one wheelwright; New Salem, with one carpenter, one cooper, one blacksmith, one wheelwright, and one clergyman; and New Bedford, a milltown, with four carpenters, one blacksmith, one merchant, one cabinet-maker, and five millwrights. New Philadelphia's occupational distribution, in fact, was comparable to that of Florence, which had a population of 99.[20]

On the basis of information available from these various sources, a graphic illustration of New Philadelphia's residential and business locations can be reconstructed. The first lots purchased in 1837 and 1838 became the center of the town's population settlement. Subsequent purchasers bought lots within that area on King Street and Broad Way in blocks, 3, 4, and 7. These lots fronted the two roads that ran through New Philadelphia. They also provided access to the nearest farm population settlement in Hadley township. Thus, unlike many frontier towns, New Philadelphia initially developed on two main streets rather than one. Table 10 lists the businesses and occupations in New Philadelphia and the names of the people who were involved in those activities. Figure 8, a plat of New Philadelphia, suggests the location of these activities. The wheelwright shop was probably established on King Street in block 7 or block 8. The property of Pottle, the cabinet-maker, fronted King Street and Broad Way. Although the Pike County Town Lot Index does not show Rawlin, the wheelwright, as a property owner, he is listed in the dwelling that the census-taker visited after securing information from Pottle. Then, too, S. Clark, the brother of Alexander Clark, the blacksmith, had purchased lots 7 and 8 on block 15, fronting Green Street, just south of the cabinet-maker's property on block 6. Being manufactories bound to each other because of their related activities, that proximity would have been advantageous for their businesses. The wheelwright made and repaired wheels, carriages, and wagons, activities that must have depended sometimes on the skills of the blacksmith and the cabinet-maker. Farmers with their ox- or horse-drawn wagons used the services of

Table 10. Occupational Distribution of New Philadelphia
Townspeople, 1850

Occupation	Name	Location[1]
Shoemaker	S. Burdick	Block 4, S 1/2 of lot 1
Merchant	D.A. Kittle	Block 4, N 1/2 of lot 1
Cabinet-maker	James Pottle	Block 6, lots 1, 2, 7, 8
		Block 7, lots 1-8
Wheelwright	J. Rawlin	Unknown
Baptist teacher	C.S. Luce	Block 8, lots 1, 2
Shoemaker	A. Taylor	Unknown
Postmaster	C.S. Luce	Block 8, lots 1, 2
Cabinet-maker	Solomon McWorter	Unknown[2]
Blacksmith	Alexander Clark	Block 15, lots 1, 2
Postmaster	Calvin Arnold	Block 8, lots 1, 2

SOURCES: U.S., Bureau of the Census, "Population Schedules of the Seventh Census of the United States, 1850, Illinois, Pike County," T4SR5W [Hadley township]; and Pike County Deed Record Book Town Lot Index, "Philadelphia," pp. 46-61, 269-71, Pike County Courthouse, Pittsfield, Ill.

1. For location, see Figure 8, p. 134.

2. Solomon McWorter probably pursued his cabinet-making activities in James Pottle's establishment, in which he held a partnership.

both the wheelwright and the blacksmith, who, in addition to repairing axles, also shoed horses and repaired farm tools.

New Philadelphia was also a stagecoach stop.[21] In his study of the Illinois frontier in the 1850s, Johnson explained that about every ten miles along the stage route there was a stage stand, consisting of a tavern and a large stable for housing and caring for the horses.[22] Until New Salem was laid out in 1847, New Philadelphia was the first town on the road after the stage left Griggsville traveling west toward the Mississippi River. The distance between the towns was about twelve miles. Luce, the postmaster, owned lots 1 and 2 in block 8, fronting King Street, one block east from where the cabinet-maker was located. The stagecoaches were often repaired at the stage stands by the local blacksmiths and wheelwrights. Considering the nature of the roads, it is not surprising that the vehicles were constantly breaking down. Luce is recorded as having rented Free Frank's land to pasture the horses used by the stagecoach line, suggesting an even greater likelihood that the manufacturing activity in New Philadelphia was on King Street west of Broad Way. Pike County records also suggest that there were other businesses in New Philadelphia owned by people whose homes were elsewhere. The merchant Churchill, for example, resided in Kinderhook

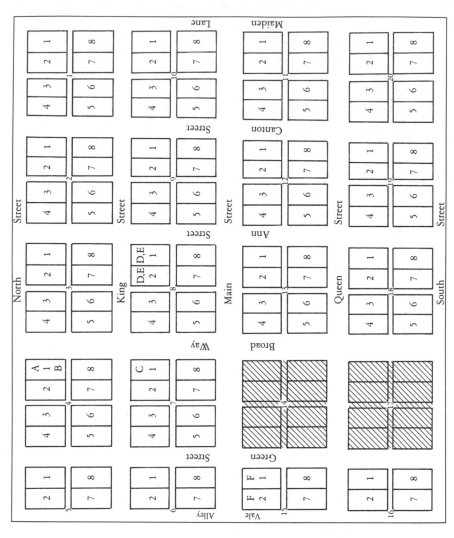

Fig. 8. The location of New Philadelphia's businesses and services: A, merchant (Kittle); B, shoemaker (Burdick); C, cabinet-maker (Pottle) (all of blocks 6 and 7); D, postmaster (Luce, later Arnold); E, Baptist teacher (Luce); F, blacksmith (A. Clark). The locations of Rawlin's wheelwright shop and Taylor's shoemaking shop are unknown. The shaded area shows the proposed site of the Free Will Baptist Seminary. Each lot in the town measured 60 x 120 feet.

Table 11. New Philadelphia Post Office Records, 1849-1853

Postmaster	Date of Appointment	Compensation		Net Proceeds	
		1851	1853	1851	1853
C.S. Luce	June 15, 1849	$12.88	$5.16[1]	$14.55	$5.45[1]
Calvin Arnold	Jan. 27, 1853		2.61[2]		3.41[2]
TOTAL			$7.77		$8.86

SOURCE: "Register of Appointments of Postmasters," U.S. Post Office Department Records, Washington, D.C., National Archives, Record Group 27, 18:156.
1. Compensation and net proceeds for two quarters.
2. Compensation and net proceeds for one quarter. Fourth quarter data not given.

and so would not have been listed as a resident of New Philadelphia in the 1850 census.

Although the federal census provides information on occupations, unless the occupation was in itself a craft trade, such as a blacksmith or wheelwright, or a profession, such as a physician, lawyer, teacher, or minister, it is difficult to determine the variety of other services or occupations provided in a small frontier town at that time. The existence of a post office in New Philadelphia is one example. Neither the federal nor the state census shows one located there, but records of the U.S. Post Office Department indicate that a post office was established in New Philadelphia in 1849. Information about the New Philadelphia Post Office is presented in Table 11. The proceeds and compensation seem minimal, but few of the approximately 1,400 post offices in Illinois during this period generated any great amount of revenue. For some there were no returns at all, and there were many in which the proceeds were less than five dollars.[23]

The New Philadelphia Post Office existed until November 25, 1853. That it was established is one indication of New Philadelphia's importance in the early 1850s. A demonstrated need for the service had to be established, based on the existence of a sufficient number of potential patrons, before a post office was opened. According to federal postal regulations, the usual procedure at that time required that "citizens of a community who desire the establishment of a post office submit a request to the Post Office Department, stating on what grounds they base their opinion that a new post office should be established, the number of patrons who would be benefitted, the names proposed, etc." The regulations also noted that "the new post office is established if it is deemed necessary for the convenience of the postal patrons."[24] The petitioners did not have to be white, but since there were few blacks in the area to be serviced by this station, most probably were white. Until 1865 federal law prohibited blacks from carrying mail and from handling it except under the supervision of whites.[25] This meant that a white had to be the New Philadelphia postmaster. With a majority white population in New Philadelphia and Hadley township, if the general sentiment had been decidedly against a post office being established in the town, probably one would not have existed. Moreover, with blacks being excluded from handling the mail, Free Frank's family was deprived of an additional source of income. His sons could read and one of them could otherwise have served as the postmaster of New Philadelphia.

In addition to selling towns lots and encouraging town business, the most significant activity in which Free Frank was involved for promoting the development of New Philadelphia at this time was his plan to build a private school which would also serve as a church. It was to be called the Free Will Baptist Seminary. In 1848 Free Frank arranged for its construction, donated two full blocks in the town for its site, and arranged for funds to be subscribed to buy equipment and other materials. Prior to this time Free Frank had rented the existing New Philadelphia public schoolhouse for use by his grandchildren and the other black children, who were proscribed by law from attending state-supported public schools. The preamble to the act establishing free public schools indicates that the legislators were aware of the importance of education as a tool in preserving freedom:

To enjoy our rights and liberties, we must understand them; their security and protection ought to be the first object of a free people, and it is a well established fact that no nation has ever continued long in the enjoyment of civil and political freedom, which was not both virtuous and enlightened; and believing that the advancement of literature always has been, and ever will be the means of developing more fully the rights of man, that the mind of every citizen in a republic, is the common property of society, and constitutes the basis of its strength and happiness; it is therefore considered the peculiar duty of a free government, like ours, to encourage and extend the improvement and cultivation of the intellectual energies of the whole.[26]

However, as to providing education for the "whole," section 1 of the act specifically states that the schools "shall be open and free to every class of white citizen between the ages of five and twenty-one years." Interestingly, at the very time when Free Frank was acting to have a school built, the Illinois General Assembly, while writing a new constitution, was debating the issue of whether black children should be allowed to attend the public schools. The vote in 1849 was for exclusion. That Free Frank made provisions to have a school built at this time is revealing. Perhaps this black town proprietor had anticipated the General Assembly's vote.

The Free Will Baptist Seminary would be an imposing structure for a frontier town. It was to be constructed from stone quarried on the lots desig-

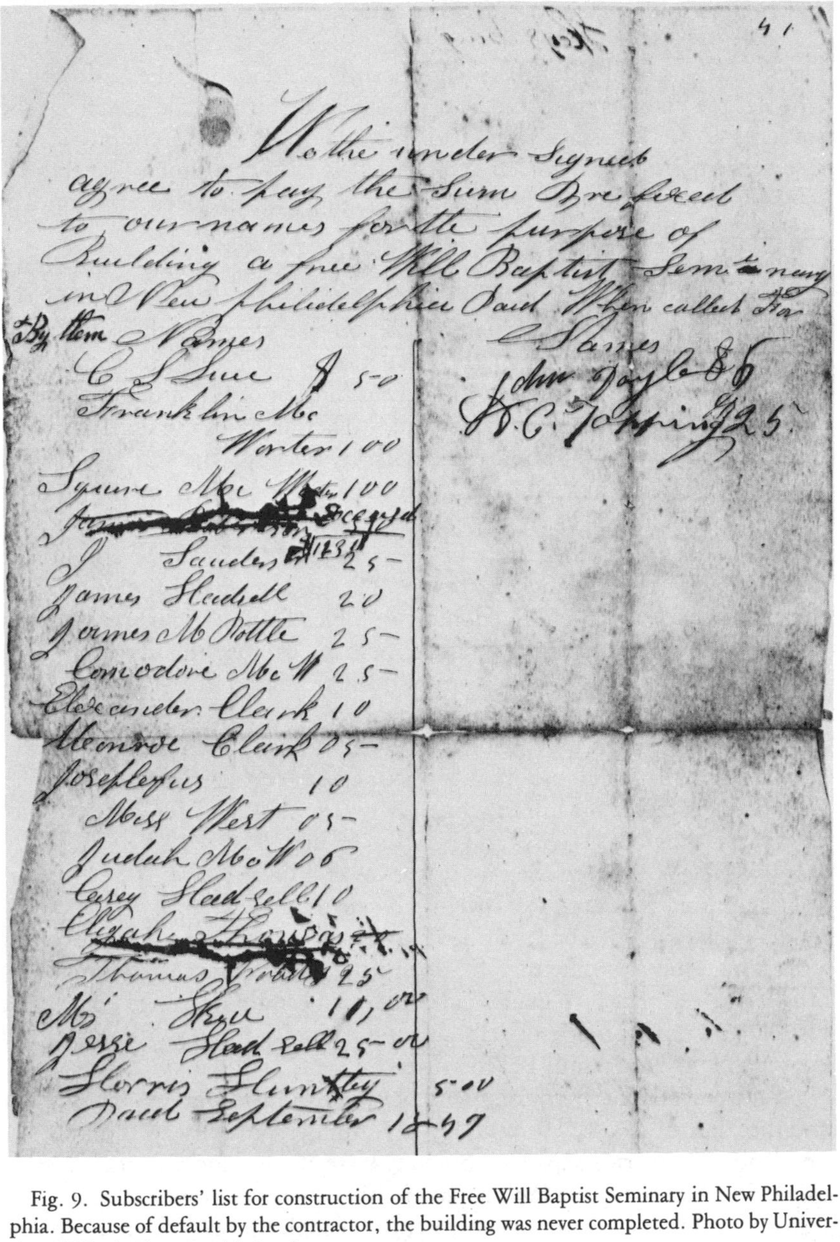

Fig. 9. Subscribers' list for construction of the Free Will Baptist Seminary in New Philadelphia. Because of default by the contractor, the building was never completed. Photo by University of Illinois Photographic Services.

nated for the school's site. Most significantly, in donating the land for the school, Free Frank emphasized that it was "to be for the sole benefit of the students of the Seminary without distinction of person." Certainly in this case he demonstrated a greater responsiveness than the Illinois General Assembly to the purpose of schools as encouraging "the intellectual energies of the whole."

The proposed construction of a Free Will Baptist Seminary is important in yet another way. The Free Will Baptists were the most radical of all Christian denominations in their open opposition to slavery and their liberal racial attitudes. As early as 1827 the church organization had moved to "ordain Negroes to the ministry, a significant forecast of the strong position it was to take against slavery in later years." Then in 1843 the denomination organized the Free Will Baptist Anti-Slavery Society. The sect also carried out its missionary work with zeal, proselytizing especially in the frontier areas. The first Free Will Baptist church in the Pike County area was organized in Quincy. Later there were branches of this "Quarterly Meeting," the major church, in Barry and Pittsfield.[27] The basic tenets of the denomination were perseverance and freedom of will. Free Frank and Lucy were members of the Free Will Baptist Church, perhaps because this denomination not only advocated perseverance without compromise, but also because of its open stand against slavery. Benjamin Quarles, in his discussion of black religious participation in antebellum America, writes: "Significantly, the denominations that held the most attraction for Negroes were those which were democratically organized, thus giving the rank and file a substantial voice in the religious exercises and business affairs."[28]

The Free Will Baptist Seminary was never built, however. Construction was begun, but the contractors eventually abandoned all work on the building. Free Frank sued. The resulting court case was significant, for it involved a black man suing a white man for defaulting on a contract.[29] The court records also reveal that Free Frank had achieved a certain degree of respect for his role as a town proprietor. His activities improved the conditions of life not only for his own family but for others, as well.

Faulty contractual arrangements between the two parties—Free Frank and the contractors C.S. Luce and D.C. Topping—precipitated the court action. First of all, two separate contracts were made: one was the deed in which Free Frank in good faith agreed to give the contractors a certain number of town lots if they would construct the school; the second was a promissory note. The implied agreement in both, as it was later established in court, was that the contractors were to be given the lots if construction of the school was completed in two years; if not, the contractors would owe Free Frank $90 for the lots. Unfortunately neither of the documents was explicit in these details, and the testimony of the litigants and witnesses was not part of the records of the Pike County Court. The deed in which Free Frank transferred title of the lots to Luce and Topping made no distinction between the lots the contractors were to receive as payment and those on which the school was to be built. Subsequently, Luce would attempt to establish that he was entitled to all of the lots. The following is an excerpt from the deed, followed by the promissory note. Both were submitted to the court as evidence.

This Indenture made this first day of December in the year one thousand Eight hundred and forty Eight Between Francis [Free Frank] McWorter and Lucy his wife of the first Part and C S Luce and D. H. Topping of the Second Part Both Parties of Pike Co and State of Illinois Wittnesses that the said Francis McWorter and Lucy his Wife witness that for and in consideration of the Sum of five dollars Paid by C S Luce and D L Toppin [*sic*] of the county of Pike and State of Illinois Party of the Second Part the Reciept of which is hereby acknowledged have granted Bargained and Sold and by these Presance do grant Bargain Sell convey and convey unto the said Party of the Second Part and there successors in office forever to be for the sole benefit of the Students of the Seminary at New Philadelphia Without distinction of person, a certain tract of land known and Described as all the lots in Block Seventeen and fourteen except lot four and Block Eleven five six seven and eight and in Block twelve seven eight and Block nine ten one and two seven and eight and all of the lots in Block twenty all in the town of New Philadelphia.

The promissory note reads:

New Philadelphia December the first 1848 For value Received I promise to pay Frank McWorter the sum on ninty dollars in two years from date without interest.

C.S. Luce

D.C. Topping[30]

In the absence of evidence to the contrary, it would appear that Luce and Topping had entered into the contract with good intentions: Free Frank's subscription list for the seminary shows that both agreed to contribute. The document is prefaced by the statement: "We the undersigned agree to pay the Sum We've fixed to our names for the purpose of Building a free Will Baptist Seminary in New Philadelphia Paid When called for by them." Luce is recorded as promising to pay $50 and Topping $25. Free Frank himself pledged $100. Squire McWorter, Commodore McWorter, Judah McWorter, Alexander Clark, and Monroe Clark are the other blacks on the subscription list. Over $400 was pledged altogether. One person, listed at the bottom, indicates that he paid the promised sum in September 1849. Construction was begun in the spring of 1849 and continued intermittently the following year, but six months before the scheduled completion

date Luce drew up a list of debts owed him by Free Frank, showing a total of
$60.90. The list in its entirety read:

June 19th 1850

Francis McWorter Owes to C.S. Luce

For	fixing one boot	.50
"	mending one shoe	.40
"	one pair of women's shoes	.50
"	mending one shoe	.35
"	" " "	.25
"	" " " pair of boots	1.00
"	work on a feed trough or pulley	1.00
"	helping hold four or five colts	1.00
"	fixing one pair boots	1.00
"	one pair of women's shoes	1.50
"	three pair of shoes	4.00
"	school bell kept by myself	6.00
"	the use of the school house 9 months	2.00
"	postage on three letters	.30
"	paper	.65
"	" "	2.75
"	Damage in not fulfilling contract on lots	12.00
"	Mys of hauling storm Damage	12.00
"	48 Bushels of corn at 25	12.00
		60.90 [sic]

Free Frank was not intimidated, however, and in the spring of 1851 initiated
proceedings against Luce. The latter, perhaps fearing that he might not win
the suit, later arranged to buy those lots for which he had promised to pay
$90. That deed shows the sale date as one day before the hearing. Then, sur-
prisingly, on the same day that he purchased the lots, Luce submitted a formal complaint to the court which said: "Christopher S. Luce being duly
sworn states on oath that he fears he cannot have a fair and impartial trial
before Arthur F. Bill Esqr." The justice of the peace was replaced, but Free
Frank, who had an attorney, requested a jury trial. The records of the proceedings show that on the day of the trial in open court, the "parties appear
and ready for trial whereupon plaintiff Free Frank demands a jury of six men
to try said cause. Jury warrant passed served by the constable who returned
the same with the following persons as jurors. . . ."

Since Luce had purchased the town lots, the court did not act on the
debt for $90, but did act on Luce's charges that Free Frank owed him
$60.90. The jury found for Luce: "After hearing the evidence and argu-

ments of counsel returned the verdict as follows the Jury finds a verdict for the defendant for fifteen dollars and 66/100 and cost of suits. Judgment moved in favor of defendant in said sum of fifteen dollars and 66/100 and costs of suit. . . . April 17, 1851." Outraged that he would have to pay that amount, Free Frank, who was now seventy-four, filed an appeal on May 3 and the trial was set for the first Monday in October. Obviously Luce had not considered Free Frank's deep inner core. Despite his age, the septuagenarian was still tough and unyielding, especially under the most obdurate pressure. Moreover, as subsequent events show, with cold and calculating objectivity and a judgment tempered by experience gained in his relations with whites, Free Frank also moved to repossess the lots he had sold Luce, but first he submitted to the court a list of debts owed him by Luce:

C.S. Luce Owes to Frank McWorter

For	Wood for burning Brick	$ 6.00
"	" " family use	5.00
"	Corn—63 bushels at 25 cts per bushel	15.00
"	Pasturing horses	3.00
"	Hauling one load of lumber from mill	1.00
"	Hauling one load of lumber from Rockport	2.00
"	Lumber for Schoolhouse	3.00
"	Six bushels of apples 50 cts per bushel	3.00
"	Fourteen pounds of soap 8 ct per lb	1.12
"	Hauling Timber for School and dwelling house	4.00
"	Timber taken off lots Damages etc.	10.00
"	Wool roles 3 lbs at $37\frac{1}{2}$ cts per lb	$1.12\frac{1}{2}$
"	Costs of [lawsuit]	10.10
"	Hauling pork to Quincy	.50
	Total	$64.84\frac{1}{2}$

No item on the list involved a large sum, but together they added up to a relatively substantial amount of money. The list is interesting in that it reveals the kinds of goods and the variety of services that the Free Frank family provided to others, indicating in poignant detail the family's intense efforts to earn money. During a twenty-year period beginning with his settlement in Pike County in 1831, the fees from these activities, in addition to profits from the sale of farm produce, cattle, farmland, and town lots, enabled Free Frank to earn over $10,000 to purchase his family from slavery. Since Free Frank had not charged Luce for his services earlier, the lists suggest that the two men were in the habit of trading goods and services. Luce, however, had apparently disregarded the benefits he received from the arrangement.

In addition to filing a countersuit, Free Frank also asked for an arbitra-

tion hearing, over the objection of his own attorney. In a letter expressing
his inability to be present at the trial, Free Frank's counsel advised: "I am
not very favorable to arbitration when I have a good case at hand." The attorney's letter in its entirety is included in the court records. Arbitration had
both advantages and disadvantages: it would be held in New Philadelphia as
requested by Free Frank, the arbitrators would be chosen by mutual consent
of the parties, and the decision of the arbitrators would be final—there
could be no appeal.[31] Among the arbitrators chosen was J.B. Donaldson,
who had served as both a county judge and a probate judge. Free Frank's attorney, C.L. Higbee, was also a prominent member of the Pike County community, as well as a highly respected member of the bar. He had served as a
circuit court judge for eighteen years and then became a judge of the appellate court.[32]

Once the arbitrators were selected and Luce had posted his bond, witnesses were summoned. Virtually all were people who had pledged to contribute to the building of the seminary, but the black contributors were not
called to testify. Illinois's Black Code proscribed their testimony against
whites. Notwithstanding, after hearing the evidence from New Philadelphia
and Hadley township whites, the arbitrators decided in favor of Free Frank,
or perhaps against Luce. Free Frank, as we have seen, had established a rep-
utation in Pike County as a "reputable, worthy citizen, kind, benevolent,
and honest."[33] Perhaps, too, the arbitrators could not help but admire this
black man, an ex-slave, as a strong and cunning adversary, however grudg-
ing that admiration may have been. Doubtless Free Frank, with his subtle
display of self-confidence and determination, used political tact and juristic
finesse in the prosecution of his case. After all, he could argue that the construction of the Free Will Baptist Seminary would have benefited the whites
of New Philadelphia and Hadley township, as well as the blacks. That the
seminary was not constructed was perhaps as much a loss to them as it was to
Free Frank.

The arbitrators' decision provides a brief review of the contractual arrangements made between the two parties:

Whereas the said Frank McWorter holds the joint promisory note of hand of the said
C.S. Luce and D.C. Toping for the sum of ninty dollars due two years after date and
dated December 1st A.D. 1848 payable to said McWorter, and for and in consideration of said note of ninty dollars as aforesaid, it appears that the said McWorter sold
and conveyed to the said C.S. Luce and D.C. Toping eighteen lots in the Town of
New Philadelphia in the County of Pike and State of Illinois which said lots were
blended and included in a deed with other lots in the aforesaid Town of New Philadelphia, donated by the said McWorter towards the construction of a Seminary in
the town aforesaid, which more fully appears by reference to said Deed dated De-

cember 1st AD 1848 and whereas said Deed does not designate which lots were sold from those donated, and it appears by the evidence in this cause that the Seminary aforesaid was to be completed in the term of two years from the date of said Deed, or otherwise the Deed aforesaid was to be canceled and anuled and whereas the time has expired and the Seminary has not been completed but, has been entirely abandoned.

Then, in a surprising decision, the arbitrators returned all of the lots to Free Frank, saying, "We the arbitrators aforesaid do award and decide that the said note for ninety dollars and the Deed aforesaid are hereby recinded, canceled and anuled" and "that the said McWorter is entitled to and may take possession of all said lots together with all the rock quarried and unquarried on said premises and possess and occupy the same as fully and completely as if the Deed aforesaid had never been executed."

The arbitrators next acted on the matter of the debts Free Frank said Luce owed him, stating that "upon hearing the evidence in relation to the private accounts of the parties respectively, we determine and decide, that the same shall be considered balanced without allowance to either." Free Frank was then ordered to pay one-third of the court costs and Luce the remainder. Although Free Frank won back his lots, the Free Will Baptist Seminary was never constructed, obviously a great disappointment to the town proprietor. His efforts to establish an educational institution were important in his attempt to promote the development of New Philadelphia. Construction of the seminary would certainly have provided more advanced educational instruction for black children in the area, and would surely have attracted additional people to settle in the town. Doubtless Free Frank was still determined that a Free Will Seminary should be built, but time became a factor. In the past Free Frank's strategy had required years of determination and perseverance, but in 1851 he had only three more years to live.

Significantly, Free Frank's ability to take court action against Luce resulted from his petition to the Illinois General Assembly in 1836 to have his name changed and to be empowered "to sue and be sued." The case is also significant in another way, for it brings into relief Christopher Luce's attempts to secure as much property in the town as he could. Had Luce succeeded in winning the case, he would have owned almost half of the town lots in New Philadelphia (see Tables 8 and 9). As a white man, Luce would also have been in a stronger position than Free Frank to direct the town's growth. Illinois laws generally operated to limit potentially profitable economic activities of blacks, especially of a black who would be a town proprietor. While the Illinois Town Platting Act did not preclude blacks from founding towns, the state's Town Incorporation Act specifically limited the right to incorporate a town to whites: "Whenever the white males over the

age of twenty-one years, being residents of any town in this state containing
not less than one hundred and fifty inhabitants, shall wish to become incorporated for the better regulations of their police, it shall be lawful for the
said residents, who may have resided six months therein, or who shall be the
owner of any freehold property therein, to assemble" and carry out the requisite functions to establish a town.[34]

Town incorporation had advantages. Aggressive town proprietors, especially if supported by enthusiastic local businessmen, could push for state action that would force the relocation of old roads or the building of new ones,
as well as the establishment of state institutions such as asylums, jails,
schools, and colleges in their towns. State monies were allocated in a variety
of other ways to incorporated towns, thus indirectly encouraging their
growth. Town proprietors invariably held local government offices which
were empowered by law to collect taxes. Luce, being white, could have used
the Town Incorporation Act to his advantage in promoting New Philadelphia's growth had he become the major property holder. With the 1851 arbitration hearing, however, Free Frank put a stop to Luce's plans to gain
control over New Philadelphia. The defaulted contractor subsequently left
the town after having lived there for thirteen years. The arbitrators' decision
forced by Free Frank was obviously the only way this black man without political rights could demonstrate that he had a "vote of confidence" in his
role as town proprietor.

That whites would choose to live in New Philadelphia when there were
at least twenty other Pike County towns in which to settle, points as much to
the spirit of productive enterprise generated by its proprietor as to the
town's potential for economic growth. For by 1850, considering the town's
occupational distribution, its population, and the general business and social activities which took place there, New Philadelphia had become an established agricultural service center. While its estimated population was
only 58, New Philadelphia was still the only town in Hadley township, and
the entire township population was 1,170.[35] The presence of the wheelwright, cabinet-making, and two shoemaking shops, the blacksmith shop, a
general store, a stagecoach stand, and a post office suggests that the population in New Philadelphia's hinterland supported these business enterprises.
The frequent trips of Hadley township farmers to New Philadelphia to get
their mail, to have wagons and other farm equipment repaired, to shop at
the general store, and to patronize the local "grocery," must have given the
town an aura of activity that the townspeople alone could not have provided. Farmers from other areas passing through on the New Philadelphia-
Rockport road, hauling their produce to Cincinnati Landing, not only
helped to enliven the town atmosphere, but also contributed to its develop-

ing economy, as did stagecoach passengers and others who traveled through the town.

The New Philadelphia schoolhouse was also an important center in the town. As the Free Frank-Luce court records show, Free Frank rented the schoolhouse for the instruction of the town's black children. He had a deep desire for education, and receipts in his papers indicate that in the 1850s he paid for lessons in reading and writing. The building may also have served as a lyceum. Even on the frontier, as Johnson explains, "one of the institutions of the village was its Lyceum, the sessions which occurred once a week during cool weather, in the schoolhouse." A lyceum would have enhanced the cultural and intellectual life of the town. On the Illinois frontier during this period, topics such as the following were intensely discussed or debated in the village lyceum: "Resolved that African slavery should be abolished in the United States. . . . that polygamy is a greater evil than African slavery . . . that the repeal of the Missouri Compromise is a menace to the perpetuity of the national union . . . that there is more satisfaction in pursuit than in possession. . . ."[36] In addition, Free Frank may also have rented the school as a meeting house for religious activities. During this period, as Johnson said, "there were comparatively few church buildings really worthy of that name and if a church was not available, then a schoolhouse would be utilized, provided one could be had." The schoolhouse also served for public business, such as the Free Frank-Luce arbitration hearings, which were held there.

Certainly by 1850 New Philadelphia was in many ways representative of small frontier towns in Illinois. It had the air of a flourishing market town and, as a center of Hadley's social and cultural life, would be a factor in attracting prospective settlers to the township. Its occupational structure and its physical and spatial development were also representative of early Illinois market centers. The streets, buildings, and houses differed little from those in other frontier towns of that period. Most of the buildings were simple but neat log cabins with sheds in the back for chickens and cows, and some lots were surrounded by picket fences. Vegetable gardens were planted on these lots, which fronted streets and sidewalks that were dirty and dusty during dry weather and muddy when wet. The sidewalks were really only dirt footpaths that paralleled the stagecoach, carriage, and wagon tracks, but all of the buildings were within walking distance, since these towns were invariably small.[37]

Tax receipts give some indication of the value of town lots during this time. Two examples are Free Frank's New Philadelphia tax receipts for 1848 and 1853; although the total tax bill for his town lots increased from $54.19 to $59.97, the value of some lots declined over the years. In 1848 the assessed valuation of lots 1-8 in block 1 was $16.00, or $2.00 per lot. In 1853, the same lots were assessed for $1.80 each. These receipts provide only one indication of the value of town lots. A tax receipt belonging to Christopher Luce shows that the assessed value of his lots ranged from $10.00 to $100.00. Tax receipts from 1855 and 1856 for lots in block 13 owned by Free Frank's son provide another indication. In 1848, when Free Frank owned block 13, it was valued at $16, but in 1855 it was valued at $266, and in 1856 at $356. The increase in the assessed valuation reflected improvements, primarily the addition of dwelling houses or businesses. Whether or not the real value of the lots was what the county assessed can be determined by the tax base at that time. In most cases property was assessed at a lower rate than its fair market value.

When considering New Philadelphia's development by 1850, it is important to recognize that within fourteen years of its founding, both merchants and tradesmen were attracted to the town. They purchased lots and established businesses that provided the goods and services necessary to support a settled farm population. Because of its trade, the town was important enough by 1850 to be placed on maps in travel guides and business directories which had national circulation.[38] However, as Johnson found, "with the advent of the early fifties the real pioneer days in Illinois were nearing their end." So while it is highly significant that a black man founded a town in antebellum Illinois, the study of New Philadelphia's origin and development is important also from the perspective of the history of town founding on the Illinois frontier.[39] These towns played an important role in the growth of Illinois from a relatively poor, undeveloped frontier state to a major agricultural and industrial center of the nation. Thus the founder of New Philadelphia, a man of uncommon drive and determination, would have had historical significance, even if he had not been black and a former slave.

CHAPTER EIGHT

The Achievement of a Dream

> As he [Free Frank] could save up money sufficient, he
> would return to Kentucky and buy one or more of his chil-
> dren. This he continued until he had bought all of his liv-
> ing children, and two of his grandchildren, the whole, in-
> cluding himself and wife, costing over ten thousand dol-
> lars . . . at the time of his death, which occurred in 1854,
> there remained four of his grandchildren in slavery, for the
> purchase of whom he made provision in his will, which
> was carried out to the letter, by his son Solomon.[1]

Free Frank's activities to earn money for his family's freedom, while at the
same time working to promote New Philadelphia's growth, were carried out
in a period of increasing legal proscription of blacks. Illinois's new 1848 constitution included a proviso that would allow the statutory exclusion of free
blacks; it would also be illegal for slaveowners to bring their slaves into the
state for the purpose of freeing them.[2] Finally passed in 1853, the law provided that a fine of $100 to $500 would be imposed on any person who
brought free blacks into the state, and that if a free black came on his own,
he would be arrested and deported.[3] Both provisions of the 1853 law would
affect Free Frank: his purpose in establishing New Philadelphia had been to
provide a place of settlement not only for his family as he purchased them
from slavery, but also for other blacks who might want to settle in Illinois.

    Although Illinois was nominally a free state, legislation limited the free-
dom of blacks and curtailed their economic capabilities. Without political
rights, their legal status differed little from that of their brothers in chains
who lived in the slave South. Illinois from the beginning had attempted to
prevent the settlement of free blacks, and it was not until 1850 that the federal census showed no listings of blacks as slaves in the state. The 1853 act,
then, would be received with a great deal of apprehension by Illinois's black
population, including Free Frank, who was now seventy-six years old. Certainly for the former slave, the black anti-immigration law only confirmed
that there would never be a time or place where people of African descent
would be accorded as full a measure of freedom as that allowed white Americans.

    Long before, Free Frank had expressed disillusionment with the condi-
tions of freedom allowed free blacks in Illinois. Solomon's 1835 emancipation deed had referred to the United States rather than the state of Illinois as

the guarantor of his son's freedom. Yet eight years later, in 1843, Free Frank said nothing about guarantees when he purchased his daughter Sally. The clerk only recorded that "Frank McWorter produced to said Court an instrument of writing purporting to be a deed of conveyance ["conveyance" was scratched out and changed to "emancipating"] and setting free Sally McWorter. . . ."[4] At the time of Sally's purchase, Free Frank had lived in Illinois for thirteen years. Doubtless his experiences there had showed him that guarantees of freedom were a specious reality to be enjoyed only to the extent that manumitted blacks could transcend the designs of the society and make their own kind of freedom within the constraints of the society in which they lived.

Illinois's 1853 black exclusion act was only one of the final steps in a series of legislative acts designed to make the state all-white. Racial hostility intensified during the 1850s, the "Decade of Crisis," as Illinois legislators found growing support from their constituents. If the state should move to exclude them altogether, free blacks would be able to offer little opposition. Free Frank's activities in buying his family from slavery, freeing them, and then bringing them to settle in New Philadelphia thus were made even more precarious by the 1853 legislation. Whether his family would retain their freedom remained a persistent and fearful question.

The presence of slavery, as well as the threat from slave catchers and "nigger stealers," were very real in Pike County from the time Free Frank settled there. Because of Pike's location on the Mississippi River, the county became a stopping point for fugitive slaves in their escape to freedom. Massie explains that "many honored old citizens were often very severely censured because they sheltered and fed the runaway negroes." But there were even more people in Pike County who actively, perhaps even eagerly, participated in the capture of fugitive slaves: "Oftentimes a negro would be captured and the captor receive $50 or $100, and be looked upon as a great hero by many for his bravery in capturing a poor fugitive from slavery."[5] Lurid newspaper accounts often provided information on fugitive slaves apprehended in Pike County. One article in 1847, for example, reported that "two Negroes, slaves, were taken up in the north eastern part of the county on the 22nd inst. [who] . . . acknowledged themselves to be runaways and that their masters lived in Marion County Mo. . . . The blacks were lodged in our county jail until Tuesday last, when their owners took them hence paying $200 reward."[6] Another Pike County newspaper article reported in graphic detail the capture of a slave mother and her daughter:

A Novel Scene

On Saturday last, at the door of the Court House in Pittsfield, a scene new to many citizens was witnessed. We drew near the crowd and noticed a negro woman nearly, or quite blind; and a negro girl 10 or 12 years of age, exposed at public sale for jail fees. The service of the girl was sold at one dollar per month; the term of one year as we understood; no bidders for the blind woman, who we understood was the mother of the child.

These blacks were taken up . . . near Perry, as runaway slaves, and no owner having appeared to claim them within the time allowed by law, they were exposed to public sale by the Sheriff for the expenses of their involuntary confinement, costs. . . .

The mother will have to go to the poor house and become a county charge. [And the capturer] . . . will have the satisfaction, if any it be, of separating a mother and child and of imposing a constantly accruing bill of expenses upon our county.[7]

Very few people, of course, openly admitted at the time that they helped fugitives. Such admissions would lessen the chances of the slaves' making a successful escape through Pike County, and those who helped them escape would jeopardize their own freedom, since assisting fugitives was a violation of federal law.

Free Frank's farm and New Philadelphia were located on two of the major roads that ran through Pike County. Fugitive slaves, always cautious, seldom traveled the open roads, but these roads did serve as guides as they moved across the county. The Free Frank family remained constantly prepared to provide aid to the fugitives. Solomon's son John later recalled that "before the war of 1860 he [Solomon] was connected with the so-called Underground Railway and assisted at the risk of his life and liberty in helping many slaves on their way to the freedom that Canada at that time offered."[8] The McWorter family not only gave the fugitives specific instructions on how to get to Canada, but in many instances Free Frank's sons accompanied the fugitives to Canada to insure that they would get there safely. Frank Jr. had fled to Canada as a fugitive in 1826 and lived there until 1829. His brothers Squire, Solomon, and Commodore also traveled to Canada to assist fugitives.[9]

In the family's underground railroad activities, every effort was taken to help the fugitives avoid detection. According to the family oral history as recalled by Free Frank's great-granddaughter, Ellen McWorter Yates, when Free Frank built his first cabin he deliberately selected a site underlain by granite, which he used as the walls for his cellar. One of the cellar walls opened to a room which the family dug out to be used as a hiding place for fugitives. When there was time, the fugitives were taken to Hadley Creek to prevent any trace of their desperate flight. When they hid in the cellar room behind the stone door they could not be detected by the dogs which slave catchers invariably used. The family was artful in throwing the slave catchers off guard, even inviting them to supper, Mrs. Yates recalled. Assured by Free Frank's calm demeanor and anxious to believe that a free black family would not risk their own freedom, perhaps even apprehensive that they might be poisoned, the slave catchers were always quick to move on in their chase.[10]

It seems likely that the Free Frank family even provided shoes for the fugitives. New Philadelphia had two shoemakers, out of a total of fifteen in Pike County, with a population of 23,351 in 1850. Unless the people of Hadley township had an unusual interest in being well-shod in comparison wih the rest of Pike's population, there is no reasonable explanation for the settlement of two shoemakers in a town of only fifty-eight people.[11] In addition, even Luce, the postmaster and erstwhile building contractor, did frequent shoe repairs for Free Frank.

Slaves invariably escaped with only the clothes on their backs, and the article of clothing most needed by the time they reached the North was shoes. In his discussion of the clothing allotment provided slaves, Genovese says that "no article of slave clothing called forth so much complaint as the shoes." Even in the worst weather many slaves worked barefoot because uncomfortable shoes, often made of sheepskin, cardboard, or sometimes wood, did not fit and were extremely painful when worn. Their discomfort was such that freedmen frequently recalled that during their bondage they had fervently prayed most for three things—"for the end of tribulation and the end of beatings and for shoes that fit our feet." Complaints increased during the late antebellum period, notes Genovese, when fewer plantation holders provided for a division of craft labor that included slave shoemakers. On the market, a pair of New England-made "Negro shoes" for slaves cost from $1.00 to $1.25.[12]

As the 1850 court records show, Luce charged from $.25 to $1.00 to repair shoes; $1.50 to make women's shoes; and $4.00 for making three pairs of shoes, an average of $1.33 per pair.[13] These debts were incurred in only one year, and by 1850 Luce had lived in New Philadelphia for at least seven years. While there are no records to indicate how long Taylor, one of the two listed shoemakers, had been in business in New Philadelphia, Burdick, the other shoemaker, had lived there since 1846 when he purchased his New Philadelphia town lot.[14] Thus what appears to be a flourishing center of shoemaking activity in New Philadelphia is revealing. Massie emphasized that "Pike County had a few stations on what was known as the underground railroad in slavery times."[15] If indeed the family provided shoes for fugitives, this activity also suggests, as with the family's construction of the hidden cellar room, that Free Frank was systematic in his efforts to provide aid to runaway slaves to assure their successful escape. Doubtless a significant number of fugitives made their way safely through Pike County with the assistance of the family. Solomon's work as a cabinet-maker and the odd jobs performed by the family, such as those seen in an 1850 receipt, when Solomon was paid for "halling a load of BedSteads to Grigsville," and in the court records in which Free Frank charged Luce for "Hauling one load of lumber from Rockport" and "Hauling pork to Quincy," provided the family with a perfect cover for transporting slave fugitives through and out of Pike County.[16]

Paradoxically, while the Free Frank family was assisting slaves in their escape to freedom, some Pike County whites seemed just as eager in their efforts to assist free blacks out of the county. Beginning in the late 1840s, four local branches of the American Colonization Society were organized in Pike County: the Pike County Colonization Society branch, the Perry and Pittsfield branches, and a branch at Griggsville. The society's objectives were expressed in the by-laws of the Pittsfield branch: "The object to which its efforts should be exclusively directed is the colonizing in Liberia with their own consent, the free people of color in the United States."[17] The Perry branch, organized in 1847 as an auxiliary to the Pike County Colonization Society branch, received a great degree of support from the townspeople. It was reported that at the first meeting "an opportunity was offered for those favorable to the cause to become members of the society, and upon examination there was found to be 52 persons [over 25 percent of the town's 1850 adult population] who had subscribed liberally and become members of the society."[18]

The specific responses of Pike County's blacks to the society's activities are unknown, but in Springfield, the state capital, some blacks were reportedly willing to consider emigration. The *Pike County Free Press* in 1847 wrote that "the exertions of the Rev. Mr. Snow and other colonization men, have aroused the Free Africans in Illinois to take part in this society's plans" and that "th[e] Baptist Colored Society have appointed Mr. Ball, a respectable African of Springfield, Illinois, an agent for them and he intends visiting Liberia in Africa to report to his people whether they should go there." The article also noted that some whites seemed reluctant to support the society principally because "the Africans do not favor the plan of colonizing them." The Springfield branch of the society therefore launched an intensive drive to recruit new members who would be more supportive of their goals. In particular, "our friends in Griggsville" were told that the society "would be glad to see them at the next meeting."[19] This activity is somewhat ironic, since by 1850 Pike's forty-three blacks constituted less than .025 percent of the county's population of 18,862.

The considerable support Pike County whites gave the Democratic Party provides yet another perspective for assessing the racial attitude that existed in the Illinois community where Free Frank lived. Except in the election of

1840, Democratic candidates were victorious, and in 1840 the Whigs were said to have carried the election only because, as Chapman noted, "Mormons in the county, and they were numerous, voted for Harrison."[20] Tom L. McLaughlin, in a study of white reactions to the idea of the equality of Afro-Americans, concluded that "the counties identified with the Democratic Party resisted Negro equality much more so than did the non-Democratic parties (Whig and Republican) from 1836-1860." McLaughlin's study also shows that during this period the two major parties took opposing positions "on the Negro question, with the Democrats becoming less tolerant and the non-Democratic parties more tolerant."[21] The Democratic Party was especially active in the area where Free Frank lived. While Pike County Whigs were in a minority, they exerted considerable influence, not only in Pittsfield but also in Barry, the township adjacent to Hadley. In their efforts to gain political strength in this area, some Pike County Democratic politicians in 1845 attempted to create a new county, "the effect of which would be to set off about all the Democratic majority in this county." Hadley was singled out as one of the three townships to be included in this new, politically based Democratic county if those efforts succeeded.[22]

In Pike County, it appears that from the mid-1840s on few people, even Whigs, cared to be identified with any issues related to the "Negro question," especially abolitionism. The campaign activities preceding a county election in 1846 are singularly revealing. One of the candidates for sheriff, a Whig, was accused of being an abolitionist.[23] The charge was so damaging to his political aspirations that his supporters found it necessary to publish a statement signed by prominent Pike County whites certifying that "from our personal knowledge he is no abolitionist and that the report of his being such is found on falsehood and circulated for slanderous purposes."[24] Any Pike County candidate who purported to have abolitionist sympathies received only minimal support. Out of 2,916 votes cast in the 1846 election, the results were: "9 abolitionist votes taken in Pike County . . . six at Barry, two at Atlas, and one at New Hartford."[25] While the Whigs might take a moderate position on abolition, their sympathies did not extend to promoting equal rights for blacks, as indicated in an 1849 newspaper commentary, which reported that "In the State Senate yesterday, upon the question of admitting black children to participation in the benefits of the school fund, every Whig in the Senate voted to exclude them. When we reflect that Illinois Whigery had for several years past been 'billing and cooing' with abolitionism, to secure their vote for Whig candidates, we are at a loss to account for this untimely desertion of their quondam allies. Probably the near approach of the advent of a slaveholding president, elected by the Whigs."[26]

The presidential election returns for 1848 to 1860 also reveal Pike

County voters continuing support for political parties that expressed open opposition to black equality or abolitionist activities. McLaughlin's analysis of the returns for 1848 shows that, "the counties which gave a high percentage vote to the Free Soil Party in the 1848 presidential election were more favorable to Negro equality than those that showed little or no support for the anti-slavery party."[27] In Pike County the returns showed 1,401 votes for Zachary Taylor (Whig), 1,633 votes for Lewis Cass (Democrat), and only 186 for Martin Van Buren (Free Soiler).[28] In the strongly contested presidential election of 1856, McLaughlin found that "the counties reflecting the highest percentage of 'nativism' . . . were considerably more against Negroes than the counties which gave little or no support to the American party."[29] Pike County's election returns for 1856 show that James Buchanan (Democrat) received 2,163 votes, John C. Fremont (Republican) received 1,053 votes, and Millard Fillmore (American) received 1,010. The 1860 election, in contrast, would suggest that Pike County whites were becoming less anti-black in their attitudes: the Republican candidate, Abraham Lincoln, received 2,553 votes, while the Democrat, Stephen Douglas, won 3,016 votes.[30] Overall, however, with the political support given the Democratic Party, the election returns for 1848, 1856, and 1860 show a decidedly anti-black attitude in Pike County, according to McLaughlin's analysis.[31]

Even in their religious affiliations, Pike County whites belonged primarily to those churches which did not take a strong position against slavery. McLaughlin found that counties that were strongly Baptist "appear less hostile to Negroes than those with Presbyterian, Methodist, and Roman Catholic 'religious denominational preference.'" An examination of the religious affiliation of Pike County citizens listed in the 1850 census reveals that there were 1,290 Baptists as compared with a total of 550 Presbyterians and 1,200 Methodists. While there were no members of the Roman Catholic church in Pike County listed, the census showed 500 members of the Christian Church, 700 in the Congregational Church, and 400 in the Free Church. The sixteen churches in the county had total property valued at $18,700. Interestingly, only two Free Churches were listed in Illinois at this time, one in Pike County and one in Cook County.[32]

From this analysis of white attitudes, it seems obvious that pioneer blacks on the Pike County frontier were never far removed from open expressions of racism. The sparse black population in the New Philadelphia area, however, found it more difficult to engage in open protest than blacks in urban areas. In the established towns and cities greater opportunity existed for blacks to participate in organized protests against slavery, political repression, economic discrimination, and legal disabilities. In the smaller communities, although participation in any protest activity outside the church was violently proscribed, some advances were still made in strengthening the black community. In a relatively restricted way, Free Frank's activities as a town founder, particularly his efforts to build the Free Will Baptist Seminary, can be viewed as a form of protest, an indication of his desire for self-determination. As Litwack explains in detailing the varied forms of antebellum black protest, "Experience had taught the Negro that only constant pressure for immediate change, rather than a passive trust in gradualism would produce results."[33]

The proposed construction of the New Philadelphia Free Will Baptist Seminary would have marked the beginning of an institutional basis for Pike County's black community. A school and its chapel that would serve as a church would have provided cohesion and strength for the county's black population, who by 1850 numbered forty-three, thirty-three of whom lived in or around New Philadelphia. When the African Methodist Episcopal church was organized in Alton in 1839, three couples and one single man comprised its founding members.[34] Certainly Free Frank's efforts in 1848 to arrange for the seminary's construction were remarkable. New Philadelphia had been in existence only twelve years. Many family members still remained in slavery, and a depression had ended only three years before. Yet Free Frank, his family, and other Pike County blacks subscribed to underwrite the costs of building the seminary and to provide funds for purchasing the necessary materials required for its operation as a school and church.

Unfortunately the Free Will Baptist Seminary was never built. The contractor's attempt to gain control of the town only confirmed what Free Frank had experienced once before when the Kentucky frontier came to a close: that whites would attempt to usurp the economic activities of blacks. Although New Philadelphia's white community decided for Free Frank in the arbitration hearing, and whites also contributed to the construction of the seminary, considering the anti-black sentiments expressed in Pike, these were decidedly minority feelings, at best. So while the central location of Free Frank's farm and of New Philadelphia in Pike County helps to explain his economic success, his activities as a town proprietor and commercial farmer were carried on in a community where overwhelming evidence indicates persistent expressions of antiblack attitudes.

Despite such opposition, throughout this period Free Frank continued to promote the development of New Philadelphia with the sale of his town lots, and also continued his farming activities. In each of these activities he had the help of his four sons: his two slave-born sons, Frank Jr. and Solomon, who by 1850 were forty-five and thirty-five respectively; and his two freeborn sons, Squire, who was thirty-three, and Commodore, who was twenty-seven. Together they worked at farming the land and improving

Table 12. Taxes on Free Frank's Farmland for 1853

No. of Acres	Section	Township	Range	Valuation	Amount of Taxes
160	SE 22	4S	5W	$2,304	$39.70
20	W 1/2 NW NW 26	4S	5W	72	1.24
40	SW NW 26	4S	5W	144	2.48
40	NE SW 26	4S	5W	144	1.04
40	NW SW 26	4S	5W	144	1.04
40	SW SW 26	4S	5W	144	1.04
35	E part N 1/2 NE 27	4S	5W	155	2.72
	Total Land Value and Taxes			$3,107	$49.26
	Personal Property			622	10.71
	Total valuation and taxes			$3,729	$59.97

SOURCE: Free Frank [McWorter] Papers.

some of their holdings for sale. Tax receipts show that Free Frank's farmland from 1840-1841 to 1853-1854 increased in value. Both Free Frank and his sons sold their improved farmland to earn money to buy the family's freedom. Whereas Free Frank alone had purchased six tracts of Illinois land between 1830 and 1839, amounting to 660 acres, including the 80-acre tract on which New Philadelphia was platted, by 1853 he had only 375 acres remaining (see Table 12), and at the time of his death in 1854, had only 335 acres. Pike County deed records show that Free Frank sold his first tract of land in 1836, ten acres for $50; he had paid $1.25 per acre for this land. In 1841 Squire sold ten acres of his land for $200 and Solomon in 1847 sold ten acres of his improved farmland for $250.[35]

For free blacks, these were substantial holdings. By 1850, only 7.5 percent of the nation's 439,494 free blacks owned real property.[36] Illinois's black property ownership was comparable. At that time, Illinois's black population of 5,436 was dispersed throughout most of the state, but the greatest concentration was in the southern and western parts of the state. With the exception of Jo Daviess County, where the Galena lead mines were located, with 218 free blacks, most free blacks in that area had settled in and around towns on the routes which new settlers took as they entered from the southern part of Illinois. St. Claire County on the Mississippi River, where East St. Louis is now located, had the greatest number of blacks, 583, followed by Madison County, with 446 blacks, including the 170 who lived in Alton. Cook County's black population of 383, including 323 in Chicago, ranked third.[37] In that city only nine blacks owned real property, ranging in value from $400 to $10,000.[38] Zucker's study of property ownership in eight

Illinois counties (all but two, Jo Daviess and Cook, were located in southern and western Illinois, where almost one-third of the state's black population lived, some 1,800), shows that only 14 percent of that total number owned real property. Assuming an average family of five, however, only 135 black heads of household owned property. Even then, 6 percent of that number, a mere seven families, owned real property valued at $600 or more.[39] Pike County's black population in 1850 was only 43, but it ranked twenty-fifth among Illinois's ninety-nine counties in the number of blacks. In Pike, three black heads of household, in addition to Free Frank and his sons, had purchased real property in farmland before 1840. By 1850 three other black heads of household had acquired real property, in New Philadelphia town lots.

By 1850 the Free Frank family owned over 600 acres of land valued at more than $7,000. For Illinois's free black population, these were substantial holdings. But they were small compared with what Paul Gates describes as the "bonanza farms," established by white pioneers where "investments ranged from a few thousand to hundreds of thousands of dollars, and for a score or more, to over one or two millions." Their holdings ranged from 15,000 to 40,000 acres by the time of the Civil War.[40] The acquisition of property by Illinois blacks was difficult. In Zucker's occupational distribution of black males in 1850, almost half (46 percent) were shown as unemployed. Only 10 percent of this group were listed as farmers, including both laborers and owners.[41] With the frontier period coming to a close in Illinois by the 1850s, little land was available for purchase at the prices Free Frank had paid in the 1830s. With the 1841 Preemption Act, attempts were made to exclude free blacks entirely from acquiring public land. As Curry notes, "In an aggressively capitalistic society, economic advancement was closely tied to property ownership."[42] Confronted by even more limitations on their freedom after 1850, and in the face of high unemployment and limited financial resources, Illinois blacks found it difficult to acquire property during this decade.[43]

Free Frank's land purchases in the 1830s had resulted from federal laws that did not discourage the sale of public land to blacks nor exclude them from preemption, although proscriptive legislation severely limited their opportunities to acquire property. It was because of his land ownership—money obtained from the sale of farmland and New Philadelphia town lots, in addition to his farming activities—that Free Frank was able to purchase thirteen family members from slavery while in Illinois. Solomon's purchase for $550 was made with money earned only four years after Free Frank settled in the state. Sally's purchase in 1843, eight years after Solomon's, was remarkable because the money for it was earned during the depths of a depression. Once the depression ended, Free Frank expanded his economic activities, and before 1850 was able to purchase his daughter Juda, his firstborn child and the last of his children to remain a slave.

Free Frank's efforts to free his family did not end with the purchase of his children, however. While they were slaves, both Sally and Juda had children. As an initial step toward buying his grandchildren, on August 16, 1846, at the age of sixty-nine, Free Frank made out his will, stipulating that "I reserve enough to buy my grandchildren in bondage six in number at a reasonable price." Thus, if Free Frank should die before their purchase, provisions for his grandchildren's freedom would be somewhat assured.[44] This will was one final example of the careful planning that this resolute and determined man took as he struggled to buy his family from slavery.

Free Frank continued with his activities to earn money, and by 1850 he had purchased three more family members: two grandchildren and the wife of his son Squire. By the late 1840s his sons were accompanying him as he returned to Pulaski, for in 1847 Free Frank was seventy years old. It was on one of these trips to Pulaski County that Squire met his wife, Louisa, whom he later helped to escape to Canada. Free Frank purchased her freedom, for without freedom papers Louisa would have been subject to reenslavement had she attempted to settle in Illinois with her husband. Thus, in a period of seven years, from 1843 to 1850, Free Frank purchased freedom for five family members.[45]

Yet other family members remained in slavery, and Free Frank lived in constant fear that they would be sold. He was aided by the support and encouragement of Pulaski County blacks, particularly his old friend Galen Gibson.[46] In his correspondence Gibson provided information on Free Frank's slave family, and also on the activities of their slaveholders, particularly Obediah Denham. Over twenty years had passed since the Kentucky court trials, but it seems that Denham remained as determined as ever to subvert Free Frank's goals by constant threats that he would sell the family. Powerless to prevent Denham from carrying out his threats, Free Frank worked desperately to secure their freedom. By the 1850s, Denham seemed even more determined to sell the family away from Kentucky. Always the possibility existed that if they were sold they would be relocated where their freedom could never be secured.

In a letter dated January 1854, Galen Gibson wrote to Solomon that Denham had refused to sell Free Frank's granddaughter Charlotte (Sally's daughter) to his son William Denham. Later communication reveals that William wanted to keep her in the Denham family until Frank could buy her, whereas Obediah wanted to sell her to another slaveholder. Gibson's letter has significance from yet another perspective. It provides a specific example of the fictive kinship relations, identified in plantation slave communities, that also persisted over time among blacks in general farming slave communities. It also reveals the affectionate regard and feelings of mutual obligation that transcended the distinctions between slave and free black. In his discussion of black familial relationships during slavery, Gutman indicates that "fictive, or quasi, kin played yet other roles in developing slave communities, *binding unrelated adults to one another* and thereby infusing enlarged slave communities with conceptions of obligations that flowed initially from kin obligations rooted in blood and marriage. The obligations to a brother or a niece were transformed into the obligations toward a fellow slave or a fellow slave's child, and behavior first determined by familial and kin obligation became enlarged social obligation."[47]

By 1854 nine family members had been purchased from slavery, but Galen Gibson expresses concern at this time as to whether Solomon will return to Pulaski County, and Sally's daughter wonders if she will ever see her family again. Their concern may reflect the anxiety caused by passage of the Illinois anti-immigration law, which had gone into effect the previous year, and the uncertainty of how it would affect the members of the family yet remaining as slaves in Pulaski County.

Somerset Ky, January 1854

Mr. Solomon McQuarter
Dear Sir
I this evening take the opportunity to address you a few lines to let you know that I am well   Wm Denham has not bought Charlotte yet he is not agoing to Buy her   She will give him Satisfaction about it. I wish you would come as Soon as you could between this and the first of March   they wish to know whether you can come by that time or Know Old Obediah says he cannot keep her no longer than that time

Lucy Ann [Charlotte's sister] requests me to tell her mother [Sally] that she is well and is hoping of seeing her yet   she wants her to write to her soon   She sends her best respects to Aunt Juda and hopes she will see her yet

Fayette is well at this time   he is married   he has been married better than a year to Emitime Hayes   he sends his best respects to Aunt Sally and all the rest

Aunt Mary and all the rest of her family are well   She sends her best respects to all   Aunt Ersey send her best respects to Aunt Sally and Aunt Juda and she is well at this time hoping she will hear from her soon

Hilda is well and sends her best respects to all

Caroline is well and sends her best respects to all   Tell Aunt Sally that I am well   hoping these lines may find her enjoying the same health I should like to hear how she is getting to [a]long   tell Aunt Juda I am well at this time.

Write soon as you can   Write whether you ever expect to come back here again or not   I should be very glad to see you in Pulaski once more   I shall not write no more until I receive an answer to this. I would have wrote sooner than this but I was waiting to Receive a letter from him [Free Frank]   the next opportunity I will try and do better

Farewell

Yours Forever

Galen Gibson[48]

Unfortunately, Free Frank would never see Charlotte or his great-granddaughter or Sally's other five children free. On September 7, 1854, the black pioneer died at the age of seventy-seven. He had not lived to see the achievement of his dream that his entire family be freed from slavery. Even as he lay dying, his final concern was that there be little delay in the probate of his estate so that the money would be available to purchase the family members remaining in slavery. Only one day before his death several land transactions were made, preventing much of his property from being encumbered by lengthy estate proceedings. Solomon, the executor, began immediately to carry out his father's plan that the rest of the family be free. As it was, the estate was not settled until almost four years later, although only three months after Free Frank's death a letter from William Denham made it imperative that Solomon make some kind of arrangement for the immediate purchase of Charlotte and her daughter. Denham wrote with somewhat restrained urgency that there was every likelihood that they would be sold.

As Galen Gibson had written, Charlotte had been insistent that William purchase her from his father, whereas old Obediah seemed adamant that she be sold. Yet a reading of William Denham's December 1854 letter suggests a somewhat personal concern on William's part: "His description of Charlotte's daughter," one person has reflected, "seems more like that of a proud father than anything else."[49] As Galen had written the previous January, Obediah had threatened to sell her by March of that year. That he had not done so almost a year later perhaps could be attributed as much to his reluctance to sell his own granddaughter as a desire to prevent a breach in the already strained relations with his son, as revealed in William's letter to Solomon:

1854 December the 30   Somerset Ky

dear Sir   I take my pen in hand this morning with Sorrow in my hart to let you no that I Cannot prevent my father from Selling Sharlet   I have kept him from Selling hur for too years   I Can doo nothing more with him   if you want hur you had Better Come quick   you ned not tak of the River being frose up   if you want Sharlet Come Right [a]long

I Right this unbe[known] to my father; you Can by hur for $850, or 900 hur and hur Child   I think Carlet has got as purty A Child and as Smart as I Ever have

Seen white or Black and it is all most white   I feel anctious you wuld Come and Buy
hur   the Children is all weell   the male is a bout to start and I must Come to a
close   Beshore to Come on Right Soon.
    your friend

                                                William Denham[50]

Solomon, however, was unable to secure Charlotte's freedom until
1857. By this time she had had another child, a fact revealed in a letter from
William Denham to Solomon written in July 1860, in which William asked
Solomon to send him a copy of the bill of sale "for Sharlet and hur Children." Their purchase price was $993.61.[51]

Charlotte and her two children were not the only family members purchased after Free Frank's death. The court records of the probate of the estate in January 1857 reveal that an additional $3,030 was appropriated on
June 28, 1856, for Sally to buy her other children and grandchildren from
slavery:

. . . that said Will of said Testator Frank McWorter bore date 15 August AD.
1846—that said Testator himself was a colored or yellow man & had once been a
slave, but had been emancipated and that the said Grand Children of said Frank
whom he directed to be purchased as aforesaid slaves in Kentucky at the time of
making said Will & continued so to be for some time after the death of said Testator,
until under & by provision in said Will your Petitioner directed the Mother [Sally] of
said Grand Children who was herself a Free Woman of Color to buy said Grand Children of said Frank from their masters in Kentucky, which was accordingly done at an
expense of Three thousand and thirty dollars with interest at ten percent from June
28, 1856 which sum has been allowed to said Sarah [Sally] McWorter by the County
Court aforesaid against said Frank McWorter's estate and is now due and un-
paid. . . .[52]

The sale of the family's farmland and New Philadelphia town lots was
one way Solomon was able to secure some of the money to buy their freedom. In 1857 he sold the 120-acre tract that Commodore had purchased in
1836. Commodore had paid $900 for the tract, making the final payment in
1852. While an 1857 tax receipt shows the assessed valuation of the land as
$2,560, Solomon, desperate for money, took the best price he could get and
sold it for $1,000. New Philadelphia town lots were sold also; Table 13
shows the value of these lots as compared to what they had been worth in
1848.

As a result of Solomon's efforts in carrying out the will, a total of seven
grandchildren and great-grandchildren of Free Frank were purchased from
slavery within three years after his death. Table 14 lists the fifteen family
members, in addition to Free Frank himself, who were purchased as a result

Table 13. Assessed Valuation of New Philadelphia Town Lots in
1848, and Prices of Town Lots Sold for Estate Settlement in 1858

Block	Lots	Assessed Valuation, 1848	Price Paid, 1858
1	1-8	$16.00	$ 8.00
2	1-8	16.00	20.00
5	1, 2, 7, 8	40.00	15.00
9	1, 2	24.00	20.00
10	1-8	16.00	36.00
11	3-8	52.00	36.00
12	1-8	16.00	41.00
14	1-8	16.00	26.00
19	1-8	16.00	60.00
20	1-8	16.00	35.00

SOURCES: Pike County Deed Record Book, 53:675, Pike County Courthouse,
Pittsfield, Ill.; 1848 tax receipt, in Free Frank [McWorter] Papers.

of his lifetime of work. An estimated total of more than $14,000 was paid
for the family's freedom from money earned by this black pioneer entrepreneur from the business activities he established on the frontier communities
where he lived in Kentucky and Illinois. [53]

In the development of those wilderness communities, Free Frank's economic activities had actually paralleled those of white pioneer entrepreneurs, although, with proscriptive legislation and severe racial constraints,
the successful development of his enterprises had required an entrepreneurial expertise far beyond that demanded of white entrepreneurs. The latter,
with virtually unlimited freedom in the use of their productive energies, and
with free access to the vast resources of the nation's wilderness frontiers, often
acted without restraint. The release of their creative energies to develop new
enterprises as they challenged the wilderness was encouraged by an unfet-
tered freedom. Despite racial constraints, the diversity of Free Frank's enterprises reflected the pattern of the pioneer entrepreneur described by Arthur
Cole who, "having launched one business enterprise, becomes involved in
the economic development of the town or regions, and to facilitate the operation of the first line of business he enters a second line, then a third, until
he winds up with a diversity of enterprises under his control." [54]

Free Frank, moreover, achieved a success far beyond that which distinguished many white entrepreneurs. The profits he earned while participat-
ing in the newly developing economies of America's antebellum frontiers
enabled him to buy his family from slavery. Even in a racist society that sys-

Table 14. Free Frank Family Members Purchased, 1817-1857

Date of Purchase	Name	Relationship to Free Frank	Price
1817	Lucy	Wife	$ 800[1]
1819	Free Frank		800[2]
1829	Frank Jr.	Son	2,500 (est.)[3]
1835	Solomon	Son	500[4]
1843	Sally [Sarah]	Daughter	950[5]
By 1850	Juda [Judah, Julia]	Daughter	4,380 (est.)[6]
	Commodore	Grandson	
	Permilia	Granddaughter	
	Louisa	Daughter-in-law	
By 1856	Calvin	Grandson	3,030[7]
	Calvin	Grandson	
	Robert	Grandson	
	Lucy Ann	Granddaughter	
By 1857	Charlotte	Granddaughter	993.61[8]
	Child of Charlotte	Great Grandchild	
	Child of Charlotte	Great Grandchild	

1. Pulaski County Real Estate Conveyances, Book 3: 228; Certificate of Good Character for Free Frank, Sept. 7, 1830, Free Frank [McWorter] Papers; *Atlas Map of Pike County,* p. 54.

2. Pulaski County Real Estate Conveyances, Book 4: 138; Certificate of Good Character for Free Frank, Sept. 7, 1830, Free Frank [McWorter] Papers; *Atlas Map of Pike County,* p. 54.

3. Pulaski County Real Estate Conveyances, Book 7: 55-56.

4. Ibid., Book 8: 199-200.

5. Ibid., Book 12: 379-80.

6. *Pike County Atlas,* p. 54; John E. McWorter to Rev. P.B. West, Aug. 31, 1919, mimeographed; Arthur McWorter to Thelma McWorter Kirkpatrick [Wheaton], Jan. 1937; and Thelma Elise McWorter, "Free Frank of Pike County, Ill." (Chicago, *ca.* 1937, mimeographed), all in Free Frank [McWorter] Papers.

7. Pike County Circuit Court Records, *Solomon, Exr. of Frank McWorter* v. *Lucy McWorter widow et al.* (1857), case no. 8850.

8. Pike County Inventories, Appraisements, Bills, etc., 1866-1869, pp. 28-29, Pike County Courthouse, Pittsfield, Ill.

tematically institutionalized the economic subordination of blacks, where laws, customs, and traditions discouraged black access to the use of private property, Free Frank's business activities can be understood within the Schumpeterian frame of a creative capitalist. Monetary gain is not the only motivating force, nor the only measure of success, explains Joseph Schumpeter, but also "the will to conquer, the impulse to fight, to prove oneself superior to others, to succeed for the sake, not of the fruits of success but of success itself."[55] That Free Frank survived for seventy-seven years the bitter hardships, the disappointments, the limitations imposed on his life by a society that operated continuously and perniciously to defeat his efforts, attests to the strength and indomitable will of this black man in his determination to buy his family from slavery. By 1857, while over forty years had passed since Free Frank first purchased Lucy in 1817, this black pioneer had succeeded. Four generations of his family had been purchased from slavery. Free Frank's dream that his family would be free finally became a reality. In the final analysis, however, blacks who purchased their freedom found that the social costs of freedom were not included in the price of manumission.

Epilogue

Mr. McWorter was a live, enterprising man, a reputable worthy citizen, kind, benevolent and honest. He labored hard to free his posterity from the galling yoke of southern slavery.[1]

The 1850s marked an end to the saga of Free Frank—an Afro-American freedom fighter, a man who struggled a lifetime to liberate his family, determined that they would be free. Even after his death in 1854, Free Frank's determination and the intensity of his efforts were still felt in Pike County, as evidenced by the indulgence of the county court. Even before the estate was finally settled, Solomon was allowed to purchase those family members still remaining in slavery. By 1860 it appeared that all the family was free.

Solomon, who had been his father's business partner, had never married. On countless occasions he had remarked, according to the family tradition, that his children would never be brought up in a country where they were marked for slavery. With the Emancipation Proclamation's promise of freedom, feeling that surely this was the beginning of the end of slavery, Solomon married. His young bride, Frances Coleman from Springfield, Illinois, was twenty years old and Solomon was nearly fifty when they married on September 29, 1863, during the Civil War.[2] Only one of Free Frank's descendants, his grandson Squire, served in the Union army.[3] And, with the exception of Solomon, who was now head of the family, all of Free Frank's sons had died before 1860—Frank Jr. in 1851 at the age of forty-six, Squire in 1855 at the age of thirty-eight, and Commodore in 1855 at the age of thirty-two.

Throughout the Civil War, Free Frank's New Philadelphia experienced its period of greatest growth. Black migration, not only from the South but also from the west, principally Missouri, contributed, although only briefly to an increase in the town's population.[4] With its predominantly black population, New Philadelphia, according to Norman Crockett, would be classed as an all-black town: "a separate community containing a population of at least 90 percent black." Despite this definition, three of the five all-black towns in Crockett's study were founded by whites: Nicodemus, Kansas, founded in 1879; Langston, Oklahoma, founded in 1891; and Boley, Oklahoma, founded in 1904.[5] W. Sherman Savage broadens the definition of a black town, however, giving consideration to places founded by blacks and settled by a biracial population. In his discussion of the origin of Douglas-ville, Texas, founded in 1853 by a black man, John Douglas, Savage explains that at first it was "a village where many slave owners left their slaves before the Civil War." After 1865, however, whites also settled in the town, soon comprising over half of the population, and Savage classes it as a black town "only because of its founder and the blacks who settled around him and in the areas which the town serves."[6] From Savage's perspective, ante-bellum New Philadelphia, although initially settled by whites as well as blacks, would be classed as a black town. Its founder, promoter, proprietor, and developer, Free Frank, was black. The black population of New Philadelphia's hinterland patronized the town's businesses, and the Hadley township black community's social and cultural life was centered in New Philadelphia.

After the Civil War, New Philadelphia's population settlement pattern and occupational distribution showed striking similarities to those found in the all-black towns discussed by Crockett. Instead of the gradual addition of new townspeople that distinguished its pre-Civil War settlement pattern, the town's new settlers after 1865—the merchants, craftsmen, and profes-sionals—all "arrived at approximately the same time." Another occupa-tional characteristic that New Philadelphia shared with Crockett's all-black towns was that "a large number of residents lived inside the town limits but earned their livelihood during the day by farming land they owned or rented in the surrounding countryside." Crockett also noted that "many persons of each town were acquainted with, if indeed not distantly related to, one an-other before they arrived."[7] The 1870 and 1880 federal manuscript census, the Pike County Deed Record Book Town Lot Index, and oral history sources point to the familial relationships and fictive kinship ties of many New Phil-adelphia townspeople after the Civil War.

While the Hadley township black population would show a steady in-crease, even into the early years of the twentieth century, New Philadelphia as a town did not survive. In 1869, when the railroad came through Pike County for the first time, it bypassed Free Frank's town. Just as the proposed construction of the Illinois-Michigan Canal had led to the establishment and growth of Pike County towns in the mid-1830s, so the construction of the railroads brought about the founding and growth of new Pike towns and vil-lages from the late 1860s through the 1870s. Simultaneously, the railroads contributed to the decline of those towns whose survival depended on wagon roads which facilitated the transportation of farm produce to the rivers for shipment to outside markets. New Philadelphia's location on an important county road leading to the Mississippi River, with its flourishing steamboat trade, had contributed to the town's success before the Civil War,

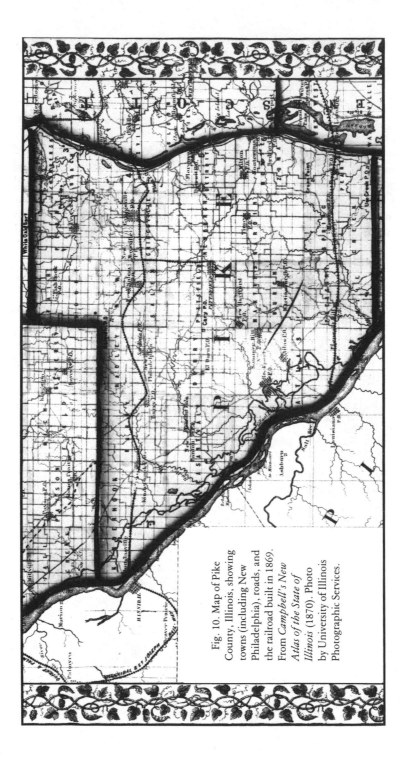

Fig. 10. Map of Pike County, Illinois, showing towns (including New Philadelphia), roads, and the railroad built in 1869. From *Campbell's New Atlas of the State of Illinois* (1870). Photo by University of Illinois Photographic Services.

but from 1869 on, "the railroad passing it a mile distant and other towns springing up . . . killed it."[8] Figure 10 shows the location of the railroad station in relation to New Philadelphia. In Hadley township two new settlements were established, Hadley Village (or Hadley Station) in 1870 and Arden in the late 1880s. These places were not platted as towns and were similar to the agricultural settlements established before the Civil War. With few businesses to encourage the development of a viable town economy, none of these communities reached a population of fifty. During their brief periods of existence, Hadley Village was serviced by the post office at Barry, Arden was serviced by the Baylis post office, and, with its decline as a town, New Philadelphia residents were served by the Cool Bank post office.[9]

New Philadelphia had thrived as an agricultural market center because Hadley township farmers supported the businesses and craft trades located there. After 1869, however, instead of going to or through New Philadelphia, they took their produce to Hadley Station or to other towns in the area with railroad facilities, such as Barry, four miles directly west of New Philadelphia. Barry, like New Philadelphia, was platted in 1836, but its growth after 1845, encouraged first by the location of county roads in the 1840s and then by the railroad in 1869, was much greater. By the time of the Civil War, Pike County had developed into a highly productive agricultural community, and those towns which early on had concentrated on processing agricultural commodities as the basis for their economy survived the coming of the railroads. In Barry, Griggsville, Perry, El Dara, Kinderhook, and even Pittsfield, the county seat, woolen mills, flour mills, and tobacco factories had been established.[10] New Philadelphia was one of several Pike County towns without agricultural processing plants. Except for a blacksmith shop and a wagon manufactory, once the railroad bypassed New Philadelphia, the town's businessmen and tradesmen relocated to other towns or turned to farming.[11] Even Free Frank's grandson Squire, who returned to Pike County in 1866 after serving with the 38th Regiment of the United States Colored Troops in Brazos, Texas, opened up his blacksmith shop at Hadley Station in 1870 rather than in New Philadelphia.[12]

Without railroad facilities, New Philadelphia declined rapidly as a market center. As several old Pike County settlers remarked in the early 1870s, "The Hannibal and Naples railroad did not run through the town, which has greatly ruined its trade."[13] In 1885 Free Frank's son-in-law, Ansel Vond, Lucy Ann's husband, who owned a substantial number of New Philadelphia town lots, secured a county order divesting him of his ownership in that property.[14] The loss of New Philadelphia's population and an increase in town lot taxes precipitated Vond's action. The reversion of New Philadelphia town lots to farmland would also increase the value of this land for fu-

Descendants (Partial) of Free Frank and Lucy McWorter

*Free Frank
1777-1854 ——— m. 1799 ——— *Lucy
1771-1870

*Juda
1800-1906
m. William Armstead
(Nov. 12, 1853)

*Frank
1804-1851
m. Mary Ann
(1846?)
b. 1828

*Sally
1811-1891

*Solomon
1815-1879
m. Frances Jane Coleman
(Sept. 29, 1863)
1843-1925

Squire
1817-1855
m. *Louisa Clark
(May 7, 1843)
1826-1883

Commodore
1823-1855
No offspring

Lucy Ann
1825-1902
m. Ansel Vond

---

*Calvin
b. 1836

*Commodore
b. 1844

*Robert
b. 1850

Mary
b. 1847

Lucy
b. 1850

*Lucy Ann

*Calvin
b. 1838

*Permilia
b. 1839

*Charlotte
b. 1840

*child
b. 1850(?)

*child
b. 1850(?)

John
b. 1864, d. bef. 1937
m. Edmonia (---)

Mary
b. 1865, d. bef. 1937
m. (---) Washington

Julia
b. 1866, d. bef. 1937
m. (---) Coleman

Lucy
b. 1869
m. (---) North

Francis
b. 1872
m. Sadie (---)

Arthur
1875-1950
m. Ophelia Walker (1905)
1884-1914

Reuben
b. 1879

Eunice
b. and d. 1877

Lucy Jane
b. 1845

Squire
b. 1847

George
b. 1849

Eliza Ann
b. 1853

Mary
b. 1859

Thelma
1907-
m. Allen James Kirkpatrick
(1933) 1898-1948

Bernice
1909-
m. (1) Victor Dunn
m. (2) John Hawkins

Ellen
1910-
m. James Yates

Festus
1912-1980
m. Alice Broady

Cordell
1914-
m. Robertine Donato

Allen
1939-

Juliet
1940-

David
1943-

Marye
1945-

---

*Purchased from slavery with Free Frank's earnings.

SOURCES: Birth dates for generation III (with the exception of Solomon's descendants) are from the 1850 and 1860 federal manuscript censuses. Information on Juda's and Squire's marriages is from Agnes DuVal Keller and Roberta Liles Zachery, comps., *The Marriage Records of Pike County, Illinois* (Portland, Ore., and Shafter, Calif., 1974) (mimeographed), in University of Illinois Historical Survey Library, Urbana, Ill.

ture sale. Legislative approval through the Illinois General Assembly was required before town lots could be vacated; that was granted in 1885.[15] This action thus symbolized the end of New Philadelphia's distinct status as a town, although its site remained as a central place for the social activities of New Philadelphia's remaining residents and much of the Hadley township farm population. According to the Chapman history of Pike County, by 1880 "Hadley township was well supplied with churches and schools, which indicate that high moral and intellectual standard of the people."[16] The New Philadelphia schoolhouse continued to serve the Hadley township population until 1936, but with the ease and access afforded by the railroads, as early as 1870 many people, both black and white, began to leave not only New Philadelphia but also Hadley township.

Hadley's population, which increased steadily up to 1880, declined from 1,254 to 1,007 by 1890.[17] Of the black population who left, some moved to the larger towns in Pike County, such as Barry and Pittsfield. Others moved to Quincy, Alton, Jacksonville, Springfield, and Decatur, Illinois, or to St. Louis, Hannibal, and Columbia, Missouri. A few New Philadelphia and Hadley township blacks moved to Kansas, Oklahoma, and as far west as Colorado. The black population who remained at Hadley township continued to work at farming.[18]

The site on which New Philadelphia was established is now farmland owned by the descendants of the shoemaker Burdick, who purchased his first New Philadelphia town lot in 1846: "The schoolhouse which was the last remnant of the town itself was torn down several years ago." A shed which was once a blacksmith shop located near the town still remains.[19] By 1983, almost one hundred and fifty years after the town's founding, only a wooden sign remains, fronting a blacktop road which marks the former location of New Philadelphia, indicating: "Here is the site of New Philadelphia, a town founded in 1836 by Free Frank, a former slave."[20]

In his will Free Frank had provided that after his grandchildren were purchased his property was to be divided equally among his children.[21] Young Frank had died in 1851, and Squire and Commodore both died in 1855. As a result, Solomon, Lucy Ann, Juda, and Sally became the owners of Free Frank's land. Solomon increased his holdings, and by 1872, according to the Pike County *Atlas,* was "extensively engaged in farming and raising stock, and there are few men in Pike County who are succeeding better than he." The *Atlas* continued by saying, "Solomon's education is rather limited, but he is a man of good natural abilities, and very industrious, and is prospering well. He is now the owner of five hundred acres of first class land, well stocked with cattle, hogs, horses and mules."[22] When he died in 1879 Solomon owned 300 acres of farmland valued at $11,200, and thirty-six New Philadelphia town lots valued at $693.[23]

Solomon and his wife Frances had eight children. By the early 1900s only two of their four sons, Arthur and Francis, remained in Hadley township, farming the family land. His sons Reuben and John had moved to St. Louis at the turn of the century. Reuben became a mail clerk and John, a mail carrier. John also was an inventor who acquired three United States patents. One of his first patents, granted in 1914, was for an "Aeroplane." His other two, granted in 1914 and 1922, were for a "flying machine," actually a helicopter, since it was designed to "ascend vertically from the ground" and have "lateral motion [which] may be controlled by the operator even when the machine is hovering." With his third patent, McWorter was listed as an assignor to the Autoplane Company of America of St. Louis.[24]

Of Solomon's four daughters, one, Eunice, died in infancy. Another, Mary McWorter Washington, remained in Pike County and was both a farmer and a school teacher. Lucy McWorter North moved to Alton, where she too was a farmer and school teacher. Julia McWorter Coleman moved to Columbia, Missouri, and taught school. By 1937, as Arthur said, "The four living [himself, Lucy, Francis, and Reuben], is the only grandchildren [of] Free Frank's alive."[25] With the exception of Mary Washington's stepson LeMoyne Washington, who remained in Pike County and now lives in Barry, Arthur McWorter, my grandfather, was the last of Free Frank's descendants to leave Pike County. He was born in 1875 and in 1905 married Ophelia Elise Walker, also born in Pike County. They had five children before she died in 1914. My mother, Thelma Elise McWorter, who was born in 1907, was their first child. While most of the family's farm holdings were lost during the Great Depression, Arthur continued to farm the remaining land until he moved to Chicago in 1949. He died one year later at the age of seventy-five. Had the family been able to retain the original 800 acres acquired by Free Frank, with Pike County farmland prices now averaging at least $3,000 per acre, their holdings would be worth a substantial fortune of $2.4 million.[26]

Free Frank did not leave his children monetary wealth, but he did leave a legacy for his descendants—a desire for education. In the third generation of the Free Frank family, four of Solomon's children earned normal school teaching certificates from Lincoln University in Missouri. Three of Free Frank's descendants in the fourth generation, Solomon's grandchildren, were the first to acquire college degrees, all in social work, attending the University of Chicago, Fisk University, and Tennessee State University. In the fifth generation (the first to be born in the city), of Solomon's ten great-grandchildren, eight have earned college degrees, including four Ph.Ds: in the fields of mathematics (University of Toronto), sociology (University of Chicago), electrical engineering (Purdue University), and history (University of Chicago). Three have acquired master's degrees: in sociology (University

Fig. 11. Arthur McWorter (1875-1950), son of Solomon and Frances Coleman McWorter, grandson of Free Frank and grandfather of the author. Photographed about 1900.

Fig. 12. Thelma McWorter Kirkpatrick Wheaton (b. 1907), daughter of Arthur and Ophelia Walker McWorter; she initiated this study of her great-grandfather while a student at Fisk University. Portrait painted in 1933 by George Neal.

Photos courtesy of Thelma McWorter Kirkpatrick Wheaton.

of Chicago), architecture (Case Western Reserve University), and social work (University of Chicago). One has a bachelor's degree in business administration (Roosevelt University). And in the sixth generation of Free Frank's descendants, two have received BA's (University of Illinois at Chicago and Loyola University of Chicago), with plans to go into law and business. Three are undergraduates in business administration, accounting, and computer technology.

That Free Frank's life is now a matter of historical record can be attributed to his great-granddaughter, Thelma McWorter Wheaton, the first of his descendants to attempt a scholarly study of his life. Her early efforts as the family historian led to a fortuitous set of circumstances which ultimately resulted in the survival of those Free Frank Papers now available. As a student at Fisk University in the late 1920s, while taking a class with the eminent black sociologist Charles S. Johnson, she was struck by the difficulty he pointed to of reconstructing the history of black people during slavery because of the absence of written records. After informing Professor Johnson of her family records, Thelma returned home and begged her grandmother to be allowed to take to school just a few of the papers which were carefully stored in the attic. Shortly after her return to campus, she received word that the farmhouse where she was born, and where Free Frank had lived, had been destroyed by fire.[27] Only those papers which she had with her at Fisk survived to document the life of a black man who was born a slave and whose whole life was a struggle to be free.

Free Frank's life and his unrelenting efforts to free his family are a part of the legacy he left his descendants. His grandson John, Solomon's first child, wrote in 1919:

When I think of what my own family has suffered, the suffering endured by millions of other former slaves, and the hardships endured at the present time by their descendants I am made to wonder what can be the Divine purpose of it all. I see one portion of the human family enslave and persecute another portion and that too in violation of the known laws of God and the highest ideals of man yet the persecutor at the present time is apparently enjoying the special favor of God. How can this fair land of ours ever fully atone for the crime of human slavery? Is it possible for this nation as now constituted to ever rid itself of the curse and blight of race prejudice, a thing that is now shaking to the very foundation the principal nation of the earth: We are passing through a crisis and the destiny of the civilizations of today is in the hands of "Divine Providence"—an expression I remember my father used very frequently.[28]

The death of Free Frank's wife Lucy in 1871, as she approached her one-hundredth birthday, and the death of Solomon in 1879 marked an end to one phase of the history of a black family that had its beginnings at the end of the eighteenth century, in 1799, when Free Frank and Lucy took each other as man and wife. Juda, their first slave-born child, lived until 1906, dying only a few months before her one hundred and sixth birthday and less than a year before the birth of her grand-niece, Thelma Elise McWorter, who was raised by her paternal grandmother, Solomon's wife—thus showing the continuity, the strength, and the persistence of this Afro-American family as it has struggled to survive and succeed in this nation.[29]

Notes

CHAPTER ONE

1. Arthur McWorter to Thelma McWorter Kirkpatrick [Wheaton], January 1937, in the Free Frank [McWorter] Papers in the possession of Thelma McWorter Kirkpatrick Wheaton, Chicago, Illinois (hereafter cited as FFP). Free Frank's son Solomon, who was born a slave in 1815, was Arthur's father. Arthur McWorter was born in 1875; his daughter Thelma was born in 1907.

2. The first record that gives an indication of Free Frank's age is U.S., Bureau of the Census, "Population Schedules of the Fourth Census of the United States, 1820, Kentucky, Pulaski County" (Washington, D.C.: National Archives and Records Service, Manuscript Microcopy M-33, reel 27). His name is listed as Free Frank and his age is checked off in the column "45 and over." The second record is idem, "Population Schedules of the Fifth Census of the United States, 1830, Kentucky, Pulaski County" (Manuscript Microcopy M-19, reel 41), which lists him as Frank Denham (Denham was the surname of the former owner of Free Frank's wife Lucy), and his age is checked off in the "of 36 and under 55" age group column. In the 1840 census, he is listed as Frank McWorter and is checked off in the "55 and under 100" age group; see idem, "Population Schedules of the Sixth Census of the United States, 1840, Illinois, Pike County" (Manuscript Microcopy M-704, reel 67). The federal census of 1850 was the first to request a specific age. Here Free Frank's age is listed as seventy-three; see idem, "Population Schedules of the Seventh Census of the United States, 1850, Illinois, Pike County" (Manuscript Microcopy M-432, reel 124). His birthplace is shown in U.S., Bureau of the Census, "Population Schedules of the Sixth Census of the United States, 1840, Illinois, Pike County"; and idem, "Population Schedules of the Seventh Census of the United States, 1850, Illinois, Pike County"; both list South Carolina as Free Frank's birthplace. Both his birth date and birthplace are recorded on his still extant gravestone in the New Philadelphia cemetery in Pike County, Illinois. The Free Frank family oral history and written records gave Union County as his birthplace (see FFP).

3. See Alan Kulikoff, "The Origins of Afro-American Society in Tidewater Maryland and Virginia, 1700-1790," *William and Mary Quarterly*, 3d ser., 35, no. 2 (1978): 259: "In the 1730s and 1740s proportionately more black immigrants went to the piedmont than to the tidewater, and after 1755 nearly every African found his new home in a piedmont county." For South Carolina, see W. Robert Higgins, "Charleston: Terminus and Entrepot of the Colonial Slave Trade," in Martin L. Kilson and Robert I. Rotberg, eds., *The African Diaspora* (Cambridge: Harvard Univ. Press, 1976), pp. 115-27; and W. Robert Higgins, "The Geographical Origins of Negro Slaves in Colonial South Carolina," *South Atlantic Quarterly* 70 (1971): 14-27.

4. Arthur McWorter to Thelma McWorter Kirkpatrick, 1937, FFP.

5. Pulaski County Real Estate Conveyances, Book 4, Pulaski County Courthouse, Somerset, Ky., pp. 134, 138; Free Frank's certificate of good character (hereafter referred to as Character Reference Statement), Sept. 7, 1830, in FFP; and Pike County Circuit Court Records, *Frank McWorter* v. *C.C. Luce and D.C. Topping* (1851), case no. 3787, Pike County Courthouse, Pittsfield, Ill. McWherter, McWhortor, McWhorton, and McWhorter are the different spellings found in the various government documents and private papers that refer to the slave-

holder. In this book, except for quoted passages employing a different spelling, the spelling McWhorter is used for the slaveholder George and his family.

6. Arthur McWorter to Thelma McWorter Kirkpatrick, 1973, FFP.

7. For information on racial attitudes expressed by former slaves, see John Blassingame, "Using the Testimony of Ex-Slaves: Approaches and Problems," *Journal of Southern History* 41, no. 4 (1975): 473-92: George P. Rawick, ed., *The American Slave: A Composite Autobiography,* 19 vols. (Westport, Conn.: Greenwood, 1972); and Leon Litwack, *Been in the Storm So Long: The Aftermath of Slavery* (New York: Knopf, 1979).

8. John E. McWorter to Rev. P.B. West, Aug. 31, 1919, FFP.

9. Richard Hooker, ed., *The Carolina Backcountry on the Eve of the Revolution: The Journal and Other Writings of Charles Woodmason, Anglican Itinerant* (Chapel Hill: Univ. of North Carolina Press, 1953), p. 227.

10. Moses Roper, *A Narrative of the Adventures and Escape of Moses Roper from American Slavery,* 5th ed. (London: Harvey and Darton, 1843), pp. 9-10.

11. Winthrop Jordan, *White over Black: American Attitudes toward the Negro, 1550-1812* (Chapel Hill: Univ. of North Carolina Press, 1968), pp. 147, 150-54.

12. Peter H. Wood, *Black Majority: Negroes in Colonial South Carolina from 1670 through the Stono Rebellion* (New York: W.W. Norton, 1974), p. 120.

13. Kulikoff, "Origins of Afro-American Society," pp. 255-58.

14. John W. Blassingame, ed., *Slave Testimony: Two Centuries of Letters, Speeches, Interviews and Autobiographies* (Baton Rouge: Louisiana State Univ. Press, 1977), pp. xiii, xviii, xli. Also see David Thomas Bailey, "A Divided Prism: Two Sources of Black Testimony in Slavery," *Journal of Southern History* 46, no. 3 (1980): 381-404; C. Vann Woodward, "History from Slavery Sources," *American Historical Review* 79 (1974): 470-81; Benjamin A. Botkin, "The Slave as His Own Interpreter," *Library of Congress Quarterly Journal of Current Acquisitions* 2 (1944): 37-63; John B. Cade, "Out of the Mouths of Ex-Slaves," *Journal of Negro History* 20 (1935): 294-337.

15. Arthur McWorter to Thelma McWorter Kirkpatrick, 1937, FFP.

16. See Robert H. Abzug, *Passionate Liberator: Theodore Dwight Weld and the Dilemma of Reform* (New York: Oxford Univ. Press, 1980), pp. 10-11, where he discusses his attempts to reconstruct Weld's childhood experiences from family memories. Abzug cautions that his attempt to rely on the psychoanalytic concept of "screen memories" creates difficulties, and admits that "one might rightly wonder whether such evidence can be the stuff of good history." Yet, for the insights gained, he feels that his method of historical reconstruction should be given consideration. In his discussion, Abzug relied on "Screen Memories" (1899) in Sigmund Freud, *Collected Papers,* ed. Strachy, 5 (New York, 1957): 47-69.

17. John W. Blassingame, *The Slave Community: Plantation Life in the Antebellum South,* rev. and enlarged ed. (New York: Oxford Univ. Press, 1979), pp. 190-91. Also see Martia Graham Goodson, "The Slave Narrative Collection: A Tool for Reconstructing Afro-American Women's History," *Western Journal of Black Studies* 3, no. 2 (1979): 116-22; Darlene C. Hine, "Female Slave Resistance: The Economics of Sex," *Western Journal of Black Studies* 3, no. 3 (1979): 123-27; and Deborah G. White, "Ain't I a Woman? Female Slaves in the Antebellum South" (Ph.D. diss., Univ. of Illinois–Chicago Circle, 1979); and Angela Davis, "Reflections on the Black Woman's Role in the Community of Slaves," *Black Scholar* 3, no. 9 (1971): 2-15.

18. Blassingame, *Slave Community,* p. 183.

19. Wood, *Black Majority,* p. 107; also see Edward McCrady, "Slavery in the Province of South Carolina," *Annual Report of the American Historical Association for the Year 1895* (Washington, D.C., 1896), pp. 631-73; and John Donald Duncan, "Servitude and Slavery in Colonial South Carolina, 1670-1776" (Ph.D. diss., Emory, Univ., 1971).

CHAPTER TWO

1. James G. Leyburn, *The Scotch-Irish: A Social History* (Chapel Hill: Univ. of North Carolina Press, 1962), p. 148.

2. The information on the McWhorter family was obtained from colonial and state records in the South Carolina Department of Archives and History, Columbia; the University of South Carolina at Columbia; Union County Court Records, Union; the Union County Historical Museum, Union; the George McWhorter Family Papers at the Kentucky State Historical Society, Frankfort; Pulaski County Court Records, Somerset, Kentucky; and Kentucky Secretary of State, Land Office, Frankfort.

3. Leyburn, *Scotch-Irish*, pp. 219, 220, 323, 324.

4. David Ramsay, *The History of South Carolina from Its First Settlement in 1670 to the Year 1808*, 2 vols. (Charleston: D. Longworth, 1809), 2:178.

5. Hooker, *Carolina Backcountry*, p. 99.

6. Richard Brown, *The South Carolina Regulators* (Cambridge: Harvard Univ. Press, 1963), pp. 17-18, 27-28, 31.

7. For information on South Carolina's population during the colonial and Revolutionary War periods, see Evarts B. Greene and Virginia D. Harrington, *American Population before the Federal Census of 1790* (New York: Columbia Univ. Press, 1932); and Frank J. Klingberg, *An Appraisal of the Negro in Colonial South Carolina: A Study in Americanization* (Washington, D.C.: Associated Publishers, 1941), pp. 1-2; Klingberg states that his compilations of the 1775 figures show approximately 100,000 blacks and 60,000 whites.

8. For a discussion of slave runaways and maroon communities in South Carolina, see Daniel Meaders, "South Carolina Fugitives as Viewed through Local Colonial Newspapers with Emphasis on Runaway Notices, 1732-1801," *Journal of Negro History* 60 (Apr. 1975): 288-319; Herbert Aptheker, *American Negro Slave Revolts* (New York: International Publishers, 1943); idem, "Maroons within the Present Limits of the United States," *Journal of Negro History* 24 (Apr. 1939): 167-74; idem, "Additional Data on American Maroons," *Journal of Negro History* 33 (Oct. 1947): 452-60. Also see Richard Price, ed., *Maroon Societies: Rebel Slave Communities in the Americas* (Garden City, N.Y.: Anchor Press, 1973).

9. Sara Sullivan Ervin, *South Carolinians in the Revolution: With Service and Miscellaneous Data* (Baltimore: Genealogical Publishing Co., 1949; rpt. with additions, 1965), pp. 80-81. See Edward McCrady, *The History of South Carolina in the Revolution, 1780-83* (New York: Macmillan, 1902), pp. 744-50, who lists the battles in which Sumter was commander.

10. Robert V. Remini, *Andrew Jackson* (New York: Twayne, 1966), p. 18.

11. For a brief discussion of the Revolutionary War in the back country, see Russell F. Weigley, *The Partisan War: The South Carolina Campaign of 1780-1782* (Columbia: Univ. of South Carolina Press, 1970).

12. Ray Allen Billington, *Westward Expansion: A History of the American Frontier* (New York: Macmillan, 1960), p. 189.

13. Herbert Aptheker, "The Negro in the American Revolution," in *Essays in the History of the American Negro* (New York: International Publishers, 1945), p. 106; Mary Frances Berry, *Black Resistance/White Law: A History of Constitutional Racism in America* (New York: Appleton-Century-Crofts, 1971), pp. 3-5. Also see Benjamin Quarles, *The Negro in the American Revolution* (Chapel Hill: Univ. of North Carolina Press, 1961); and Sidney Kaplan, *The Black Presence in the Era of the American Revolution, 1770-1800* (Greenwich, Conn.: New York Graphic Society, 1973); Michael Mullin, "British Caribbean and North American Slaves in an Era of War and Revolution, 1775-1800," in Jeffrey J. Crow and Larry E. Tise, eds., *The Southern Experience in the American Revolution* (Chapel Hill: Univ. of North Carolina Press, 1978). On blacks who fought with the British, see James W. St. G. Walker, "Blacks as Amer-

ican Loyalists: The Slaves' War for Independence," *Historical Reflections/Reflexions Historique* 2 (1975): 51-67.

14. Remini, *Jackson*, p. 14.

15. R. Lamb, *An Original and Authentic Journal of Occurrences during the Late American War, from Its Commencement to the Year 1783* (Dublin, 1809), pp. 293-94. Also see F. Nwabuez, "Chattel Slavery as the Nightmare of the American Revolutionaries," *William and Mary Quarterly* 37, no. 1 (1980): 3-28.

16. Blassingame, *Slave Community*, p. 185.

17. Eugene Genovese, *Roll Jordan Roll: The World the Slaves Made* (New York: Random House, 1974), pp. 502-03. Also see Kenneth F. Kiple and Virginia H. Kiple, "Slave Child Mortality: Some Nutritional Aspects to a Perennial Puzzle," *Journal of Social History* 10 (1977): 284-309.

18. For a general discussion of the South Carolina up-country frontier during this period, see Ramsay, *History of South Carolina*; D. Hugh Bacat, "The South Carolina Up Country at the End of the Revolution," *American Historical Review* 28 (1923): 682-98; David L. Coon, "The Development of Market Agriculture in South Carolina, 1670-1785" (Ph.D. diss., Univ. of Illinois, Urbana-Champaign, 1972); Ulrich B. Phillips, *American Negro Slavery: A Survey of the Supply, Employment and Control of Negro Labor as Determined by the Plantation Regime* (New York, 1918; rpt., Baton Rouge: Louisiana State Univ. Press, 1966), p. 156.

19. U.S., Bureau of the Census, *First Census of the United States, 1790, South Carolina: Heads of Families* (Washington, D.C., 1908), p. 298; for specific information on George McWhorter and his brother John, see p. 92.

20. See Willard Rouse Jillson, *The Kentucky Land Grants* (Baltimore: Genealogical Publishing Co., 1971), p. 5.

21. Harry Toulmin, *A Description of Kentucky in North America* (1792; rpt., Lexington: Univ. of Kentucky Press, 1945), pp. 96-97.

22. Thomas Perkins Abernethy, *Three Virginia Frontiers* (Gloucester, Mass: Peter Smith, 1940), p. 65. Also see Lewis Collins, *Historical Sketches of Kentucky* (Maysville, Ky. 1848), pp. 18-27; and Willard Rouse Jillson, *Old Kentucky Entries and Deeds* (Baltimore: Genealogical Publishing Co., 1971). All provide a brief survey of the early migration and settlement in Kentucky.

23. C.S. Moorehead and Mason Brown, eds., *A Digest of the Statute Laws of Kentucky, of a Public and Permanent Nature,* 2 vols. (Frankfort: A.G. Hodges, 1834), 2:924.

24. Pulaski County Tax Lists, Kentucky State Historical Society, Frankfort, provide information on the location of George McWhorter's landholdings.

25. *Atlas Map of Pike County, Illinois* (Davenport, Iowa: Andreas Lyter, 1872), p. 54.

26. Thomas D. Clark, *A History of Kentucky* (New York: Prentice Hall, 1937), p. 275.

27. Abernethy, *Three Virginia Frontiers*, p. 79.

28. Collins, *Historical Sketches of Kentucky*, p. 408.

29. "A List of Taxable Property Taken in by Urbin Ewing, Comm. for Lincoln County, 1796," Kentucky State Archives, Frankfort.

30. Alma Owens Tibbals, *A History of Pulaski County, Kentucky* (Bagdad, Ky.: Grace Owens Moore, 1952), pp. 6-7, 66. For general descriptions of this area, see also Willard Rouse Jillson, *Pioneer Kentucky: . . . to the Year 1800* (Frankfort, Ky.: State Journal Co., 1934), pp. 130-31.

31. William Littel and Jacob Swigert, eds., *A Digest of the Statute Law of Kentucky . . . to the May Session, 1822,* 2 vols. (Frankfort, Ky.: Kendall & Russell, 1822), 2:736.

32. Thomas D. Clark, *Kentucky: Land of Contrast* (New York: Harper & Row, 1968), p. 109.

33. William Savage, *Observations on Emigration to the United States of America* (London: Sherwood, Neely & Jones, 1819), p. 37.

34. Maria T. Daviess, *History of Mercer and Boyle Counties* (Harrodsburg, Ky.: Harrodsburg Herald, 1924), pp. 41, 108.

35. W.H. Perrin, *Kentucky: A History of the State* (Louisville: F.A. Battery, 1887), p. 637.

36. Reginald Horsman, *The Frontier in the Formative Years, 1783-1815* (New York: Holt, Rinehart and Winston, 1970), p. 127.

37. J. Winston Coleman, Jr., *Slavery Times in Kentucky* (Chapel Hill: Univ. of North Carolina Press, 1940), p. 15.

38. William Littell, ed., *The Statute Law of Kentucky to 1816, Comprehending Also the Laws of Virginia and Acts of Parliament in Force in This Commonwealth,* 5 vols. (Frankfort, Ky.: Hunter, 1809-1819), 2:114.

39. John Hope Franklin, *The Militant South, 1800-1861* (Cambridge: Harvard Univ. Press, 1956). In frontier areas, however, it was not unusual during the initial settlement period for slaves to have weapons and join in defense of the settlements. See Wood, *Black Majority,* pp. 125-30. Wood notes that the main issue with arming slaves was whether they "could be contained in the usage of the weapons." Pioneer slaves were also charged with hunting, not only for food but also to kill animals that threatened the livestock.

40. Clarice Ramey, "History of Pulaski County" (Master's thesis, Univ. of Kentucky, 1935), pp. 69-71.

41. Pulaski County Tax List of 1799, Kentucky State Historical Society, Frankfort.

42. Littell and Swigert, *Digest of the Statute Law of Kentucky,* 2: 1151.

43. Ibid., 2:1150.

44. Ibid., 2:1151.

45. Tibbals, *History of Pulaski County,* pp. 90-91.

46. Francis Fredric, *Slave Life in Virginia and Kentucky* (London: n.p., 1863), pp. 48-49.

47. Chas. C. Chapman, *History of Pike County, Illinois* (Chicago: C.C. Chapman, 1880), p. 739.

48. U.S., Bureau of the Census, "Population Schedules of the Seventh Census of the United States, 1850, Illinois, Pike County," lists Virginia as Lucy McWorter's birthplace; her age is listed as seventy-three. However, her gravestone is marked, "Lucy McWorter wife of F. McWorter born in 1771 d. Aug. 23, 1870."

49. Pulaski County Real Estate Conveyances, Book 3, p. 228. Also see Denham Family Papers, Kentucky State Historical Society, Frankfort. See Pulaski County Court records for listings of his landholdings.

50. Coleman, *Slavery,* p. 57.

51. Chapman, *History of Pike County,* p. 739.

52. Juda was an African female name. Henig Cohen, "Slave Names in Colonial South Carolina," *American Speech* 28, no. 2 (1952): 106. See also Lorenzo Turner, *Africanisms in the Gullah Dialect* (Chicago: Univ. of Chicago Press, 1949), p. 214, Table XX, "Checklist of African Names from the South Carolina *Gazette,* 1732-1775."

53. *Atlas Map of Pike County,* p. 54.

54. Studies which discuss the various ways slave families augmented their meager existence to survive as a unit include Herbert G. Gutman, *The Black Family in Slavery and Freedom, 1750-1925* (New York: Pantheon Books, 1976); Blassingame, *Slave Community*; Leslie Owens, *This Species of Property: Slave Life and Culture in the Old South* (New York: Oxford Univ. Press, 1976); and Genovese, *Roll Jordan Roll.*

55. This description was provided by Free Frank's great-granddaughter, Thelma McWor-

ter Wheaton, who grew up in the Pike County house built by Free Frank. Her sisters Ellen McWorter Yates and Bernice McWorter Hawkins, who also lived there, agreed with this description. Thelma Wheaton attended Fisk University (B.A., 1929) and Case Western Reserve University (M.A., 1931). From the 1920s she has taken an interest in reconstructing Free Frank's history.

56. Chapman, *History of Pike County*, p. 739.

57. Coleman, *Slavery*, p. 17.

58. Wood, *Black Majority*, p. 105.

59. Ira Berlin, *Slaves without Masters: The Free Negro in the Antebellum South* (New York: Random House, Pantheon Books, 1974), p. 154.

60. Herbert Aptheker, "Buying Freedom," in *To Be Free: Studies in American Negro History* (New York: International Publishers, 1948), p. 31.

CHAPTER THREE

1. *Atlas Map of Pike County*, p. 54.

2. Elijah Iles, *Sketches of Early Life and Times in Kentucky, Missouri and Illinois* (Springfield, Ill.: Springfield Printing Co., 1883), pp. 63-64.

3. François Michaux, *Travels to the Westward of the Allegany Mountains, in the States of the Ohio, Kentucky and Tennessee . . . in the Year 1802*, trans. B. Lambert (London: J. Mawman, 1805), p. 76.

4. Littell and Swigert, *Digest of the Statute Law of Kentucky*, 2:752-53.

5. Savage, *Observations on Emigration*, pp. 18-19.

6. Gilbert Imlay, *A Topographical Description of the Western Territory of North America*, 3d ed. (London: J. Debrett, 1797), p. 168.

7. Kenneth M. Stampp, *The Peculiar Institution: Slavery in the Ante-Bellum South* (New York: Alfred A. Knopf, 1956), pp. 391-92.

8. Pulaski County Order Book 1, Pulaski County Courthouse, Somerset, Ky., p. 345 (the date was Oct. 2, 1802); Jillson, *Kentucky Land Grants*, p. 377. This land was located on Cold Weather and Frozen creeks.

9. Robert Williams Fogel and Stanley L. Engerman, *Time on the Cross: The Economics of American Negro Slavery* (Boston: Little, Brown & Co., 1974), p. 41.

10. Thomas Perkins Abernethy, *From Frontier to Plantation in Tennessee: A Study in Frontier Democracy*, Southern Historical Publications, no 12 (University, Ala.: Univ. of Alabama Press, 1967), p. 207.

11. Tibbals, *History of Pulaski County*, p. 66.

12. Pulaski County Order Book 1, pp. 3, 22, 34-35.

13. Fogel and Engerman, *Time on the Cross*, p. 41.

14. Clark, *History of Kentucky*, pp. 275-77.

15. *Atlas Map of Pike County*, p. 54. For an excellent discussion and analysis of slave-hiring in a rural community, see Sarah S. Hughes, "Slaves for Hire: The Allocation of Black Labor in Elizabeth City County, Virginia, 1782-1810," *William and Mary Quarterly* 35 (1978): 260-86. Fogel and Engerman, *Time on the Cross*, p. 56, point out that some 6 percent of the slave labor force in rural areas were hired out.

16. Coleman, *Slavery*, p. 124.

17. For studies of the slave hiring process, see Richard Morris, "The Measure of Bondage in the Slave States," *Mississippi Valley Historical Review* 41 (1954): 219-40; Clement Eaton, "Slave-Hiring in the Upper South: A Step Toward Freedom," *Mississippi Valley Historical Re-*

view 46 (1960): 663-78; Robert S. Starobin, *Industrial Slavery in the Old South* (New York: Oxford Univ. Press, 1970); Frederic Bancroft, *Slave Trading in the Old South* (New York: Frederick Angar, 1931), p. 162. Also see Edna Chappel McKenzie, "Self-Hire among Slaves, 1820-1860: Institutional Variation or Aberration" (Ph.D. diss., Univ. of Pittsburgh, 1973).

18. See Littell, *Statute Law of Kentucky*, 1:116-17; and Littell and Swigert, *Digest of the Statute Law of Kentucky*, 2:1159-60, for full provisions of the 1802 law.

19. Lewis Cecil Gray, *History of Agriculture in the Southern United States to 1860*, 2 vols., Carnegie Institution Publication no. 430 (Washington, D.C.: Carnegie Institution, 1933), 1:488-92, provides some discussion of slave economic activities on the southwestern frontiers.

20. *Atlas Map of Pike County*, p. 54.

21. George McWhorter is not found in the Pulaski County manuscript census for 1810; he is listed in Wayne County. See F. Volkel, "An Index to the 1810 Federal Census of Kentucky," Kentucky State Historical Society, Frankfort. Also see U.S., Bureau of the Census, "Population Schedules of the Third Census of the United States, 1810, Kentucky, Pulaski County" (Washington, D.C.: National Archives and Records Service, Manuscript Microcopy M-252, reel 8). See Pulaski County Real Estate Conveyances, Book 4, pp. 134-35, which gives McWhorter's location in 1815.

22. Coleman, *Slavery*, p. 57.

23. Genovese, *Roll Jordan Roll*, pp. 391-92, provides examples of slaves who were hired out as punishment for their behavior; Wood, in *Black Majority*, p. 105, explains that on the frontier slaves "who were merely obedient and submissive would have been a useless luxury."

24. Frederick Douglass, *Life and Times of Frederick Douglass Written by Himself: His Early Life as a Slave, His Escape from Bondage, and His Complete History* (London: Collier-Macmillan, 1962 [1892]), pp. 189-92. Douglass as a slave hired out in 1836 to work in the Baltimore shipyard. On becoming a skilled caulker, Douglass wrote, "I was now of some pecuniary value to my master. During the busy season I was bringing six and seven dollars per week. I have sometimes brought him as much as nine dollars a week, for wages were a dollar and a half per day."

25. Berlin, *Slaves without Masters*, p. 155.

26. Fogel and Engerman, *Time on the Cross*, p. 151.

27. See Gray, *History of Agriculture*, 1:542, 557-59; 2:663-64, 708-09, 730-31, 776; Fogel and Engerman, *Time on the Cross*, p. 208; and Genovese, *Roll Jordan Roll*, pp. 567-68. Also see Forrest McDonald and Grady McWhiney, "The South from Self-Sufficiency to Peonage: An Interpretation," *American History Review* 85, no 5 (Dec. 1980): 1098-1101, for discussion of work load in terms of man-hours in settled agricultural areas in the antebellum South; and Carville Earl and Ronald Hoffman, "The Foundations of the Modern Economy: Agriculture and the Costs of Labor in the United States and England, 1800-1860," *American Historical Review* 85, no. 5 (Dec. 1980): 1063, for the rural work year in the South. "The norm was nine to twelve months." On tobacco cultivation, see Stampp, *Peculiar Institution*, pp. 48-51.

28. Bancroft, *Slave Trading*, p. 153. Also see John Hope Franklin, "Slaves Virtually Free in Ante-Bellum North Carolina," *Journal of Negro History* 28 (1943): 284-310.

29. Collins, *Historical Sketches of Kentucky*, pp. 500-501. See also J. Leander Bishop, *A History of American Manufactures from 1608-1860*, 3 vols. (Philadelphia: Edward Young, 1868), 2:203-04; and Horace Carter Hovey, *The Mammoth Cave of Kentucky*, rev. ed. (Louisville: John P. Morton, 1912), p. 16.

30. Collins, in *Historical Sketches of Kentucky*, p. 160, says that crude niter was "found in most of the caves [in Kentucky] which are so numerous in the cavernous limestones." See also

Alma Owens Tibbals, "Notes for a History of Pulaski County, Kentucky," Alma Owens Tibbals Papers, Margaret I. King Library, University of Kentucky, Lexington, p. 6.

31. Clark, *History of Kentucky*, p. 246: Collins, *Historical Sketches of Kentucky*, pp. 500-501; Horace C. Hovey, "Our Saltpeter Caves in Time of War," *Scientific American* 76 (1897): 291.

32. Michaux, *Travels*, p. 58.

33. "American Manufactures," *Niles Weekly Register*, June 6, 1812, p. 227.

34. Hovey, "Our Saltpeter Caves," p. 291.

35. R.W. Bird, "The Mammoth Cave," *American Monthly Magazine* 9 (1837): 434.

36. *Atlas Map of Pike County*, p. 54.

37. Samuel Brown, "A Description of a Cave on Crooked Creek, with Remarks and Observations on Nitre and Gunpowder," *American Philosophical Society Transactions* 6 (1806): 236.

38. Collins, *Historical Sketches of Kentucky*, pp. 160, 501.

39. Hovey, *Mammoth Cave*, p. 16. For additional information, see Burton Faust, "The History of Saltpeter Mining in Mammoth Cave, Kentucky," *Filson Club History Quarterly* 41: (1967); 5-17, 127-40, 227-62, 323-52; Ebenezer Merriam, "Mammoth Cave," *New York Municipal Gazette* 1 (1844): 3; Samuel W. Thomas, Eugene H. Conner, and Harold Meloy, "A History of Mammoth Cave Emphasizing Tourist Development and Medical Experimentation under Dr. John Croghan," *Register of the Kentucky Historical Society* 68 (1970): 319-25; John H. Farnham, "Mammoth Cave," *Transactions of the American Antiquarian Society* 1 (1830): 3; Edward F. Lee, *Notes on the Mammoth Cave* (Cincinnati, 1835). See also Carol A. Hill and Duane DePaepe, "Saltpeter Mining in Kentucky Caves," *Register of the Kentucky Historical Society* 77 (Autumn 1979): 247-62.

40. For information on the basic items Free Frank used to produce saltpeter, see Pulaski County Real Estate Conveyances, Book 7-I, pp. 55-56.

41. Berlin, *Slaves without Masters*, pp. 234-35. See also Stampp, *Peculiar Institution*, pp. 61, 71; Starobin, *Industrial Slavery*, pp. 22-26; and the excellent study by Ronald L. Lewis, *Coal, Iron, and Slaves: Industrial Slavery in Maryland and Virginia, 1785-1865* (Westport, Conn.: Greenwood, 1979), for blacks engaged in mining.

42. Allan G. Bogue, "Social Theory and the Pioneer," in Allan G. Bogue, Thomas D. Phillips, and James E. Wright, eds., *The West of the American People* (Itasca, Ill.: F.E. Peacock, 1970), p. 534.

43. See Rolla Milton Tryon, *Household Manufactures in the United States, 1640-1860: A Study in Industrial History* (Chicago: Univ. of Chicago Press, 1917), p. 264.

44. For summary information on trade patterns in Pulaski County, see Ramey, "History," pp. 50-51; Tibbals, *History of Pulaski County*, pp. 74-75; and Tibbals, "Notes," p. 8.

45. Faust, "History of Saltpeter Mining," p. 252.

46. Littell, *Statute Law of Kentucky*, 2:119. Also see Kentucky, *Constitution* (1799), art. 7, sec. 1, which provides for the right of slaveowners to free their slaves.

47. Pulaski County Real Estate Conveyances, Book 4, p. 134; the date was Aug. 10, 1815.

48. Littell, *Statute Law of Kentucky*, 2:120; 3:238.

49. Pulaski County Real Estate Conveyances, Book 4, pp. 134-35.

50. Moorehead and Brown, *Digest of the Statute Laws of Kentucky*, 1:608. Also see Sumner Eliot Matison, "Manumission by Purchase," *Journal of Negro History* 33, no. 2(1948): 154-55; and Aptheker, "Buying Freedom," pp. 33-34, who notes, "Everywhere in the antebellum United States the right of a slave to accumulate, with his master's permission, his own personal property—or peculium—was recognized either by law, judicial decision, or custom. Evidence concerning this is implicit in the material already presented on the slave's right to con-

tract for his own purchase, but even where this right was not acknowledged, or specifically denied, the right to personal property was, in fact, granted."

51. Arthur McWorter to Thelma McWorter Kirkpatrick [Wheaton], January 1937, FFP.

52. Fogel and Engerman, *Time on the Cross*, p. 41. Stampp, *Peculiar Institution*, p. 36, notes, "Occasionally a small slaveholder, either temporarily or for a long period of time, left farm operations entirely in the hands of his slaves. . . . But these informal managerial arrangements were exceptional; slaves rarely enjoyed such relative autonomy."

53. Clark, *History of Kentucky*, p. 24.

54. Collins, *Historical Sketches of Kentucky*, p. 499.

55. Tibbals, *History of Pulaski County*, p. 4.

56. Littell, *Statute Law of Kentucky*, 5:54-55. The act applied to those who wished to set up salt-manufacturing works on a large scale to supply the heavy demand for this product.

57. Ramey, "History," p. 56.

58. Michaux, *Travels*, p. 78.

59. Garnett Laidlaw Eskey, *Salt: The Fifth Element* (Chicago: J.G. Ferguson, 1948), p. 55. The description was given in 1801 by the secretary of the Society for the Promotion of Agriculture, Arts and Manufacture. Also see Collins, *Historical Sketches of Kentucky*, pp. 159-60, 217, 401, for a general survey of salt-making in Kentucky; and Starobin, *Industrial Slavery*, pp. 24-25.

60. Arthur McWorter to Thelma McWorter Kirkpatrick [Wheaton], January 1937, in FFP.

61. *Atlas Map of Pike County*, p. 54.

62. Character Reference Statement, Sept. 7, 1830. See also deposition taken from Joseph Porter, Pulaski County, Ky., Mar. 14, 1856, for a Pike County (Ill.) Circuit Court case, in FFP.

63. See Table 1, above, for information on the approximate birth dates of Free Frank's and Lucy's children.

64. See Table 13 for information on family members purchased by Free Frank.

65. Pulaski County Real Estate Conveyances, Book 3, p. 228.

66. Littell, *Statute Law of Kentucky*, 1:121.

67. Moorehead and Brown, *Digest of the Statute Laws of Kentucky*, 1:609.

68. *Atlas Map of Pike County*, p. 54.

69. Tibbals, *History of Pulaski County*, p. 3.

70. Berlin, *Slaves without Masters*, p. 218.

71. *Atlas Map of Pike County*, p. 54.

72. Stanley L. Engerman to Juliet E.K. Walker, Feb. 13, 1981, University of Rochester, Rochester, N.Y.

73. August Meier to Juliet E.K. Walker, December 31, 1979, FFP.

74. Pulaski County Real Estate Conveyances, Book 4, p. 138.

75. Character Reference Statement, Sept. 7, 1830, FFP.

76. Pulaski County General Index to Real Estate Conveyances—Grantees: E-G Grantees, 1799-1934, p. 43, Pulaski County Courthouse, Somerset, Ky.; each emancipation document was recorded here.

77. Littell and Swigert, *Digest of the Statute Law of Kentucky*, 2:1152-53.

78. Gavin Wright, *The Political Economy of the Cotton South: Households, Markets, and Wealth in the Nineteenth Century* (New York: W.W. Norton, 1978), pp. 113-14.

79. Fogel and Engerman, *Time on the Cross*, p. 56.

80. Character Reference Statement, Sept. 7, 1830, FFP.

81. Coleman, *Slavery*, p. 79.

82. See Genovese, *Roll Jordan Roll*, pp. 1-7, for a discussion of slavery and the paternalis-

tic ethos. Gutman, *Black Family*, pp. 310-19, presents an opposing position on the "paternal-istic compromise," arguing that "the formative development of the slave family, kin group, and enlarged community occurred before the rapid spread and internalization of paternalist ideology in the developing plantation class." He emphasizes that before 1830 slaveowners "interacted with slaves who were the product of these earlier social and cultural developments." From this perspective, neither Free Frank nor his owners based their relationship on a paternal-istic compromise, thus pointing to the economic basis of his manumission. See Berry, *Black Resistance*, p. ix: "Those blacks who did not become involved in conspiracy and rebellion before the Civil War were not necessarily 'docile'; they lived in the grip of a system of violent control institutionalized under the Constitution."

83. U.S., Bureau of the Census, "Population Schedules of the Fourth Census of the United States, 1820, Kentucky, Pulaski County" (Manuscript Microcopy M-33, reel 27).

CHAPTER FOUR

1. Pulaski County Real Estate Conveyances, Book 7-I, p. 55.

2. *Free Frank and Lucy* v. *Denham's Administrator*, 5 Littell 330 (Ky. 1824); and *Free Lucy and Frank* v. *Denham's Administrator*, 4 Monroe 167 (Ky. 1827). For a brief review of the points of law derived from the two cases, see Helen T. Catterall, ed., *Judicial Cases Concerning American Slavery and the Negro*, vol. 1: *Cases from the Courts of England, Virginia, West Virginia, and Kentucky* (Washington, D.C.: Carnegie Institution, 1936): 304, 307; William Goodell, *The American Slave Code* (New York: American and Foreign Anti-Slavery Society, 1853), p. 93; and Jacob D. Wheeler, *A Practical Treatise on the Law of Slavery* (n.p.: Allan Pollock, Jr., 1837; rpt.: New York: Negro Universities Press of Greenwood Publishing Corp., 1968), p. 190.

3. *Free Frank and Lucy* v. *Denham's Administrator*, 5 Littell 330 (Ky. 1824).

4. Ibid.

5. Ibid.

6. *Free Lucy and Frank* v. *Denham's Administrator*, 4 Monroe 167 (Ky. 1827).

7. Denham Family Papers, Kentucky Historical Society, Frankfort.

8. See deposition taken from Joseph Porter, Pulaski County, Ky., Mar. 14, 1856, for a Pike County (Ill.) Circuit Court case, for information which indicates that Free Frank had hired out his time to William Denham.

9. *Free Frank and Lucy* v. *Denham's Administrator*, 5 Littell 330 (Ky. 1824).

10. Ibid.

11. Ibid. According to *Black's Law Dictionary*, 4th ed. (1968), p. 520, a demurrer in equity is "an allegation of a defendant, which, admitting the matters of fact alleged by the bill to be true, shows that as they are therein set forth they are insufficient for the plaintiff to proceed upon or to oblige the defendant to answer." A demurrer in pleading is "the formal mode of disputing the sufficiency in law of the pleading of the other side. In effect it is an allegation that, even if the facts as stated in the pleading to which objection is taken be true, yet their legal consequences are not such as to put the demurring party to the necessity of answering them or proceeding further with the cause." In this case the demurrer could be sustained under one or the other as construed by the judge.

12. *Free Lucy and Frank* v. *Denham's Administrator*, 4 Monroe 167 (Ky. 1827).

13. Ibid.

14. Catterall, *Cases from the Courts*, pp. 304, 307; Godell, *American Slave Code*, p. 93; Wheeler, *Law of Slavery*, p. 190; Moorehead and Brown, *Digest of the Statute Laws of Kentucky*, 1:341, under "Civil Proceedings." All discuss the procedural aspects on which the Free

Lucy case fell as it applies to the implementation of those laws. In essence, the errors were as stated at the beginning of the reported case: (1) When the case was before here plaintiff's replication to defendant's plea was held bad. (2) On the return of the case to the court below, replication was not withdrawn but another filed. (3) Where this court reverses the judgment on a replication to defendant's plea and adjudges the replication insufficient, the plaintiff must withdraw it and reply *de novo.* (4) If he filed another replication without withdrawing the one condemned, it is in error. (5) Where a cause is not ready for trial, defendant may be allowed to file an additional plea.

15. *Lapsley* v. *Brashear,* 4 Littell (Ky. 1823).

16. *Free Frank and Lucy* v. *Denham's Administrator,* 5 Littell 330 (Ky. 1824).

17. Ibid.

18. A.E. Keir Nash, "Fairness and Formalism in the Trials of Blacks in the State Supreme Courts of the Old South," *Virginia Law Review* 56 (Feb. 1970): 64-100; idem, "A More Equitable Past? Southern Supreme Courts and the Protection of the Antebellum Negro." *North Carolina Law Review* 48 (1970): 197-242. Also see Michael Meltsner, "Southern Appellate Courts: A Dead End," in Leon Friedman, ed., *Southern Justice* (New York: Pantheon, 1965), pp. 135-54.

19. See Pulaski County Real Estate Conveyances, Book 7-I, pp. 55-56, for information on the date Young Frank ran away. John E. McWorter to Rev. P.B. West, 1919 FFP: "One of my uncles [Young Frank] ran away to Canada."

20. T.H. Breen and Stephen Innes, *"Myne Owne Ground": Race and Freedom on Virginia's Eastern Shore* (New York: Oxford Univ. Press, 1980), p. 113.

21. Information on Kentucky land laws is available from Moorehead and Brown, *Digest of the Statute Laws of Kentucky,* 2:905-1103. For information on land prices in the 1820s, and especially the price of Head Right land and Treasury Warrant land, see ibid., pp. 991 and 1028, respectively. Kentucky granted land under six different claim systems: Virginia Claims, Head Right Claims, Seminary Claims, Tellico Claims, Treasury Warrant Claims, and Claims below the Tennessee River. Interestingly, only the Tellico Claims which had been quit claimed and ceded to the United States government by the Cherokee nation specifically excluded blacks from acquiring land in this region. See ibid., p. 1009, for the provision of the law passed in 1810 which stated "that it shall be lawful for every free white male or widow or other unmarried female above the age of eighteen years . . . [to] be entitled to a certificate for . . . land." The Treasury Warrant System only excluded aliens (ibid., p. 1019). The Head Right System applied to any free person (ibid., p. 926).

22. Included in Table 3 are three purchases listed in William Rouse Jillson, *The Kentucky Land Grants* (Baltimore: Genealogical Publishing Co., 1971), p. 550. One of two general land indexes, this source contains names of people who secured the initial titles to land claimed under the Kentucky Treasury Warrant System. With the exception of the 1821 transaction, the Pulaski County General Index to the Surveyor's Office lists Free Frank as the patentee in the remaining nine applications for patent surveys.

23. For Free Frank's 1829 joint land purchase with J. Harris and J. Love see Pulaski County Surveyor's Office Book 2, p. 231: "Surveyed for Free Frank James Harris and Joseph Love . . . 100 acres of land by virtue of two Kentucky Land Office Warrants of fifty acres each Nos. 16190 and 16189."

24. For Free Frank's January 20, 1827, joint land purchase with E. Farris, see Jillson, *Kentucky Land Grants,* p. 550, which shows Free Frank as the sole grantee of fifty acres. An examination of the warrant shows that it was made out to Ephraim C. Farris, but on the back of it is the notation: "Free Frank equally Interested with myself in the within land Warrant 8th January, 1827." See Kentucky Land Office Warrant no. 16466, Book W, p. 138, Kentucky Secre-

tary of State, Land Office, Frankfort. Included on the warrant was information regarding the survey, which also points to Free Frank's interest in the land: "January 20, 1827 survey for Free Frank and Ephraim C. Farris 50 acres of Land by Virtue of a Kentucky Land Office Warrant of fifty acres No. 16466." For the January 22, 1827, joint purchase with Farris, see Jillson, *Kentucky Land Grants,* p. 550, which shows that Free Frank had acquired 200 acres. Kentucky Land Office Warrants nos. 16468 and 16470, Book W, p. 139, show that the 200 acres were part of two separate tracts: "January 22-1827—Surveyed for Free Frank and Ephraim C. Farris 200 acres of Land by virtue two Kentucky Land Office Warrants of one hundred acres Each No. 16468 and 16470."

25. For Free Frank's 1821 land purchase with Free Zibe, see Kentucky Land Office Warrant no. 5805, Book U, p. 425. The warrant, dated May 30, 1821, was made out to Free Zibe. On the face of the warrant was the notation, "Executed in full on two surveys of fifty acres each." On the back of the warrant was the notation indicating the survey date: "December 29, 1821. I [assign] over the within 50 acres to Free Frank for Value Received Free Zibe."

26. See Pulaski County General Index to Real Estate Conveyance—E-G Grantees, 1799-1934, p. 43, Pulaski County Courthouse Somerset, Ky., which shows Zibe emancipated by two different owners. See Pulaski County Real Estate Conveyances, Book 4, pp. 218 and 232. Also see U.S., Bureau of the Census, "Population Schedules of the Fourth Census of the United States, 1820, Kentucky Pulaski County," which shows Zibe as head of a household of five (according to sex and age distribution, a wife and three children).

27. For information on Free Frank's individual land purchases see: for October 19, 1822 purchase, Pulaski County Surveyor's Office Book 1, p. 326, which notes, "October 19, 1822. Survey free Frank 50 acres of land by virtue of a Kentucky Land Office Warrant No. 8826." For information on the June 1823 100-acre land purchases, see Pulaski County Surveyor's Office Book 1, pp. 375 and 449. The January 1826 purchase applied to land Free Frank had purchased under Kentucky's Head Rights Claim System, in which a county land certificate was issued. See Pulaski County Surveyor's Office Book 1, p. 155, which notes: "January 9, 1826 Surveyed for Free Frank 59 acres by virtue of part of a county certificate of 300 acres no. 436." For information on the February 1826 land purchase, see Jillson, *Kentucky Land Grants,* p. 550. This land was purchased from Free Zibe. See Pulaski County Surveyor's Office Book 1, p. 524, which notes: "Surveyed for Free Frank [assignee] of Zibe Harrison 50 acres of land by virtue of Kentucky Land Office Warrant No. 5805." In 1830 Free Frank quit-claimed this fifty-acre tract purchased from Zibe for one dollar. See Pulaski County Real Estate Conveyances, Book 7-1, p. 328. For Free Frank's November 2, 1829, individual land purchase, see Pulaski County Surveyor's Office Book 2, p. 64, "November 2, 1829 survey for Free Frank . . . 50 acres of land by virtue of Kentucky Land Office Warrant of fifty acres No. 18166."

28. Moorehead and Brown, *Digest of the Statute Laws of Kentucky,* 2:1019-23.

29. Ibid., p. 1022.

30. See Pulaski County Surveyor's Office Book 1, p. 195, for information on Free Frank's land acquired under the Head Rights Claim System.

31. See Pulaski County General Index to the Surveyor's Office Books, under "Frank, Free," which shows him listed as the patentee.

32. Moorehead and Brown, *Digest of the Statute Laws of Kentucky,* 2:1022.

33. Ibid., p. 1021. Kentucky's first attempt to conform to the rectangular system of survey that had been initiated in the United States in the land ordinance of 1785 was in the state's 1797 Head Rights Claim Act, which stated that "every claim shall be surveyed as nearly in a square as the interfering claim will admit of." See Littell and Swigert, *Digest of the Statute Law of Kentucky,* 2:736. It was not until 1820 that Kentucky provided in law for the rectangular system of survey. See Moorehead and Brown, *Digest of the Statute Laws of Kentucky,* 2:1040.

34. Berlin, *Slaves without Masters,* p. 9.

35. Two important studies of free black land ownership are John Hope Franklin, *The Free Negro in North Carolina, 1790-1860* (Chapel Hill: Univ. of North Carolina Press, 1943); and Luther Porter Jackson, *Free Negro Labor and Property Holding in Virginia, 1830-1860* (New York: Appleton Century, 1942). Both make extensive use of state and county records.

36. For information on Harris, Goggin, and Wait as Kentucky legislators, see Collins, *Historical Sketches,* p. 683. Goggin, a slaveholder, is listed as a "grantor" in the Pulaski County General Index to Real Estate Conveyances—Grantees, 1799-1934, p. 43. See Tibbals, *History of Pulaski County,* pp. 56-58, for a discussion of Cyrenius Wait. Wait's sale of land to Free Frank was made Nov. 2, 1829; see Pulaski County Real Estate Conveyances, Book 2, p. 64. For Goggin's sale, also in that year, see ibid., p. 231.

37. See U.S., Bureau of the Census, "Population Schedules of the Fourth Census of the United States, 1820, Kentucky, Pulaski County," for information on the Somerset population. By 1820 only 171 people lived in the town, including almost 100 slaves and 24 white families. The occupational distribution of the town's white population showed 19 involved in commercial activities, 18 in manufacturing, and 14 in agriculture.

38. Coleman, *Slavery,* p. 201. Also see Moorehead and Brown, *Digest of the Statute Laws of Kentucky,* 2:1220-21. Under this law all whites were given the authority to seize and arrest any free black who was thought to be a migrant. In order to remain free while establishing proof of his status, the accused had to post a $500 bond. If this could not be done, he waited in jail for the trial. If his status could be proved, the accused was released and had to leave the state within twenty days or be sold as a slave. Also see Juliet E.K. Walker, "The Legal Status of Free Blacks in Early Kentucky, 1792-1825," *Filson Club History Quarterly* (forthcoming, 1983).

39. Pulaski County Order Book 1, p. 296.

40. *Danville* (Ky.) *Olive Branch,* Aug. 11, 1826.

41. *Olive Branch,* Oct. 27, 1826.

42. U.S., Bureau of the Census, "Population Schedules of the Fourth Census of the United States, 1820, Kentucky" (Washington, D.C.: National Archives and Records Service, Manuscript Microcopy M-33, reel 26).

43. Richard Griffin, *Newspaper History of a Town: A History of Danville Kentucky* (Danville: Danville Advocate-Messenger and Kentucky Advocate, 1965), pp. 174-75.

44. See U.S., Bureau of the Census, "Population Schedules of the Fourth Census of the United States, 1820, Kentucky."

45. *Olive Branch,* Oct. 6, 1826.

46. H.C. Nixon, *Lower Piedmont Country,* ed. Erskine Caldwell (New York: J.J. Little & Ives, 1946), pp. 13-14.

47. Pulaski County Real Estate Conveyances, Book 7-I, pp. 55-56. Also see Gray, *History of Agriculture,* 2:666, which discusses slave prices ranging from $800 to $2,000 for prime field hands in the new regions in 1819. Prices fell in the 1820s, but began to rise in the Southwest after 1825, averaging from $1,000 to above $1,200 for prime field hands.

48. Deposition taken from Joseph Porter, Pulaski County, Ky., Mar. 14, 1856, for a Pike County (Ill.) Circuit Court case.

49. *Olive Branch,* May 26, 1820.

50. Daviess, *History,* p. 110.

51. *Olive Branch,* May 26, 1820.

52. John Robinson, *The Testimony and Practice of the Presbyterian Church in Reference to American Slavery* (Cincinnati: J.D. Thorp, 1852), quoted in Asa Martin, *Anti-Slavery Movement in Kentucky: Prior to 1850* (Louisville: Standard Printing Co., 1918), p. 52.

53. Daviess, *History,* p. 71.

54. Speech by Henry Clay in 1829 before the American Colonization Society, published in *African Repository and Colonial Journal* 6 (1830): 12.

55. Martin, *Anti-Slavery Movement*, p. 54.

56. See Malcolm J. Rohrbough, *The Trans-Appalachian Frontier: People, Societies, and Institutions, 1775-1850* (New York: Oxford Univ. Press, 1978), p. 12: "The 'frontier' is the new land settlements, often with primitive economic, political, and social development. . . . The frontier is almost always a temporary circumstance—sometimes very brief—followed, in turn, by the rural world of nineteenth century America." For a summary of the economic and social changes in the Pennyroyal with the closing of the frontier, see Fackler, *Early Days,* p. 188; and F. Garvin Davenport, *Ante-Bellum Kentucky: A Social History, 1800-1860* (Oxford, Ohio: Mississippi Valley Press, 1943), p. 37; Everett Dick, *The Dixie Frontier: A Social History of the Southern Frontier from the First Transmontane Beginnings to the Civil War* (New York: Alfred A. Knopf, 1948), p. 87-93. Also see Frank L. Owsley, "The Patterns of Migration and Settlement on the Southern Frontier," *Journal of Southern History* 11 (1945): 147-76; and Carter G. Woodson, "Freedom and Slavery in Appalachian America," *Journal of Negro History* 1 (April 1916):. 132-50. For information on the economic activities of slaves on the urban frontier, see Richard Wade, *The Urban Frontier: The Rise of Western Cities, 1790-1830* (Cambridge: Harvard Univ. Press, 1959); and Anita S. Goodstein, "Black History on the Nashville Frontier, 1780-1810," *Tennessee History Quarterly* 38 (Winter 1979): 401-20.

57. Moorehead and Brown, *Digest of the Statute Laws of Kentucky,* 2:1162-63. The purpose of teaching black children to read was so they could read the Bible. This provision was repealed in 1843. See Kentucky, General Assembly, *Acts Passed at the Sessions of the General Assembly for the Commonwealth of Kentucky,* 1842-43 (Frankfort, 1844).

58. Deposition taken from Joseph Porter, Pulaski County, Ky., Mar. 14, 1856, for a Pike County (Ill.) Circuit Court case.

59. Pike County Deed Record Book, 23:46, Pike County Courthouse, Pittsfield, Ill. Chapman, in *History of Pike County,* p. 246, provides information on how little Military Tract Land was valued. While some soldiers were able to sell their land for $100 or more, Chapman tells of many soldiers who traded their "patent to a fine 'prairie quarter' in this county for a horse, a cow or a watch." One even traded his 160-acre tract for a pair of shoes.

60. Illinois, General Assembly, *Laws . . . Passed by the Sixth General Assembly at the Session of 1829* (Vandalia, 1830).

61. "A letter published in the *Western Luminary* in 1827 and printed in the *Genius of Universal Emancipation,* September 15, 1827," in Martin, *Anti-Slavery Movement,* p. 88n.

62. Coleman, *Slavery,* pp. 143-44.

63. William V. Pooley, *The Settlement of Illinois from 1830-1850,* Bulletin of the University of Wisconsin, History Series, no. 1 (Madison: Univ. of Wisconsin Press, 1908), p. 353.

64. Pulaski County Real Estate Conveyances, Book 7-I, p. 560.

65. Ibid., Book 7-II, p. 774.

66. Illinois, *Revised Laws* (1833), p. 463.

67. FFP.

CHAPTER FIVE

1. Chapman, *History of Pike County,* p. 739.

2. Pooley, *Settlement of Illinois,* p. 370.

3. Early Pike County settler Judge Henderson, 1874, in Jess M. Thompson, *Pike County History: As Printed in Installments in the Pike County Republican, Pittsfield, Illinois, 1935-1939* (Racine, Wis.: Preston Miller, 1967), pp. 63, 67, 134. This massive volume is a collection

of articles on Pike County history by Thompson, who was the editor of the *Pike County Republican* and whose weekly articles were based on the oral history of the descendants of early Pike County settlers, written records which were available in their family papers, and nineteenth-century published accounts. Court records of estate inventories are useful sources for information on the value of goods brought by those who settled Pike County in the early 1830s.

4. Pooley, *Settlement of Illinois*, p. 356.

5. Coleman, *Slavery in Kentucky*, p. 205.

6. For a discussion of travel routes and road conditions from Kentucky to Illinois, see Pooley, *Settlement of Illinois*, pp. 370-73; Jillson, *Pioneer Kentucky*, pp. 106-07; and Billington, *Westward Expansion*, pp. 294-95.

7. Thompson, *Pike County History*, pp. 134-38.

8. *Illinois Advocate*, July 10, 1832. This newspaper was published in Edwardsville at this time, then moved to Vandalia in December 1832.

9. Thompson, *Pike County History*, pp. 136-38.

10. Chapman, *History of Pike County*, pp. 215-16.

11. Ibid., p. 326.

12. Rebecca Burlend, *A True Picture of Emigration: Or Fourteen Years in the Interior of North America* (London: G. Berger, 1848) ed. with a preface by Milo Milton Quaife (Chicago: Lakeside Press, 1936), pp. 42-43. Burlend's book provides the only published record of Pike County in the early 1830s. For general accounts of the Illinois frontier, including Pike County, see John M. Peck, *A Gazetteer of Illinois: In Three Parts* (Jacksonville, Il: R. Goudy, 1834); Samuel Augustus Mitchell, *Illinois in 1837: A Sketch . . . of the State of Illinois* (Philadelphia: S.A. Mitchell, 1837); Lewis C. Beck, *A Gazetteer of the State of Illinois and Missouri* (1823); Timothy Flint, *The History and Geography of the Mississippi Valley* (1832); and John M. Peck, *A New Guide for Emigrants to the West* (1836).

13. See Illinois, *Revised Laws* (1833), pp. 457-62, for the black code entitled "An Act Respecting Free Negroes and Mulattoes, Servants and Slaves." For a general review of the code in force, see Elmer Gertz, "The Black Laws of Illinois," *Journal of the Illinois State Historical Society* 56 (Autumn 1963): 454-73; and Mason Fishback, "Illinois Legislation on Slavery and Free Negroes, 1818-1865," *Transactions of the Illinois State Historical Society*, no. 9 (1904): 414-32.

14. Chapman, History of Pike County, p. 446. While lifetime servitude was contrary to the Illinois Constitution, legally it was permissible to indenture black males for up to thirty-five years and females for up to thirty-two years. Indentures, however, were sometimes made for longer terms—on some occasions for as long as ninety-nine years. Hence indentured servitude while it existed in Illinois was only a subterfuge for slavery. See Illinois, Constitution (1818), art. 6, secs. 1, 3, and 5; art. 5, secs. 3 and 5. Judicial recognition was given to indentured servitude in the *Phoebe* v. *William Jay* case, which examined the issue of the right to hold blacks as indentured servants under the Illinois Constitution. See *Phoebe* v. *William Jay*, 1 Breese 268 (Ill. 1828); and *Nance* v. *Howard,* 1 Breese 242 (Ill. 1828). Both cases were decided at the same session. For a review of Illinois slavery and the courts, see Norman Dwight Harris, *History of Negro Slavery in Illinois and of the Slavery Agitation in That State* (Chicago: A.C. McClurg, 1906). For general information on slavery in Illinois salt mines, see George W. Smith, "The Salines of Southern Illinois," *Transactions of the Illinois State Historical Society,* no. 9 (1904): pp. 245-58.

15. Randall Parrish, *Historic Illinois* (Chicago: A.C. McClurg, 1905), p. 322. The law regarding kidnapping, effective as of 1825, can be reviewed in Illinois, *Revised Laws* (1833), p. 180. See Harris, *Negro Slavery in Illinois,* pp. 14, 32, 54-56.

16. Illinois, Constitution (1818), art. 2, sec. 27, for example, states: "In all elections, all white male inhabitants above the age of twenty-one . . . shall enjoy the right of an elector."

Ibid., art. 5, sec. 1, states that "the militia . . . shall consist of all free male able-bodied persons, negroes, mulattoes and Indians excepted." Also see Illinois, *Revised Laws* (1833), Criminal Code, sec. 16: "No black or mulatto person, or Indian, shall be permitted to give evidence in favor, or against, any white person whatsoever"; and ibid., Jurors, sec. 1: "All free white male taxable inhabitants . . . shall be considered . . . to serve on all grand and petit juries."

17. Illinois, *Revised Laws* (1833), p. 556.

18. Illinois, General Assembly, Senate, *Journal*, 1828-1829, pp. 182-83.

19. Illinois, *Revised Laws* (1833), p. 463.

20. Ibid., pp. 464-65.

21. Thompson, *Pike County History*, p. 152.

22. Chapman, *History of Pike County*, p. 739. Also see "A History of Pike County," *Pike County Free Press*, Jan. 21, 1847.

23. Chapman, *History of Pike County*, pp. 216-17.

24. U.S., Bureau of the Census, "Population Schedules of the Fifth Census of the United States, 1830, Illinois, Pike County" (Washington, D.C.: National Archives and Records Service, Manuscript Microcopy M-19, reel 24).

25. Theodore L. Carlson, *The Illinois Military Tract: A Study of Land Occupation, Utilization and Tenure* (Urbana: Univ. of Illinois Press, 1951), pp. 1-9. The Military Tract was land set aside by the federal government as bounty payment for soldiers of the War of 1812. The entire tract covered 5,360,000 acres, but only 3,500,000 acres were reserved for the soldiers. The tract was located between the Illinois and Mississippi rivers, extending north 169 miles from their confluence.

26. Chapman, *History of Pike County*, pp. 246-47.

27. Carlson, *Illinois Military Tract*, p. 27. For additional information on land surveys relating specifically to Illinois and the Military Tract, see Zadislav Matousek, *The Beginning of Illinois Surveys* (Springfield: Phillips Brothers, 1971), which is a reprint of the article first published in the archive issue of *Illinois Libraries* 53, no. 1 (1971).

28. E. Dana, *Description of the Bounty Lands in the State of Illinois* (Cincinnati: Looker Reynolds & Co., 1819), pp. 14-15. Other sources of information on this system in the 1830s were Peck, *Gazetteer of Illinois*, pp. 92-101; Mitchell, *Illinois in 1837*, pp. 51-55; and Burlend, *Picture of Emigration*, pp. 52-53.

29. Federal Field Notes 263 (Dec. 12, 1816): 16, Illinois State Archives, Springfield. T4SR5W4PM is the description of a tract of land in the fourth township south of the base line and five townships west of the fourth principal meridian, which is the federal survey description of Hadley township. Within the township, Free Frank's land was located in the southeast quarter (SE 1/4) of section 22. One-quarter section is 160 acres. All land in the public domain was decribed in this manner in federal land records, Ilinois state censuses, Pike County records, newspapers, atlases, and county histories. Sometimes the name of the township is not given, so that familiarity with the federal land description is important when researching land records. For an initial overview of federal land policies, including a discussion of the survey system, see Payson Jackson Treat, *The National Land System, 1785-1820* (New York: Russell & Russell, 1910); Benjamin Horace Hibbard, *A History of the Public Land Policies* (New York: Peter Smith, 1939); and Vernon Carstensen, ed., *The Public Land: Studies in the History of the Public Domain* (Madison: Univ. of Wisconsin Press, 1939).

30. Peck, *Gazetter of Illinois*, pp. 11-12, gives a more detailed description.

31. Surveyor's Map of Hadley Township, 1830, Illinois State Archives, Springfield.

32. Dana, *Description of the Bounty Lands*, p. 22.

33. *Pike County Free Press*, Jan. 21, 1841, stated that Hadley Creek watered several townships, including "4 south 5 west [Hadley]; 4 south, 6 west [Barry] and 5 south 7 west [Pleasant Vale]."

34. Peck, *Gazetteer of Illinois,* p. 249.

35. Chapman, *History of Pike County,* p. 216.

36. *Atlas Map of Pike County,* p. 54.

37. Ibid., p. 100.

38. Captain Melville D. Massie, *Past and Present of Pike County, Illinois* (Chicago: S.J. Clarke, 1906), p. 136.

39. Carlson, *Illinois Military Tract,* p. 23.

40. Burlend, *Picture of Emigration,* pp. 48-49.

41. Interview with Ellen McWorter Yates, great-granddaughter of Free Frank, Kansas City, Mo., April 1974.

42. The *Illinois Advocate* and its successor, the *Illinois Advocate and State Register,* carried numerous advertisements for runaway slaves from as far away as Virginia, North Carolina, Alabama, Tennessee, and Mississippi, and as close as Missouri, who were thought to be hiding out in Illinois. See, for example, *Illinois Advocate,* Apr. 6, 1832; Apr. 21, 1832; Nov. 13, 1832; Dec. 11, 1832; Jan. 5, 1833; Jan. 26, 1833; May 18, 1833; and June 22, 1833. In the *Illinois Advocate and State Register,* see Sept. 7, 1833; Feb. 3, 1834; May 3, 1834; Sept. 3, 1834; Oct. 8, 1834; Dec. 3, 1834; and Aug. 12, 1835.

43. For a study of Black Hawk's life, see Donald Jackson, ed., *Black Hawk: An Autuobiography* (Urbana: Univ. of Illinois Press, 1964).

44. *Illinois Advocate,* Dec. 2, 1831.

45. Carlson, *Illinois Military Tract,* p. 67.

46. Theodore Calvin Pease, *The Frontier State, 1818-1848* (Chicago: A.C. McClurg, 1922), p. 159.

47. Thompson, *Pike County History,* p. 55.

48. Pease, *Frontier State,* p. 171.

49. *Illinois Advocate,* Dec. 2, 1831.

50. Carlson, *Illinois Military Tract,* p. 135.

51. Mitchell, *Illinois in 1837,* pp. 44, 70.

52. Burlend, *Picture of Emigration,* pp. 107-08.

53. Pooley, *Settlement of Illinois,* p. 544.

54. Carlson, *Illinois Military Tract,* p. 137.

55. Massie, *Past and Present of Pike County,* p. 136.

56. Chapman, *History of Pike County,* pp. 739-40.

57. *Atlas Map of Pike County,* p. 51.

58. *Pike County News,* June 3, 1979.

59. See Illinois, General Assembly, Senate, *Journal,* 1828-1829, pp. 182-83.

60. *Illinois Advocate,* Dec. 23, 1831.

61. Ibid., Jan. 19, 1833.

62. Ibid., July 20, 1833.

63. Harris, *Negro Slavery in Illinois,* p. 54. Also see Henry W. Farnam, *Chapters in the History of Social Legislation in the United States to 1860* (Washington, D.C.: Carnegie Institute, 1938), p. 219, who notes that "Illinois seems to have been peculiarly fearful of the Negro element."

64. *Atlas Map of Pike County,* p. 54.

65. Mitchell, *Illinois in 1837,* p. 41.

66. Peck, *Gazetteer of Illinois,* pp. 40-42.

67. Burlend, *Picture of Emigration,* pp. 75-76.

68. *Pike County Free Press,* Jan. 21, 1841.

69. Carlson, *Illinois Military Tract,* p. 129. See also Margaret B. Bogue, "The Cattlemen's Domain," in *Patterns from the Sod,* Collections of the Illinois State Historical Society,

vol. 24, Land Series, vol. 1 (Springfield: Illinois State Historical Society, 1959), pp. 48-84.

70. Peck, *Gazetteer of Illinois,* pp. 41-43.

71. Ibid., pp. 41-42.

72. Pike County Commissioners Records (1832-1838), 2:144. Pike County Courthouse, Pittsfield, Ill. *Illinois Advocate and State Register,* March 1, 1834.

73. Illinois, *Revised Laws* (1833).

74. Mitchell, *Illinois in 1837,* pp. 41-43.

75. Pike County Commissioners Records (1832-1838), 2:73.

76. Illinois, General Assembly, House, *Journal,* 1835-1836.

77. Illinois, *Revised Laws* (1833), p. 183. In Pike County, Hadley township was in the Sixth Road District. See Pike County Commissioners Records (1832-1838), 2:306, where the county commissioners ordered that men need only perform two days' labor on the public road within the district, whereas Illinois state law required five days' labor. See Illinois, General Assembly, House, *Journal,* 1835-1836.

78. Pike County Commissioners Records (1832-1838), 2:174, 177, 178-79. Information is provided here on roads that were later built and by which Free Frank could get to either the Illinois or the Mississippi River.

79. Pulaski County Real Estate Conveyances, Book 8, pp. 199-200.

80. Peck, *Gazetteer of Illinois,* p. 110.

CHAPTER SIX

1. Pike County Deed Record Book, 9:182, Pike County Courthouse, Pittsfield, Ill.

2. Ibid., 23:46.

3. See U.S., Congress, House, *General Public Acts of Congress, Respecting the Sale and Dispostion of the Public Lands. . . ,* 2 vols. (Washington, D.C., 1838); idem, *Laws of the United States of a Local or Temporary Character, and Exhibiting the Entire Legislation of Congress upon Which the Public Land Titles in Each State and Territory Have Depended,* House Misc. Doc. 45, 47th Cong., 2nd sess. (1881), parts 2-3; idem, *The Public Domain: History and Statistics,* prepared by the Public Lands Commission, House Misc. Doc. 45, 47th Cong., 2nd sess. (1881), part 4; and Thomas Donaldson, comp., *The Public Domain: Its History, with Statistics* (Washington, D.C.: G.P.O., 1884).

4. Paul W. Gates, "Frontier Estate Builders and Farm Laborers," in Walker D. Wyman and Clifton B. Kroeber, eds., *The Frontier in Perspective* (Madison: Univ. of Wisconsin Press, 1965), p. 152. Also see Ray Allen Billington, "The Origin of the Land Speculator as a Frontier Type," *Agricultural History* 19 (October 1945): 203-12; and Paul W. Gates, "Land Speculator in Western Development," *Pennsylvania Magazine of History and Biography* 66 (1942): 314-33.

5. Federal Field Notes, 263:16; and Dana, *Description of the Bounty Lands,* p. 22.

6. Federal Tract Book S: Quincy, Township 4S Range 5 West, 710:17-22, Illinois State Archives, Springfield.

7. "Petition for Bounty Lands for Freedmen, Dec. 16, 1818," in *Bounty Land Revenues,* vol. 4 of *New American State Papers: Public Lands* (Wilmington, Del.: Scholarly Resources, 1973), p. 66.

8. *Official Opinions of the Attorneys General of the United States* (40 vols: Washington, D.C., 1791-1948), 1:602-03.

9. "Petition for Bounty Lands," pp. 65-66.

10. Illinois, General Assembly, Senate, *Journal,* 1828-1829, pp. 182-83.

11. "Report on Proposed Changes in Distribution of Proceeds from Public Land Sales," in *Bounty Land Revenues,* p. 291.

12. Ibid., p. 276. Also see Berry, *Black Resistance*, pp. 20-22, for discussion of the impact of slave resistance on federal policies supporting black settlement in the Northwest Territory.

13. Carlson, *Illinois Military Tract*, pp. 43-49.

14. Thomas LeDuc, "History and Appraisal of U.S. Land Policy to 1862," in *Land Use Policy and Problems in the United States*, ed. Howard W. Ottoson (Lincoln: Univ. of Nebraska Press, 1963), p. 9.

15. Peck, *Gazetteer of Illinois*, p. 110.

16. LeDuc, in "History and Appraisal," p. 11, points out: "We know, for example, that in Illinois in the 1820's thousands of rural male voters owned no land." Also see Carlson, *Illinois Military Tract*, pp. 43-49.

17. LeDuc, "History and Appraisal," p. 9.

18. U.S., Congress, *American State Papers*, Class VIII, *Public Lands* (Washington, D.C., 1832-1861), 5:401.

19. LeDuc, "History and Appraisal," p. 9.

20. Carlson, *Illinois Military Tract*, p. 6; for a detailed discussion of the land offices, see also Malcolm S. Rohrbough, *The Land Office Business: The Settlement and Administration of American Public Lands, 1789-1837* (New York: Oxford Univ. Press, 1968). Chapman, *History of Pike County*, p. 797. Also see Hibbard, *History of the Public Land Policies*, pp. 198-208.

21. Chapman, *History of Pike County*, p. 797; also see Carlson, *Illinois Military Tract*, p. 29.

22. See Pike County Deed Record Book, 23:46, for a copy of the land deed.

23. See Peck, *Gazetteer of Illinois*, pp. 23-24, for the 1834 Pike County population; and Mitchell, *Illinois in 1837*, p. 49, for the 1835 Pike County population.

24. John W. Reps, *The Making of Urban America: A History of City Planning in the United States* (Princeton: Princeton Univ. Press, 1965), p. 360. For additional information on town platting in Illinois and other states during this period, see ibid., pp. 300-302, 357-58, 382-88. Also see idem, *Cities of the American West: A History of Frontier Urban Planning* (Princeton: Princeton Univ. Press, 1979).

25. Juliet E.K. Walker, "The Origin of Agricultural Towns in Nineteenth Century Western Illinois: Pike County, 1823-1877," *Journal of the Illinois State Historical Society* (forthcoming, 1983).

26. Chapman, *History of Pike County*, pp. 449-50.

27. Carlson, *Illinois Military Tract*, pp. 87-88.

28. The relevant law can be found in Illinois, *Revised Laws* (1833), pp. 599-602, "An Act Providing for the Recording of Town Plats."

29. Pike County Deed Record Book, 9:182. Maps and plats made by the county surveyor had no legal effect unless they were recorded by the county clerk. Free Frank's plat of New Philadelphia was similar to the plats of most Illinois towns. See Karl Lohman, *Cities and Towns of Illinois—A Handbook of Community Facts* (Urbana: Univ. of Illinois Press, 1941), p. 26. Reps, *Urban America*, p. 302, points out that "the gridiron spread across the country as the natural tool of the land speculator. No other plan was so easy to survey, and no other system of planning yielded so many uniform lots, easy to describe in deeds or to sell from the auctioneer's block."

30. Chapman, *History of Pike County*, pp. 650-51.

31. Illinois, *Revised Laws* (1833), p. 460.

32. The bill as it was initially submitted can be found in the Illinois State Archives, Springfield, as Enrolled Law No. 2031, H.R. No. 1813, Box 48. William Ross, one of the fourteen Pike County residents who had signed Free Frank's certificate of good character, was one of the two state senators from Pike County who sat in the General Assembly. He submitted the petition.

33. Gutman, *Black Family*, pp. 213-32.

34. Litwack, *Been in the Storm So Long*. Also see Gutman, *Black Family*, for information on surnames as a factor that promoted the reuniting of black families after the Civil War; and Mary Frances Berry and John W. Blassingame, *Long Memory: The Black Experience in America* (New York: Oxford Univ. Press, 1982), pp. 75-76.

35. Illinois, General Assembly, *Laws . . . Passed by the Tenth General Assembly, December, 1836*, p. 175, "An Act to change the name of Free Frank."

36. Certificate of Good Character for Free Frank, Pittsfield, Ill., May 17, 1837, FFP.

37. Interview with Thelma McWorter Wheaton, May 8, 1974, Chicago, Ill.

38. For the distance between Pike County towns, see Chapman, *History of Pike County*, p. 914. F.S. Hudson, in *A Geography of Settlements* (London: MacDonald and Evans, 1970), p. 167, discusses the spatial pattern that characterized the location and distribution of Pike County towns, which in their origin and development reflected on aspect of the central-place theory of town location. Hudson (pp. 117-18) says this pattern is characteristic of "a prosperous area, e.g., the U.S. Middle West, . . . where small market towns normally form a close, fairly even pattern. . . . These towns are 'central places' whose main function is to provide services for people living in the surrounding areas. . . . Clearly they form a hierarchy of location in terms of accessibility, measured by both travel time and transportation costs."

39. In addition to the plat, which shows when a town was vacated, this information can be obtained from Illinois, General Assembly, Senate, *Journal Index*, 1831-1850, vol. 1, part 3.

40. Pooley, *Settlement of Illinois*, p. 433.

41. Illinois, General Assembly, House, *Journal*, 1835-1836. See also Pike County Commissioners Records (1832-1838), 2:73, for information on the Meacham's Ferry-Quincy Road, which ran in a northwesterly direction.

42. Pike County Commissioners Records (1832-1838), 2:371.

43. Ibid., p. 384.

44. Ibid., p. 508. For state laws regarding road building, also see Illinois, Revised Laws (1833), pp. 539-45; and Norman Higgins Purple, ed., *A Compilation of the Statutes of the State of Illinois of a General Nature, in Force January 1, 1856*, 2 vols. (Chicago: Keen & Lee, 1856), 2:1038-59.

45. Pike County Commissioners Records (1832-1838), 2:371.

46. Ibid. (1838-1844), 3:218.

47. Ibid.

48. Chapman, *History of Pike County*, p. 98.

49. Pike County Deed Record Book, 2:260; Pike County Commissioners Records (1832-1838), 13:274.

50. Pike County Commissioners Records (1838-1844), 3:879.

51. Ibid. (1832-1838), 2:185.

52. Thompson, *Pike County History*, p. 152; Chapman, *History of Pike County*, p. 854; Pike County Commissioners Records (1832-1838), 2:550.

53. Illinois, *Revised Laws* (1833), p. 438.

54. Thompson, *Pike County History*, pp. 137-38.

55. The contemporary newspapers are full of various stories on abolitionist activities in Quincy. See also Wilbur H. Siebert, *The Underground Railroad from Slavery to Freedom* (New York: Macmillan, 1898); "Journal of the Illinois State Anti-Slavery Society" (manuscript, Chicago Historical Society) and "Minute Book of the Illinois Anti-Slavery Society" (manuscript, Chicago Historical Society). Also see Charles Noye Zucker, "The Free Negro Question: Race Relations in Ante-Bellum Illinois, 1801-1860" (Ph.D. diss., Northwestern Univ., 1972), pp. 217, 223-51.

56. Berry, *Black Resistance*, pp. 71-72. The conditions in Alton and the proslavery attitudes of the people in this region are also reviewed in Merton L. Dillon, *Elijah P. Lovejoy: Abolitionist Editor* (Urbana: Univ. of Illinois Press, 1961); Edward Beecher, *Narrative of the Riots at Alton: In Connection with the Death of Rev. Elijah P. Lovejoy* (Alton, Ill.: George Holton, 1838); and Henry Tanner, *The Martyrdom of Lovejoy—An Account of the Life, Trials and Perils of Rev. Elijah P. Lovejoy Who Was Killed by a Pro-Slavery Mob at Alton, Illinois on the Night of November 7, 1838* (Chicago: Fergus Printing Co., 1881). Also see Zucker, "Race Relations," pp. 217, 223-51.

57. Chapman, *History of Pike County*, p. 516.

58. U.S., Bureau of the Census, "Population Schedules of the Sixth Census of the United States, 1840, Illinois, Pike County" (Washington, D.C.: National Archives and Records Service, Manuscript Microcopy M-704, reel 67).

59. Pulaski County Real Estate Conveyances, Book 8, pp. 199-200.

60. For Pulaski County manumission deeds, see Pulaski County General Index to Real Estate Conveyance—Grantees— E-G Grantees, 1799-1934.

61. Leonard P. Curry, *The Free Blacks in Urban America, 1800-1850: The Shadow of the Dream* (Chicago: Univ. of Chicago Press, 1981), p. 122.

62. William Pease and Jane Pease, "Organized Negro Communities: A North American Experiment," *Journal of Negro History* 47, no. 1 (1962): 19-34.

63. Howard H. Bell, *A Survey of the Negro Convention Movement, 1830-1861* (New York: Arno Press, 1969), p. 11.

64. First Annual Convention for the Improvement of Free People of Colour, "Constitution" (Philadelphia: J.W. Allen, 1831).

65. William Pease and Jane Pease, *Black Utopia: Negro Communal Experiments in America* (Madison: Wisconsin State Historical Society, 1963), pp. 46-49.

66. American Society of the Free Persons of Colour, "Minutes and Proceedings of the Third Annual Convention of the Free People of Colour in the United States," in Howard H. Bell, ed., *Minutes and Proceedings of the National Conventions, 1830-1864* (New York: Arno Press, 1969).

67. Carter G. Woodson, *The Mind of the Negro as Reflected in Letters during the Crisis, 1800-1860* (Washington, D.C.: Associated Publishers, 1962 [1926]), p. 2.

68. Pease and Pease, *Black Utopia*, p. 23.

69. Ibid., pp. 23-24.

70. Ibid., pp. 41-44.

71. *Colored American* (New York), Aug. 18, 1838.

72. Ibid.

73. Ibid., Nov. 18, 1837.

74. Floyd J. Miller, "'The Father of Black Nationalism': Another Contender," *Civil War History* 17, no. 4 (1971): 310-19.

75. *Colored American*, Feb. 9, 16, 17, 1839.

76. Miller, "Father of Black Nationalism," p. 315.

77. Towns founded by blacks would become common after the Civil War. See Norman Crockett, *The Black Towns* (Lawrence, Kan.: Regents Press of Kansas, 1979), who identifies sixty black towns founded in the late nineteenth century. Most were located on the Kansas and Oklahoma frontiers. Free Frank's New Philadelphia, established before the Civil War, represents the first example of this form of land occupancy in the historic settlement patterns distinctive to blacks in the frontier west. Individual pioneer farm homesteads were the first and predominant form of black land occupancy. See Breen and Innes, *"Myne Owne Ground"*, pp. 5-6, 111, for their discussion of black pioneers in 17th century Virginia, who did not "hive togeth-

er," nor did they flourish by separating themselves from the rest of the county community" (p. 68). Maroon communities, also established beginning in the seventeenth century, provide a second example of black land occupancy forms. Located in the Carolinas, Virginia, Georgia, Florida, Louisiana, and Alabama, these isolated and quite often fortified settlements were established by fugitive slaves. See Kenneth Porter, *The Negro on the American Frontier* (New York: Arno Press, 1971) p. 209; Herbert Aptheker "Slave Guerilla Warfare," in *To Be Free,* pp. 11-30; Gerald W. Mullin, *Flight and Rebellion: Slave Resistance in Eighteenth Century Virginia* (New York: Oxford Univ. Press, 1972), pp. 43-44; and for the nineteenth century, Berlin, *Slaves without Masters,* p. 113. "Racial islands" provide a third example of black land occupancy forms. These were rural settlements established by blacks of mixed Indian and white ancestry. Considering themselves racially distinct, many claimed only Indian heritage and sought isolation from both blacks and whites. See E. Franklin Frazier, *The Negro Family in the United States* (Chicago: Univ. of Chicago Press, 1939), pp. 221-26, 231-34. The Gouldtown settlement in southern New Jersey, established in the mid-1760s, is the first recorded example of a "racial island." Beginning in the nineteenth century the Organized Negro Community Settlements provide a fourth example of black land occupancy forms, and included utopian communitarian settlements, manumission settlements, and white philanthropic settlements. With each, black settlement was supported by whites, although in the United States less than 5,000 blacks ever lived in the settlements. See Pease and Pease, *Black Utopia*; and idem, "Organized Negro Communities"; also see J. Treadwell Davis, "Nashoba: Frances Wright's Experments in Self-Emancipation," *Southern Quarterly* 2, no. 1 (1972): 63-90; Frank F. Mathias, "John Randolph's Freedman: The Thwarting of a Will," *Journal of Southern History* 39, no. 2 (1973): 263-72; Benjamin C. Wilson, "Kentucky Kidnappers, Fugitives, and Abolitionists in Antebellum Cass County, Michigan," *Michigan History* 60, no. 4 (1976): 339-58; and Emma Lou Thornbrough, *The Negro in Indiana: A Study of a Minority* (Indianapolis: Indiana Historical Bureau, 1957). For examples of black pioneers who established farm homesteads in the antebellum frontier west, see Svend E. Holsoe, "A Portrait of a Black Midwestern Family during the Early Nineteenth Century: Edward James Roye and His Parents," *Liberian Studies Journal* 3, no 1. (1970-71): 41-52; William Loren Katz, *The Black West* (Garden City, N.Y.: Doubleday, 1971); Allan Peskin, ed., *North into Freedom: The Autobiography of John Malvin, Free Negro, 1795-1880* (Cleveland: Press of Western Reserve University, 1966); Joseph C. Carroll, "William Trail: An Indiana Pioneer [1784-1858]," *Journal of Negro History* 23, no. 4 (1938): 420-24; and W. Sherman Savage, *Blacks in the West* (Westport, Conn.: Greenwood Press, 1976), p. 103.

78. "Minutes of the National Convention of Colored Citizens: Held at Buffalo, on the 15-19th of August, 1843 for the Purpose of Considering Their Moral and Political Conditions as American Citizens," in Bell, ed., *Minutes of the Proceedings,* pp. 30-32. For black emigrationist ideology, see Floyd J. Miller, *The Search for a Black Nationality: Black Colonization and Emigration, 1787-1863* (Urbana: Univ. of Illinois Press, 1977). On Martin Delany, see Dorothy Sterling, *The Making of An Afro-American: Martin Robinson Delany, 1812-1860* (Garden City, N.Y.: Doubleday, 1971); and Victor Ullman, *Martin R. Delany: The Beginning of Black Nationalism* (Boston: Beacon Press, 1971).

79. Philip Foner, ed., *The Life and Writings of Frederick Douglass,* 4 vols. (New York: International Publishers, 1950-1955), 2:173.

80. On black newspapers, see Frederick G. Detweiler, *The Negro Press in the United States* (Chicago: Univ. of Chicago Press, 1922); Irvin Garland Penn, *The Afro-American Press* (Springfield, Mass.: Wiley Co., 1891); Armistead Pride, "A Register and History of Negro Newspapers in the United States: 1827-1950" (Ph.D. diss., Northwestern Univ., 1950). On Illinois newspapers, see Franklin W. Scott, *Newspapers and Periodicals of Illinois, 1814-1879*

(Collections of the Illinois State Historical Society, VI, Springfield), 139. Also see Dorothy Porter, *Negro Protest Pamphlets* (New York: Arno Press, 1969).

81. John E. McWorter to Rev. P.B. West, FFP.

82. U.S., Bureau of the Census, *Sixth Census of the United States: 1840, Enumeration of Inhabitants.*

83. Miles Mark Fisher, "Negro Churches in Illinois: A Fragmentary History with Emphasis on Chicago," *Journal of the Illinois State Historical Society* 61 (Autumn 1963): 552-54.

84. John E. McWorter to Rev. P.B. West, FFP.

85. Squire McWorter, Declaration for Pension for Military Service in the Civil War, 1912, National Archives, Washington, D.C.

86. *Colored American,* July 28, 1838.

87. For black thought, see Philip S. Foner, ed., *The Voice of Black America: Major Speeches by Negroes in the United States, 1797-1971* (New York: Simon and Schuster, 1972); Carter G. Woodson, ed., *Negro Orators and Their Orations* (Washington, D.C.: Associated Publishers, 1925); Dorothy Porter, *Early Negro Writing, 1760-1837* (Boston: Beacon Press, 1971); Sterling Stuckey, *The Ideological Origins of Black Nationalism* (Boston: Beacon Press, 1972). Also see Robert L. Harris, Jr., "The Free Black Response to American Racism, 1790-1863" (Ph.D. diss., Northwestern Univ., 1974).

88. Miller, "Father of Black Nationalism," p. 318.

89. Pease and Pease, "Organized Negro Communities," p. 20.

90. For responses to communal settlements in Western Illinois, see Pooley, *Settlement of Illinois,* pp. 500-538; and Carlson, *Illinois Military Tract,* pp. 73-83. For information on Mormons in Pike County, see Chapman, *History of Pike County,* pp. 104-17, 239. Chapman says there were 300 Mormons settled at "Mormontown," three miles east of Pittsfield: "They tried to work some miracles about Pittsfield, but not with very much success." While the Mormon stand on polygamy did not meet with approval, even more hostility resulted after 1844 when Joseph Smith announced his candidacy for United States president on a platform that called for the freeing of all slaves and prisoners. See George R. Gayler, "The Mormons and Politics in Illinois, 1839-1844," *Journal of the Illinois State History Society* 49 (Spring 1956): 48-66.

91. Sam Bass Warner, Jr., *The Private City: Philadelphia in Three Periods of Its Growth* (Philadelphia: Univ. of Pennsylvania Press, 1968), pp. x, 3, 9. Warner points to the unequal distribution of wealth, but adds that the city's "unique quality lay in the general prosperity of the common artisan and shopkeepers and the widely-shared entrepreneurial experiences and goals of the artisan, shopkeeper, and merchant."

92. Reps, *Town Planning in Frontier America,* pp. 220-21.

93. Wade, *Urban Frontier,* p. 322.

94. On Philadelphia's preeminent role in black life, see Franklin, *From Slavery to Freedom,* 3rd ed., pp. 153, 160, 163, 240; Curry, *Free Blacks in Urban America,* specifically his discussion on "The Negro Church in the City," pp. 174-95, "Associational Activities," pp. 196-215, and "Black Participation and Protest," pp. 216-38; and Vincent P. Franklin, *The Education of Black Philadelphia: The Social and Educational History of a Minority Community, 1900-1950* (Philadelphia: Univ. of Pennsylvania Press, 1979).

95. FFP.

96. Chapman, *History of Pike County,* p. 739.

CHAPTER SEVEN

1. Chapman, *History of Pike County,* p. 217.

2. Pooley, *Settlement of Illinois,* p. 455.

3. Pulaski County Real Estate Conveyances, Book 12, pp. 379-80.

4. See Pike County Deed Record Book Town Lot Index, "Philadelphia," pp. 46-61; and Pike County Tract Index, Hadley-Barry (T4SR5, 6W), Pike County Courthouse, Pittsfield, Ill.

5. U.S., Bureau of the Census, *Seventh Census of the United States, 1850,* p. 714, provides information on Griggsville and Barry.

6. Thompson, *Pike County History,* pp. 151-52.

7. John M. Peck, *The Traveller's Directory for Illinois* (New York: J.H. Colton, 1839), p. 9.

8. Mitchell, *Illinois in 1837,* p. 98.

9. U.S., Bureau of the Census, "Population Schedules of the Sixth Census of the United States, 1840, Illinois, Pike County." The entire county population is listed with no distinctions made regarding local towns. Consequently, it is difficult to ascertain the existence of a town unless a group of people with nonagricultural occupations are consecutively listed. Even then there are no specific listings of occupations because the census only classified occupations in seven broad categories: mining, agriculture, commerce, manufactures and trades, navigation of the ocean, navigation of canals, lakes, and rivers, and learned professions and engineers. In addition, only the names of heads of families are given; members of a household are listed according to age groupings. Thus, if members of a household worked in occupations classified under different categories, there would be no way of determining exactly who pursued a specific occupation or the exact nature of that occupation.

10. Pike County Deed Record Book, 2:60; 22:383; 27:419; 28:263.

11. Interviews with Morrison Worthington, Pittsfield, Pike County, Illinois, May 13, 1973; and with Virgil Burdick, Pike County, Illinois, May 13, 1973. Both men are descendants of early Pike County settlers who lived in the county at the time Free Frank founded New Philadelphia. The two gentlemen, who are white, are in their eighties. Virgil Burdick is the descendant of a man who lived and worked in New Philadelphia. Burdick remembers the site of New Philadelphia, which was still occupied by several families while he was a child. Morrison Worthington, a Harvard graduate and retired lawyer, is a descendant of a family who also came to Pike County in the 1830s. Worthington said that Cincinnati Landing was used by Free Frank and the other people in and around the area of New Philadelphia. He not only remembers the town of New Philadelphia, but also Free Frank's oldest daughter Juda. The Worthington family had a long history of pioneering in the Northwest. The first Worthington in Pike County was the son of Thomas Worthington, Ohio's sixth governor, who served from 1814 to 1818.

12. John Leonard Conger, *Illinois River Valley* (Chicago: J.S. Clarke, 1932), 1:438; and Massie, *Past and Present of Pike County,* p. 83.

13. Illinois, General Assembly, *Laws . . . Passed by the Eleventh General Assembly, Special Session, 1839,* pp. 129-30.

14. Pike County Commissioners Records (1834-1844), 3:123.

15. U.S., Bureau of the Census, *Seventh Census of the United States, 1850,* pp. 703-17, provides information on "Population by Subdivisions of Counties." See p. 714 for information on Pike County towns.

16. Illinois State Census, 1855, "Pike, Pulaski, Pope and Putnam Counties," p. 254, Illinois State Archives, Springfield. The 1855 Illinois State Census lists nineteen other Pike County towns and their population: Summer Hill, 32; Martinsburg, 69; New Salem, 82; New Bedford, 85; Florence, 99; Kinderhook, 103; Montezuma, 117; Atlas, 125; Detroit, 125; New Canton, 135; El Dara, 136: Milton, 176; New Hartford, 178; Chambersburg, 210; Rockport, 221; Perry, 628; Barry, 655; Pittsfield, 950; and Griggsville, 1,116.

17. FFP.

18. Ibid.

19. U.S., Bureau of the Census, "Population Schedules of the Eighth Census of the United States, 1860, Illinois, Pike County" (Washington, D.C.: National Archives and Records Service, Manuscript Microcopy M-653, reel 219).

20. U.S., Bureau of the Census, *Seventh Census of the United States, 1850,* shows that out of a total of 215,339 males counted as employed, over half—140,894—were listed as farmers. Several occupations were basic to town development on the frontier, including blacksmiths, wheelwrights, merchants, shoemakers, carpenters, and cabinetmakers. For information on Pike County towns, see Juliet E.K. Walker, "Occupational Distribution of Frontier Towns in Pike County: A Census Survey," *Western Illinois Regional Studies* 5, no. 2 (1982):146-71.

21. Interview with Morrison Worthington, Pike County, May 1973.

22. Charles B. Johnson, *Illinois in the Fifties, or a Decade of Development* (Champaign, Ill.: Flanigan-Pearson, 1918), p. 51.

23. "Register of All Officers and Agents, Civil, Military and Naval in the Service of the United States," 1851 and 1853, U.S. Post Office Department Records, National Archives, Washington, D.C., Record Group 27, 18:512 and 542, respectively.

24. "Laws and Regulations for the Government of the Post Office," 1852, U.S. Post Office Department Records, National Archives, Washington, D.C., Record Group 27, 18:5.

25. "An Act to Remove All Disqualifications of Color in Carrying the Mails," *Statutes at Large* 96, sec. 1: 515 (1863-1865).

26. Illinois, *Revised Laws* (1833), p. 556.

27. Robert C. Torbet, *A History of the Baptists,* rev. ed. (Chicago: Judson Press, 1963), pp. 259, 285, 358; Pease, *Frontier State,* pp. 415-16; Conger, *Illinois River Valley,* 1:325-31; G.A. Burgess and J.T. Ward, eds., *Free Baptist Cyclopaedia: Historical and Biographical* (Boston: Free Baptist Cyclopaedia Co., 1889), pp. 210, 289.

28. Benjamin Quarles, *Black Abolitionists* (New York: Oxford Univ. Press. 1969), p. 69.

29. Unless otherwise indicated, the source for the information on the building of the Free Will Baptist Seminary is Pike County Circuit Court Records, *Frank McWorter* v. *C.S. Luce and D.C. Topping* (1851), case no. 3787, Pike County Courthouse, Pittsfield, Ill.

30. FFP.

31. See Purple, *Compilation of the Statutes of . . . Illinois,* 1:88-90, for the law on "Arbitration and Awards."

32. Chapman, *History of Pike County,* pp. 671, 880, 882, 904.

33. Ibid., p. 739.

34. Illinois, General Assembly, *Laws . . . Passed by the Seventh General Assembly, Session, December, 1830,* pp. 82-87, "An Act to Incorporate the Inhabitants of Such Towns as May Wish to be Incorporated."

35. U.S., Bureau of the Census, "Population Schedules of the Seventh Census of the United States, 1850, Illinois, Pike County," T4SR5W (Hadley township).

36. Johnson, *Illinois in the Fifties,* p. 43.

37. Hudson, *A Geography of Settlements,* p. 81, states that "for census purposes, and other statistical records, countries have adopted their own methods of defining a town or urban area. Some use an economc criterion, some a criterion based on population numbers, others based on the form of administration. There is no uniformity, but it is curious to note that hardly any country uses population density or areal size in its definition." One definition of a town is "a settlement in which a high proportion of the gainfully employed are non-agricultural workers."

38. New Philadelphia first appeared on Illinois maps published for national distribution in 1850. See *Colton's Traveler and Tourist's Guide-Book through the United States* (New York, 1850). Also see Charles G. Colby, *Handbook of Illinois, Accompanying Morse's New*

Map of the State (New York: R. Blanchard, 1854). New Philadelphia also appears on Morse's 1858 revised map. The last map published for national distribution on which New Philadelphia appears is the map of Pike County in 1869 in *Campbell's New Atlas of the State of Illinois* (Chicago, 1870).

39. William C. Found, *A Theoretical Approach to Rural Land Use Patterns* (London: Butler and Tanner, 1973), p. ix, stresses the fact that "land-use patterns reflect the decisions of thousands of individuals and groups, and that an understanding of the patterns can be achieved only by analyzing the decision-making process." Those factors involved in Free Frank's decision to use his land as a town site provide additional information on the history of land use in nineteenth-century America.

CHAPTER EIGHT

1. *Atlas Map of Pike County*, p. 54.
2. Illinois, *Constitution* (1848), art. 14.
3. Purple, *Compilation of the Statutes of . . . Illinois*, 1:780-83, reprinting "An Act to Prevent the Immigration of Free Negroes into This State" (approved Feb. 12, 1853), from Illinois, *Laws* (1853), p. 57.
4. Pulaski County Real Estate Conveyances, Book 8, pp. 199-200.
5. Massie, *Past and Present of Pike County*, p. 132.
6. *Pike County Free Press*, July 29, 1847.
7. Ibid., Dec. 2, 1847.
8. John E. McWorter to Rev. P.B. West, Aug. 31, 1919, FFP.
9. See U.S., Bureau of the Census, "Population Schedules of the Seventh Census of the United States, 1850, Illinois, Pike County," T4SR5W (Hadley township), for information on Canada as the place of birth of Frank Jr.'s and Squire's children. Later information shows Squire Jr.'s birthplace as Illinois, but his army records show it as Canada.
10. Interview with Ellen McWorter Yates, Apr. 17, 1974, Kansas City, Mo. Although Free Frank's house was destroyed by fire in 1925, the remains of the cellar were still evident even into the early 1950s. For further discussion of the Illinois underground railroad, see Verna Cooley, "Illinois and the Underground Railroad to Canada," *Transactions of the Illinois State Historical Society*, no. 22 (1917), pp. 76-98; and Larry Gara, "The Underground Railroad in Illinois," *Journal of the Illinois State Historical Society* 56 (Autumn 1963): 508-28. Another source is Siebert, *Underground Railroad*. See also "Journal of the Illinois State Anti-Slavery Society" (manuscript, Chicago Historical Society); and "Minute Book of the Illinois Anti-Slavery Society" (manuscript, Chicago Historical Society). Also see Benjamin Quarles, *Black Abolitionists* (New York: Oxford Univ. Press, 1969). pp. 143-67, which includes Free Frank's underground railroad activities.
11. See U.S., Bureau of the Census, "Population Schedules of the Seventh Census of the United States, 1850, Illinois, Pike County," T4SR5W (Hadley township), which shows one shoemaker in Atlas, population 125; one shoemaker in Chambersburg, population 210; three shoemakers in Perry, population 628; three shoemakers in Barry, population 655; two shoemakers in Pittsfield, population 950; and three shoemakers in Griggsville, population 1,116.
12. Genovese, *Roll Jordan Roll*, pp. 551-52; and Benjamin A. Botkin, ed., *Lay My Burden Down: A Folk History* (Chicago: Univ. of Chicago Press, 1945), p. 21.
13. Pike County Circuit Court Records, *McWorter v Luce and Topping* (1851).
14. See Pike County Deed Record Book, 27: 419, for Burdick's town lot purchase in 1846.
15. Massie, *Past and Present of Pike County*, p. 132.

16. See Receipt for Payment of Services Rendered: D.A. Kittle to Solomon McWorter, August 13, 1850 in Pike County Court Records, *McWorter v Luce and Topping,* "C.S. Luce Owes to Frank McWorter," FFP.

17. *Pike County Free Press,* May 6, 1847.

18. Ibid., Feb. 24, 1848.

19. Ibid., Oct. 7, 1847.

20. Chapman, *History of Pike County,* p. 157,

21. Tom L. McLaughlin, "Popular Reactions to the Idea of Negro Equality in Twelve Non-Slaveholding States, 1846-1869: A Quantitative Analysis" (Ph.D. diss., Washington, State Univ., 1969), p. 112. Also see Richard H. Sewell, *Ballots for Freedom: Antislavery Politics, in the United States, 1837-1860* (New York: Oxford Univ. Press, 1976).

22. Broadside on "Division of Pike County," Feb. 4, 1845, in William Blair Collection, Illinois State Historical Society Library, Springfield.

23. Chapman, *History of Pike County,* p. 880.

24. *Pike County Free Press,* July 9, 1846.

25. Ibid., Aug. 20, 1846. Chapman, *History of Pike County,* p. 880, shows that the Democratic candidate received 1,540 votes and the Whig candidate, 1,376 votes.

26. *Illinois State Register,* Jan. 30, 1849. Chapman, *History of Pike County,* p. 874, said, "Properly speaking, we think the people of this county have never been political Abolitionists. They were never in favor of disturbing the constitutional rights of the people of the South, nor of clandestinely assisting their slaves to escape."

27. McLaughlin, "Popular Reactions," p. 112.

28. Chapman, *History of Pike County,* p. 880.

29. McLaughlin, "Popular Reactions," p. 112.

30. Chapman, *History of Pike County,* p. 882. For Lincoln's and Douglas's views on black equality, see Robert W. Johannsen, ed., *The Lincoln-Douglas Debates of 1858* (New York: Oxford Univ. Press, 1965); Benjamin Quarles, *Lincoln and the Negro* (New York: Oxford Univ. Press, 1962); Arvarh E. Strickland, "The Illinois Background of Lincoln's Attitude toward Slavery and the Free Negro," *Journal of the Illinois State Historical Society* 56 (Autumn 1963): 474-94. Charles H. Wesley, "Lincoln's Plan for Colonizing the Emancipated Negro," *Journal of Negro History* 4 (Jan. 1919): 7-21; William O. Douglas, *Mr. Lincoln and the Negroes: The Long Road to Equality* (New York: Atheneum, 1963); and Eric Foner, *Free Soil, Free Labor, Free Men: The Ideology of the Republican Party Before the Civil War* (New York: Oxford Univ. Press, 1970) On Stephen Douglas, see Robert W. Johannsen, *Stephen A. Douglas* (New York: Oxford Univ. Press, 1978). Both Lincoln and Douglas practiced law in Pike County. Pittsfield printer John G. Nicolay became the private secretary to President Lincoln. John Hay, Secretary of State and most famous for the American Open Door Policy with China, attended school in Pittsfield and began his career as a secretary to Lincoln. See Jay Stuart, "Father of Modern Diplomacy," *Illinois Guest* 1 (Dec. 1937): 17. Stuart says, "Pike County had a profound influence on John Hay. Although he met the rough river men who gave rise to his characters in the *Pike County Ballads,* he also became acquainted with the important lawyers of the day and heard Lincoln, Douglas, Browning, Trumbull and Yates argue cases in Court." See Chapman, *History of Pike County,* pp. 221, 238, 271, 321, 389, 396, 398-99, 513, 652, and 644, for mention of Lincoln and Douglas in Pike County.

31. McLaughlin, "Popular Reactions," p. 114. He concludes that opposition to blacks provided the basis for affiliation with the Democratic party, and that in those counties that supported the Democrats there was near unanimity in their opposition to black equality proposals. Also see Frank L. Klement, "Midwestern Opposition to Lincoln's Emancipation Policy," *Journal of Negro History* 59 (July 1964): 169-83. Klement argues that the Democratic party, with its appeal to the "common white man," found support from this group, especially those of south-

ern origin regardless of geographical location, were "enchanted by a knowledge that there was a class below them in the social and economic scale." In Hadley township, one of the three centers of Democratic strength in Pike, the majority of heads of household were of northern origin. See U.S., Bureau of the Census, "Population Schedules of the Seventh Census of the United States, 1850, Illinois, Pike County," T4SR5W, which shows eighty-five heads of household born in northern states, forty-six born in southern states, and nine in foreign countries. Most prominent Pike County whites belonged to the Whig party, including the Ross family. Pike's most prominent Democrat, Joshua Woosley, who held more offices than any other man in the county, lived in Hadley township, the second settler after Free Frank. See Chapman, *History of Pike County*, p. 753,

32. McLaughlin, "Popular Reactions," p. 113. For Pike County religious affiliation, see U.S., Bureau of the Census, *Seventh Census of the United States, 1850*, pp. 737-46. See Litwack, *North of Slavery*, pp. 187-213, and Quarles, *Black Abolitionists*, pp. 69-71, for discussion of various denominations and their relations to free blacks.

33. Litwack, *North of Slavery*, p. 104.

34. Fisher, "Negro Churches in Illinois," *Journal of the Illinois State Historical Society*, pp. 553-54.

35. For deeds of sale, see Pike County Tract Index, Hadley-Barry (T4SR5, 6W).

36. J.B.D. DeBow, *Statistical View of the United States* (Washington, D.C.: A.O.P. Nicholson, 1854), pp. 103, 191.

37. U.S., Bureau of the Census, *Seventh Census of the United States, 1850: Statistics of the United States.*

38. U.S., Bureau of the Census, "Population Schedules of the Seventh Census of the United States, Illinois, Chicago," (Washington, D.C.: National Archives and Records Service, Manuscript Microcopy M-432, reel 102).

39. Zucker, "Free Negro Question," p. 326. The eight counties and their black populations were: Jo Daviess, 218; Gallatin, 353; Alexander, 20; Madison, 449; Randolph, 383; Sangamon, 253: Knox, 38; and Cook, 378. For comparison of black property ownership, see Thornbrough, *Negro in Indiana*, pp. 139-40; she found that less than 6 percent of that state's black population, some 11,000 in 1850, owned property; the average holding was valued at $628; the total value was $412,755. Also assuming a family of five, she makes the point that 25 percent of Indiana's free black heads of household owned property. Curry, *Free Blacks in Urban America*, pp. 37-48, provides information on 1850 black property ownership in fifteen selected cities. Once land was acquired by free blacks, maintaining possession often provoked unwarranted litigation. One Indiana black settler who relocated in Ontario, Canada, reported, "I had a good deal of property there, . . . [but] it was not safe, for any loafing white might destroy or steal, and unless a white man were by to see it, I could get no redress." See Benjamin Drew, ed., *A North-Side View of Slavery: The Refugee: or The Narratives of Fugitive Slaves in Canada Related by Themselves* (Boston, 1856), pp. 272-73.

40. Gates, "Frontier Estate Builders," pp. 154-55.

41. Zucker, "Free Negro Question," pp. 324-25. By 1852 the estimated cost of farmmaking in Illinois for a forty-acre tract of undeveloped land was $550; for a forty-five acre tract of unimproved land, the cost was $930. See Clarence H. Danhof, "Farm-making Costs and the 'Safety Valve': 1850-1860," *Journal of Political Economy* 49 (June 1941): 317-59.

42. Curry, *Free Blacks in Urban America*, p. 38.

43. Litwack, *North of Slavery*, pp. 47-50, discusses the impact of the 1857 Dred Scott decision, noting that "any Negro who desired to settle on the newly opened western lands now faced not only the anti-immigration laws of various states and territories but the open hostility of the federal government." Also see Herbert Aptheker, ed., *A Documentary History of the*

Negro People in the United States (New York: Citadel Press, 1951), pp. 447-48. Aptheker notes that after 1857, on the basis of the noncitizenship status of Afro-Americans, the United States General Land Office made attempts to deny the validity of land claims staked out by blacks under the 1841 Preemption Act.

44. Pike County Circuit Court Records, *Solomon McWorter, Exr. of Frank McWorter* v. *Lucy McWorter widow et al.* (1857), case no. 8850, Pike County Courthouse, Pittsfield, Illinois.

45. See U.S., Bureau of the Census, "Population Schedules of the Seventh Census of the United States, 1850, Illinois, Pike County," T4SR5W (Hadley township), which shows the family members listed under McWorter.

46. Tibbals, *History of Pike County,* pp. 102-03, refers to Galen Gibson as a school-teacher in Pulaski County after the Civil War and a founder of an African Methodist Episcopal church in Somerset in 1868.

47. Gutman, *Black Family,* p. 220 (his italics).

48. FFP.

49. Personal communication from Gloria Valentine, March 5, 1976, Chicago, Ill.

50. FFP.

51. William Denham to Solomon McWorter, July 21, 1860, FFP. Pike County Inventories, Appraisements, Bills, etc., 1866-1869, pp. 28-29, Pike County Courthouse, Pittsfield, Ill. The price is shown in the account that Solomon presented to the court in a settlement of Free Frank's estate.

52. Pike County Circuit Court Records, *Solomon McWorter, Exr. of Frank McWorter* v. *Lucy McWorter widow et al.* (1857), case no. 8850.

53. Pulaski County General Index to Real Estate Conveyances—Grantees: E-G Grantees, 1799-1934, p. 43, shows only four McWorter manumissions: Lucy's, Free Frank's, Solomon's, and Sally's. The bill of sale for Frank Jr.'s manumission is not listed but the record is available; see Pulaski County Real Estate Conveyances, Book 7-I, p. 55. Also see Thelma Elise McWorter Kirkpatrick [Wheaton], "Free Frank McWorter of Pike County, Ill." (mimeographed; Chicago, *ca.* 1937), p. 2, FFP. Frank Jr.'s military record (in FFP) shows date of enlistment and length of service.

54. Arthur H. Cole, *Business Enterprise in Its Social Setting* (Cambridge: Harvard Univ. Press, 1959), p. 109. Also see Alfred D. Chandler, Jr., "Entrepreneurial Opportunity in Nineteenth Century America," *Explorations in Entrepreneurial History,* 2nd ser., 1 (1963): 106.

55. Joseph A. Schumpeter, *The Theory of Economic Development: An Inquiry into Profits, Capital, Credit, Interest and the Business Cycle* (Cambridge: Harvard Univ. Press, 1963), p. 93.

EPILOGUE

1. Chapman, *Pike County History,* p. 739.

2. *Atlas Map of Pike County,* p. 54.

3. For information on Ilinois black participation in the Civil War, see Victor Hicken, "The Record of Illinois' Negro Soldiers in the Civil War," *Journal of the Illinois State Historical Society* 56 (Autumn 1963): 529-51. Also see Benjamin Quarles, *The Negro in the Civil War* (Boston: Little, Brown, 1969).

4. U.S., Bureau of the Census, "Population Schedules of the Eighth Census of the United States, 1860, Illinois, Pike County," Hadley township (Washington, D.C.: National Archives and Records Service, Manuscript Microcopy M-653, reel 219); ibid., "Population Schedules of the Ninth Census of the United States, 1870, Illinois, Pike County," Hadley township (Manuscript Microcopy M-593, reel 219); and ibid., "Population Schedules of the

Ninth Census of the United States, 1870, Illinois, Pike County," Hadley township (Manuscript Microcopy M-593, reel 269); and ibid., "Population Schedules of the Tenth Census of the United States, 1880, Illinois, Pike County," Hadley township (Manuscript Microcopy M-T9, reel 243). Federal manuscript censuses are important sources for determining the place of origin of New Philadelphia's adult population, especially when the range in the ages of children and their birthplace in states other than Illinois suggest migration patterns.

5. Crockett, *Black Towns,* pp. xiii, 2, 75, 184, for Nicodemus; pp. 20, 193, for Langston; and, pp. 35-36 for Boley.

6. Savage, *Blacks in the West,* p. 103.

7. Crockett, *Black Towns,* p. 49.

8. Chapman, *History of Pike County,* pp. 740-41. Chapman (pp. 904-09) points out that railroad stations were located at sites township residents considered easily accessible, and that those who contributed the most money to underwrite costs of railroad construction in their area invariably had the controlling voice in determining the site.

9. *Atlas Map of Pike County,* p. 100; Chapman, *History of Pike County,* pp. 738-53; and George Ogle and Co., comps., *Standard Atlas of Pike County, Illinois, Including a Plat Book of the County* (Chicago, 1912). Included among the Free Frank Papers are envelopes addressed to Solomon McWorter and other family members dated in the 1870s and 1880s with a Cool Bank post office stamp.

10. Hon. William A. Grimshaw, "History of Pike County: Centennial Address, Pittsfield, Ill., July 4, 1876," p. 33, Springfield, Illinois State Historical Society Library.

11. Chapman, *History of Pike County,* pp. 741-53. While over sixty black towns were founded in the period after the Civil War to the early twentieth century, few survived. Mount Bayou, Mississippi, founded by the ex-slave Isiah Montgomery, was one town which survived into the mid-twentieth century. See Harold E. Rose, "The All-Negro Town: Its Evolution and Function," *Geographical Review* 53, no. 3 (1965): 376. Rose emphasizes that the town was successful partly because of its location in the "productive cotton lands of Bolivar County, the South's largest cotton producing county." It also thrived because of its cotton processing plants and mills and because of the large concentration of blacks in the area who patronized the town's businesses. Frederick C. Luebke, in "Ethnic Group Settlement on the Great Plains," *Western Historical Quarterly* 8, no. 4 (1977): 428, also points to population size as an important factor that determined the success or failure of a town. "The blacks on the plains, except those in Oklahoma, could not achieve the 'critical mass' necessary for the survival of agricultural communities." Additional studies that discuss aspects of black town development in newly settled frontiers after 1865 are: Nell Irwin Painter, *Exodusters: Black Migration to Kansas after Reconstruction* (New York: Alfred A. Knopf, 1977); Randall Bennett Woods, *A Black Odyssey: John Lewis Waller and the Promise of American Life, 1878-1900* (Lawrence: Regents Press of Kansas, 1981); George H. Wayne, "Negro Migrations and Colonization in Colorado—1870-1930," *Journal of the West* 15, no. 1 (1976): 110-15; Willard B. Gatewood, Jr, "Katie D. Chapman Reports on 'The Yankton Colored People,' 1889," *South Dakota History* 7, no. 1 (1976): 28-35; Kenneth Hamilton, "The Origin and Early Development of Langston, Oklahoma," *Journal of Negro History* 61, no. 3 (1977): 276; and William E. Bittle and Gilbert Geis, "Racial Self-Fulfillment and the Rise of an All-Negro Community in Oklahoma," *Phylon* 18, no. 3 (1957): 247-60.

12. "Map of Hadley Township," *Atlas Map of Pike County,* p. 100, shows the location of Squire's shop at Hadley Station.

13. Ibid., p. 10. William Ross was among those who made this comment. In 1880 the Wabash, St. Louis and Pacific Railroad assumed control over the Hannibal and Naples Road. See Chapman, *Pike County History,* pp. 904-06.

14. Pike County Miscellaneous Records, 2:496, Pike County Courthouse, Pittsfield, Ill.

15. Illinois, *Revised Statutes* (Cothran, 1885), pp. 1086-87. A town site is distinct from a town, which is a political subdivision of the state government. Under state law the right to plat a town implies the use of town lots not only for private purposes but also for public purposes. Unoccupied land not used for public purposes may be lost by abandonment of occupancy.

16. Chapman, *Pike County History*, p. 741.

17. U.S., Bureau of the Census, *Compendium of the Eleventh Census, 1890*, part 1: *Population* (Washington, D.C., 1892).

18. For their occupations, see U.S., Bureau of the Census, "Population Schedules of the Tenth Census of the U.S., 1880, Illinois, Pike County," Hadley township (Washington, D.C.: National Archives and Records Service, Manuscript Microcopy M-T9, reel 243).

19. Pike County Farm Bureau, *Triennial Atlas and Plat Book: Pike County, Illinois* (Rockford, Ill.: Rockford Map Publishers, 1969), p. 44, shows the Burdick family as owners of the land where New Philadelphia was located. Also see account of New Philadelphia history from family members and from reminiscences of descendants of Pike County Old Settlers given at a Pike County Historical Society meeting in Pittsfield, *Pike County Democrat-Times*, April 22, 1964.

20. In 1976 the Illinois Bicentennial Commission selected the site of New Philadelphia as a historic place to be designated by a bronze marker.

21. Pike County Circuit Court Records, *Solomon McWorter, Exr. of Frank McWorter* v. *Lucy McWorter widow et al.* (1857), case no. 8850, Pike County Courthouse, Pittsfield, Ill.

22. *Atlas Map of Pike County*, p. 54.

23. Pike County, Inventory Record, 1874-79, 17:2, 72, Pike County Courthouse, Pittsfield, Ill.

24. John E. McWorter's patents were no. 1,114,167, October 20, 1914; no. 1,115,710, November 3, 1914; and no, 1,438,929, December 12, 1922. See *Specifications and Drawings of Patents Issued from the United States Patent Office*, vol. 509, pt. 7 (Washington, D.C.: G.P.O., 1915); vol. 510, pt. 2 (1915); and vol. 607, pt. 6 (1923).

25. Arthur McWorter to Thelma McWorter Kirkpatrick [Wheaton], January 1937, FFP. By that time, John, Mary, and Julia were also dead.

26. From Pike County farmland prices listed in the county newspapers, including the *Pike County News*.

27. Barbara J. Flint, "Black Women and Urban Life: A Study of Social Transformation, 1910-1954," unpublished paper, provides information on Thelma McWorter Wheaton. After working her way through Fisk University, she received a fellowship to Case Western, where she received her M.A. in social work in 1931. Two years after coming to Chicago she married Allen James Kirkpatrick, a mailman from Texas and the grandson of a former slave freed after the Civil War. Since the 1930s she has been active in contributing to the institution building of Chicago's black community. Working at the Chicago YMCA, she was active in labor organizing for black women in the 1930s, a founder of the Chicago Southside Community Art Center in 1938-1939, and during World War II was president of the Illinois Housewives Association. In the 1960s she participated in the development of the DuSable Museum of African-American History, founded by Dr. Margaret Burroughs. After her husband's death in 1948, she continued her work as a teacher in the Chicago public school system until she retired in 1972. Since then she has been active in the Chicago Branch of the Association for the Study of Afro-American Life and History, while continuing her work with the Southside Community Art Center, the DuSable Museum, Alpha Kappa Alpha sorority, her church, and various civic clubs. She has been active in civil rights protests and in protests against American investments in South Africa, and has taken an active interest in world hunger, the women's rights movement, and

activities of senior citizens. She is listed in *The World Who's Who of Women,* 5th ed., pp. 116-17. She is a remarkable, highly intelligent woman who has given priority to raising her family and contributing to her community. Her activities in the black community reflect the participation of the fourth generation of women among Free Frank's descendants.

Also part of this heritage was Solomon's wife's sister, Jennie Coleman McLain, who participated in the work of the black women's club movement at the turn of the century. McLain was one of the founders and early officers in the Illinois Federation of Colored Women's Clubs. See Elizabeth Lindsay Davis, *The Story of the Illinois Federation of Colored Women's Clubs, 1900-1922* (n.p., 1922), pp. 42, 110-11.

28. John E. McWorter to Rev. P.B. West, August 31, 1919, FFP.

29. Thelma McWorter Kirkpatrick [Wheaton], "Free Frank McWorter of Pike County, Il." Chicago, *ca.* 1937 (mimeographed), FFP.

Bibliographic Note

The study of Free Frank's life is unique because of the kinds of sources used to document his activities on the antebellum frontier. His personal records (the Free Frank Papers) and government records (federal, state, and county) provided the documentary evidence to support the family's oral history. With such corroboration, those oral sources proved invaluable to the interpretation of his life. While no sources contained substantive material to assess the personal attitudes and inner reality of Free Frank, sufficient information did exist to reconstruct his experiences as a black pioneer. Specialized books, articles, and monographs focusing on federal and state land policies, slavery, westward expansion, population settlement patterns, agricultural and town development on the frontier, and black intellectual thought and social reform activities, provided valuable detailed information and extensive analyses which illuminated the information obtained from the Free Frank Papers and government records. They also offered a conceptual framework for interpreting Free Frank's life on the three frontiers where he lived, and, in particular, for assessing his activities as a pioneer entrepreneur.

Free Frank's life as a slave in South Carolina was reconstructed in part from information available about his owner, George McWhorter. Colonial government records, the 1790 federal manuscript census, and various kinds of genealogical materials found in the South Carolina, Union County, and Kentucky historical societies provided specific background information on McWhorter. Supplemented by secondary sources that detailed the impact of the Revolutionary War era on settlers in the South Carolina Piedmont, those records helped me to reconstruct the conditions of Free Frank's life from his birth in 1777 to 1795, when his owner moved to Kentucky.

Various government records provided information on Free Frank's life as a pioneer slave in Kentucky from 1795 to 1819. The Kentucky land laws and Pulaski County Deed Record Books and Real Estate Conveyances Books, for example, made it possible to determine the date when his owner settled in Kentucky. Although the 1800 federal manuscript census is not extant, information on the Pulaski County population was obtained from the 1800 Pulaski County tax list. Documents from the Free Frank Papers, particularly a deposition from a witness (a Pulaski County resident) in an 1856 Pike County, Illinois, court case, contained a general outline of Free Frank's life in Kentucky.

The 1810 federal manuscript census and Pulaski County Court probate records documented the geographical mobility of the slave owner, corroborating the family's oral history that Free Frank's owner left him in charge of the Pulaski County farm during his absence. Free Frank's 1819 manumission certificate, recorded in the Pulaski County Real Estate Conveyances Books, also showed that he continued to manage that farm after the death of his first owner and in the absence of his new owners. County deed records showed the location of the farm, and topographical surveys of this area and contemporary sources pointed to the existence of saltpeter caves in close proximity. The *Pike County* (Illinois) *Atlas* described Free Frank's salt-peter manufacturing activities while he worked as a slave who hired his own time in Kentucky. The 1819 manumission record also confirmed that Free Frank purchased his own freedom, and showed the amount he paid his owners. His 1830 Pulaski County Certificate of Good Character and the 1856 deposition affirmed the family's oral history that Free Frank also purchased his wife Lucy's freedom.

Free Frank was listed in both the 1820 and the 1830 federal manuscript censuses for Pulaski County. The 1856 deposition provided the first indication of his Kentucky landownership. The Kentucky Secretary of State and Pulaski County land records, including Deed Record Books, Real Estate Conveyances Books, and Surveyor's Office Books, showed the location, price, and number of acres he owned in Kentucky. Published compilations of judicial cases concerning antebellum blacks pointed to the Kentucky court cases in which Free Frank and Lucy were involved in the 1820s. An 1829 property transaction, recorded in the Pulaski County Real Estate Conveyances Books, showed the transfer of Free Frank's saltpeter enterprise in exchange for the freedom of his oldest son, and also confirms the family oral history that one of his sons fled to Canada as a fugitive slave. The 1856 deposition was again important in outlining Free Frank's decision to leave Kentucky, providing details on the 1830 purchase of Illinois Military Tract land and the subsequent sale of his Pulaski County farm. Those transactions were recorded in Pulaski County and Pike County records.

Pike County histories, augmented by Pike County Commissioners' Records, offered information on Free Frank's farm activities during his early years on the Illinois frontier. Pike County and federal land tract records pointed to his additional property purchases in Illinois. Those records also detailed other Hadley township land sales. The 1840, 1850, and 1860 federal censuses showed the increasing number of settlers in the township, suggesting the desirability of farmland in that area. Contemporary publications, especially newspapers and travelers' guides (although frequently exaggerated), together with personal diaries, letters, and journals, and information on the increasing frequency of steamboat landings during this period, confirmed Pike County's agricultural productivity. The increasing value of Free Frank's farmland was shown by his tax receipts, which comprise an important part of the Free Frank Papers.

The existence of New Philadelphia was documented in various Pike County records, such as deed books, surveyor's record books, and county commissioner's records, and in the 1850 federal manuscript census and the 1855 Illinois state manuscript census. Contemporary published sources provided supportive information. The 1850 federal manuscript census was particularly useful; it contained the first official count of the Hadley township population, revealing that a sufficient number of people lived in the town's hinterland to support the services offered by New Philadelphia businessmen. The occupational listings of New Philadelphia townspeople in that census indicated the kinds of businesses established in Free Frank's town. The Pike County Deed Record Books contained information on New Philadelphia town lot purchases and purchasers. By using the town plat, recorded in the county surveyor's books, in conjunction with information from other sources, it was possible to achieve a graphic reconstruction of the town, including the location of business establishments. The existence of New Philadelphia Post Office was confirmed by United States Post Office Department records.

Various documents in the Free Frank Papers allowed me to reconstruct New Philadelphia's development. Of particular interest was the subscription list of donations pledged by Hadley township and New Philadelphia residents for the building of Free Frank's Free Will Baptist Seminary. Promissory notes and receipts in that collection provided additional information on New Philadelphia business activities. Pike County records of Free Frank's 1851 court cases and arbitration hearing indicated not only his role as a town proprietor but also the family's various economic activities.

Oral interviews proved particularly important in reconstructing the history of New Philadelphia. Information obtained from Virgil Burdick and Morrison Worthington was extremely useful. Mr. Burdick, a descendant of a Pike County settler who lived in New Philadelphia in the 1840s and 1850s, was born in the late nineteenth century and grew up in the area of New Philadelphia. He gave me information on social activities that took place in the town. Mr. Worthington was an important source of information on New Philadelphia business activities. Informal conversations with other descendants of early Pike County settlers whose ancestors were contemporaries of Free Frank were sources of general information. Members of the Pike County Historical Society, particularly Grace Matteson, were extremely helpful.

Many of Free Frank's descendants who were born in Hadley township and grew up in the New Philadelphia area provided their reminiscences of Free Frank. Some of them obtained their information from their grandmother, Frances Jane McWorter, the widow of Free Frank's son Solomon, who raised five of Free Frank's great-grandchildren from early childhood. Finally, the gravestones in the New Philadelphia cemetery of Free Frank, Lucy, and their seven children who lived to adulthood, offered poignant testimony to the survival of the first and second generations of Free Frank's family, from 1771, when Lucy was born, to 1906, when the oldest daughter, Juda, died.

Free Frank's economic activities had one purpose—to buy his family's freedom. The family's oral history pointed to sixteen family members who were purchased from slavery. The 1850 and 1860 federal manuscript censuses for Pike County listed their names. Since slaves were property and manumissions were controlled by the state, some documents of transfer of slave property and instruments of manumission were shown in county records. In the instance of Free Frank's family, Pulaski County records listed only five who were manumitted. Free Frank's 1846 will and the Pike County court probate records of his estate pointed to several more family members who were purchased by Free Frank's son Solomon. Letters written by a member of the white family who owned one of Free Frank's granddaughters and her children provided additional evidence of purchases that were not recorded in Pulaski County court records. Thus information from several published sources, as well as the Free Frank Papers, corroborated this part of the family's oral history.

The bibliographic listing which follows includes only the most important primary source materials used in my research. It is divided into three major sections: the Free Frank Papers, public manuscript sources, and contemporary sources. The listing of documents from the Free Frank Papers shows the diversity of papers in that collection and a cursory review of many of the activities and experiences which characterized Free Frank's life. The listing of public manuscript sources includes county, state, and federal records for Pulaski County, Kentucky, and Pike County, Illinois. Of those, the county records were the most valuable. The contemporary published sources include government records, atlases, travelers' guides, maps, and plats. For both sections, materials are arranged to reflect the time when Free Frank lived in each state. Thus Kentucky sources precede Illinois sources.

The Free Frank [McWorter] Papers

McWhorter, Abner. Manumission paper for Free Frank. Lincoln, Tenn., September 13, 1819.

Denham to Free Frank. Bill of sale for Free Frank's son. Somerset, Ky., June 9, 1829.

Character Reference Statement for Free Frank signed by nineteen Pulaski County, Ky., citizens. September 7, 1830.

Certificate of Freedom for Lucy (Free Frank's wife). Somerset, Ky., September 8, 1830.

J.M. Higbee to Free Frank. Land deed. Pike County, Ill., July 10, 1836.

Certificate of Good Character for Free Frank signed by fourteen Pike County, Ill., citizens. May 17, 1837.

Lamb & Dunlap to Frank McWorter. Land deed. April 20, 1840.

Received of Frank McWorter. Tax receipts, 1840, 1841, 1848, and 1853.

Received of Commodore McWorter. Tax receipt, 1848.

Frank McWorter and Lucy to C.S. Luce and D.C. Topping. New Philadelphia town lots deed of sale. December 1, 1848.

C.S. Luce and D.C. Topping to Frank McWorter. Promissory note. December 1, 1848.

Received of C.S. Luce. New Philadelphia town lots tax receipt, 1849.

Subscription list for construction of the New Philadelphia Free Will Baptist Seminary, ca. 1849.

Solomon McWorter and James M. Pottle to James Wilson or bearer. Promissory note. New Philadelphia, Ill., February 1, 1850.

D.A. Kittle to Solomon McWorter. Receipt for payment for services rendered. New Philadelphia, Ill., August, 13, 1850.

Arbitrators' Award, September 25, 1851. Decision rendered at the New Philadelphia schoolhouse, case of *Frank McWorter* v. *C.S. Luce*.

Clement Adams to Commodore McWorter. Land deed. September 29, 1852.

Received of Frank McWorter. New Philadelphia town lots tax receipt, 1853.

Received of Solomon McWorter, Executor of the estate of Frank McWorter. Tax receipt, 1854.

Galen Gibson to Solomon McQuarter [McWorter]. Letter. Somerset, Ky., January 1854.

William Denham to Solomon McWorter. Letter. Somerset, Ky., December 30, 1854.

Received of S & S [Solomon and Squire] McWorter. Tax receipt, 1855.

Received of Solomon McWorter and D. Kirtwright. New Philadelphia town lots tax receipt, 1855.

Received of Solomon McWorter, Administrator for Squire McWorter. New Philadelphia town lots tax receipt, 1856.

Deposition taken from Joseph Porter, Witness in a Pike County, Ill., Circuit Court Case. Pulaski County, Ky., March 14, 1856.

Solomon McWorter to C. Adams. Land Deed. September 29, 1857.

William Denham to Solomon McWorter. Letter. Somerset, Ky., July 21, 1860.

John E. McWorter to Rev. P.B. West. Letter. St. Louis, Mo., August 31, 1919. (Mimeographed.)

Arthur McWorter to Thelma McWorter Kirkpatrick [Wheaton]. Letter. Hadley, Ill., January 1937.

Kirkpatrick [Wheaton], Thelma Elise McWorter. "Free Frank McWorter of Pike County, Ill." Chicago, ca. 1937. (Mimeographed.)

Public Manuscript Sources

COUNTY AND STATE: KENTUCKY

Kentucky Historical Society, Frankfort. Garret G. Clift. *Second Census of Kentucky—1800: Privately Compiled and Published Enumeration of Tax Papers Appearing in the 79 Manuscript Volumes Extant of Tax Lists of the 42 Counties in Existence in 1800.* Frankfort, 1954.

————. Denham Family Papers.

————. Lincoln County Tax List of 1799.

————. Pulaski County Tax Book I, 1799.

————. Pulaski County Tax List of 1799.

————. Volkel, F. "An Index to the 1810 Federal Census of Kentucky."

Margaret I. King Library, University of Kentucky, Lexington. Alma Owens Tibbals Papers.

Kentucky Secretary of State, Land Office, Frankfort. Land Warrants, nos. 5803, 5805, 16466, 16468, and 16470.

Kentucky State Archives, Frankfort. "A List of Taxable Property Taken in by Urwin Ewing, Comm. for Lincoln County, 1796."

COUNTY AND STATE: ILLINOIS

Illinois State Archives, Springfield. Enrolled Law, no. 2031, no. 2031, H.R. no. 1813, box 48.

————. Federal Field Notes. Vol. 263.

————. Federal Tract Book S: Quincy, Township 4S Range 5 West. Vol. 701.

————. Illinois State Census, 1845.

————. Illinois State Census, 1855. "Pike, Pulaski, Pope and Putnam Counties." Illinois State Historical Society Library, Springfield. William Blair Collection.

Pike County Courthouse, Pittsfield. County Circuit Court Records. *Frank McWorter v. C.S. Luce and D.C. Topping* (1851), case no. 3787.

————. County Commissioners' Records. Vol. 2 (1832-1838), and vol. 3 (1838-1844).

————. County Deed Record Books. Vols. 9, 11, 13, 17, 23, 24, 27, 28, and 53.

————. County Deed Record Book Town Lot Index.

————. County Inventories, Appraisements, Bills, etc., 1866-1869.

————. County Marriage Records.

————. County Miscellaneous Records. Vols. 1-2.

————. County Surveyor's Record Book. 1838.

————. County Tract Index, Hadley-Barry (T4SR5, 6W).

FEDERAL

National Archives and Records Service, Washington, D.C. United States, Bureau of the Census. "Population Schedules of the Fourth Census of the United States, 1820, Kentucky, Pulaski County." Manuscript Microcopy M-33, reels 26 and 27.

————. United States, Bureau of the Census. "Population Schedules of the Fifth Census of the United States, 1830, Kentucky, Pulaski County." Manuscript Microcopy M-19, reel 41.

————. United States, Bureau of the Census. "Population Schedules of the Fifth Census of the United States, 1830, Illinois, Pike County." Manuscript Microcopy M-19, reel 24.

————. United States, Bureau of the Census. "Population Schedules of the Sixth Census of the United States, 1840, Illinois, Pike County." Manuscript Microcopy M-704, reel 67.

————. United States, Bureau of the Census. "Population Schedules of the Seventh Census of the United States, 1850, Illinois, Pike County." T4SR5W (Hadley Township). Manuscript Microcopy M-432, reels 102 and 124.

————. United States, Bureau of the Census. "Population Schedules of the Eighth Census of the United States, 1860, Illinois, Pike County." Hadley Township. Manuscript Microcopy M-653, reel 219.

————. United States, Post Office Department Records. "Laws and Regulations for the Government of the Post Office," 1852; "Register of All Officers and Agents, Civil, Military and Naval in the Service of the United States," 1851 and 1853; "Register of Appointments of Postmasters." Record Group 27, vol. 18.

Contemporary Sources

STATE DOCUMENTS

Free Frank and Lucy v. Denham's Administrator. 5 Littell 330 (Ky. 1824).

Free Lucy and Frank v. *Denham's Administrator.* 4 Monroe 167 (Ky. 1827).

Kentucky, General Assembly. *Acts Passed at the Sessions of the General Assembly for the Commonwealth of Kentucky,* 1796-1797 to 1859-1860.

Littell, William, ed. *The Statute Law of Kentucky to 1816, Comprehending Also the Laws of Virginia and Acts of Parliament in Force in This Commonwealth.* 5 vols. Frankfort: W. Hunter, 1809-1819.

—— and Swigert, Jacob, eds., *A Digest of the Statute Law of Kentucky . . . to the May Session, 1822.* 2 vols. Frankfort: Kendall and Russell, 1822.

Moorehead, C.S., and Brown, Mason, eds. *A Digest of the Statute Laws of Kentucky, of a Public and Permanent Nature.* 2 vols. Frankfort: A.G. Hodges, 1834.

Illinois. *Constitution* (1818).

——. *Constitution* (1848).

——. *Revised Laws* (1833).

——. *Revised Statutes* (1845).

——. *Revised Statutes* (1885).

Illinois, General Assembly. *Laws of the State of Illinois Passed by the Sixth General Assembly at the Session of 1829.* Vandalia, 1830.

——. *Laws of the State of Illinois Passed by the Seventh General Assembly, Session, December, 1830.* Vandalia, 1830.

——. *Laws of the State of Illinois Passed by the Tenth General Assembly, December, 1836.* Vandalia, 1836.

——. *Laws of the State of Illinois Passed by the Eleventh General Assembly, Special Session, 1839.* Springfield, 1839.

——, House. *Journal,* 1835-1836.

——, Senate. *Journal,* 1828-1829.

——, Senate. *Journal Index,* 1831-1850. Vol. 1, part 3.

Purple, Norman Higgins, ed. *A Compilation of the Statutes of the State of Illinois, of a General Nature, in Force January 1, 1856.* 2 vols. Chicago: Keen and Lee, 1856.

FEDERAL DOCUMENTS

Cochran, T., ed. *The New American State Papers: Public Lands.* 13 vols. Vol. 4: *Bounty Land Revenues.* Wilmington, Del.: Scholarly Resources, Inc., 1973.

Cummings, John. *Negro Population in the United States, 1790-1915.* Prepared for the U.S. Bureau of the Census. Washington, D.C.: G.P.O., 1918.

Donaldson, Thomas, comp. *The Public Domain: Its History, with Statistics.* Washington, D.C.: G.P.O., 1884.

U.S., Bureau of the Census. *A Century of Population Growth from the First Census of the United States to the Twelfth, 1790-1900.* Washington, D.C., 1909.

——. *First Census of the United States, 1790, South Carolina: Heads of Families at the First Census Taken in the Year 1790.* Washington, D.C., 1908.

——. *Fifth Census, or Enumeration of the Inhabitants of the United States, 1830.* Washington, D.C., 1832.

——. *Compendium of the Enumeration of the Inhabitants of the United States in 1840.* Washington, D.C., 1841.

——. *Sixth Census or Enumeration of the Inhabitants of the United States in 1840.* Washington, D.C., 1841.

——. *Seventh Census of the United States, 1850: Statistics of the United States.* Washington, D.C., 1853.

——. *Population of the United States in 1860.* Washington, D.C., 1864.

————. *Statistics of the Population of the United States, Ninth Census, 1870.* Washington, D.C., 1872.

————. *Statistics of the Population of the United States, Tenth Census, 1880.* Washington, D.C., 1883.

————. *Compendium of the Eleventh Census, 1890.* Part 1: "Population." Washington, D.C., 1892.

U.S., Congress. *American State Papers: Public Lands.* Vols. 3-6. Washington, D.C., 1832-1861.

U.S., Congress, House. *General Public Acts of Congress, Respecting the Sale and Disposition of the Public Lands, with Instructions Issued, from Time to Time, by the Secretary of Treasury and Commissioner of the General Land Office, and Official Opinions of the Attorney General, on Questions Arising under the Land Laws.* 2 vols. Washington, D.C., 1838.

ATLASES, TRAVELERS' GUIDES, AND MAPS

Atlas Map of Pike County, Illinois. Davenport, Iowa: Andreas Lyter, 1872.

Campbell's New Atlas of the State of Illinois. Chicago, 1870.

Colby, Charles G. *Handbook of Illinois, Accompanying Morse's New Map of the State.* New York: R. Blanchard, 1854.

Colton's Guide Map of Illinois. Chicago, 1872.

Colton's Traveler and Tourist's Guide-Book through the United States. New York, 1850.

Cram's Railroad and Township Map of Illinois. Chicago, 1869.

George Ogle and Co., comps. *Standard Atlas of Pike County, Illinois, Including a Plat Book of the County.* Chicago, 1912.

Western Rivers Map or Travellers Guide, 1845. Newberry Library, Chicago.

Index